Just Promoted!

How to Survive and Thrive in Your First 12 Months as a Manager

Edward Betof, Ed.D.
Frederic Harwood, Ph.D.

D0914757

McGraw-Hill, Inc.
New York St. Louis San Francisco Auckland Bogotá
Caracas Lisbon London Madrid Mexico Milan
Montreal New Delhi Paris San Juan São Paulo
Singapore Sydney Tokyo Toronto

Library of Congress Cataloging-in-Publication Data

Betof, Edward
     Just promoted : how to survive and thrive in your first 12 months
as a manager / Edward Betof, Frederic Harwood.
          p.   cm.
     Includes bibliographical references and index.
     ISBN 0-07-005072-4 (cloth)   —ISBN 0-07-005073-2 (pbk.)
     1. Executive ability.   2. Executives.   3. Career changes.
I. Harwood, Federic.   II. Title.
HD38.2.B49   1992
658.4'09—dc20   91-47959
                                                                    CIP

Copyright © 1992 by McGraw-Hill, Inc. All rights reserved. Printed in the
United States of America. Except as permitted under the United States
Copyright Act of 1976, no part of this publication may be reproduced or
distributed in any form or by any means, or stored in a data base or re-
trieval system, without the prior written permission of the publisher.

1 2 3 4 5 6 7 8 9 0   DOC/DOC   9 8 7 6 5 4 3 2

ISBN 0-07-005072-4 {HC}
ISBN 0-07-005073-2 {PBK}

*The sponsoring editor for this book was Karen Hansen, the editing supervisor was
Fred Dahl, and the production supervisor was Pamela A. Pelton. It was set in
Baskerville by Carol Woolverton, Lexington, Mass.*

Printed and bound by R. R. Donnelley & Sons Company.

To Mom and Dad, Nila, Ari, and Allison
for your love, support, and encouragement
E. H. B.

To my parents, Fred L. and Charlotte Harwood,
who have been there for me always
F. H.

Contents

Preface

This book is about what happens in the first 12 months after you've been promoted to manager. You're moving up! It's about that exciting and challenging time in your professional life when you change from an *us* to a *them*, when you opt for group over individual responsibility, when you become a manager.

This is a period of professional and personal change unlike any other in your career. In a relatively short time, no more than a few months, you will negotiate the rocky, treacherous channel that separates the knowledgeable, motivated, technical phase of your career from your new role as manager and leader. No longer responsible solely for the performance and quality of your own work, you now have to figure out how to help others achieve that same level of skill, motivation, and knowledge that got you the promotion. No longer are you the master professional; now you are in charge. You will be judged on how well you manage this difficult transition. Your new responsibilities will test and change you as a person and as a professional and will likely have a lasting effect on your career as others assess your potential as a leader.

This book is primarily for those of you assuming your first or second management position, with titles such as Manager, Group Leader, Department Head, Unit Director, or Plant Manager. It is also for managers moving up in the government, education, or nonprofit sector, such as school principals or program directors. The processes are similar even if the settings are not. This book is also helpful for more experienced mid-level and senior managers, who can use it as a resource to guide and coach their managers as they assume new responsibilities. Experienced managers will also find this book helpful as a reminder of what to do as they change management assignments.

When you move up, you are really making two transitions simultaneously. The first comes to mind immediately when you pursue a promotion—the organizational and management aspects of moving into a new position. You must establish yourself in your new assignment and begin to work toward achieving an impact on your organization, now as a manager. On the surface, the obstacles may not seem especially difficult or the hurdles particularly formidable. But the barriers to success are ever present. There is much to do and much to plan for. This is a critical phase in your professional development, and your ability to perform can make or break your career.

As you move up, you also have a second transition to make, a very personal one. In their euphoria about getting the promotion, few managers adequately plan for the inevitable changes in their personal lives. In later chapters we will address the important interplay between work, personal life, and home life. The process of moving up stresses other aspects of your life. Effectively managing this interplay between key elements of your life comprises the final section of this book.

We suggest effective, practical ways for you to succeed at work and at home as you develop as a manager. This book is not a quick fix. It is not a treatise on management philosophy; nor do we emphasize a single set or cluster of isolated skills. Throughout this book, we teach from our own and from others' errors and successes in taking on management responsibility. We have drawn our suggestions from our own experiences and from the many with whom we have worked, interviewed, observed, and consulted. Their willingness to share has enriched this book with invaluable insight, and has made it a useful tool for anyone who is fortunate to have been "just promoted."

Acknowledgments

Many people played vital roles in the preparation of this book. Some provided personal encouragement, others gave much needed assistance, and others provided examples and ideas. We would like to thank Peter Giuliano, Joan Rose, Penn Waggener, and Syms Wyeth. The manuscript was read in its entirety at different stages by Carole Brand, Jim Walker, and Tom Bechet. Their numerous comments and suggestions have improved this book measurably. Carole's edits made this book eminently more readable. Thanks also to Frank Freeman, Librarian at the Center for Creative Leadership, whose resources helped us develop our bibliography, and to David Noer, Randy White, and Bob Dorn, also of CCL, whose perspective helped us realize the potential of this work for newly appointed leaders. Karen Hansen, our sponsoring editor at

McGraw-Hill, has been instrumental in helping us structure our book, keeping us on track, and nudging our creative juices.

It is sometimes difficult to recall where an idea comes from, or from whom a skill or concept was learned. It is easier to remember the network of people who affected our thinking. Foremost are the people involved in human growth, affective education and organizational development in the Philadelphia area and at Temple University in the 1970s. Seminal were Leland Howe, Mary Martha Howe-Whitworth, and Howie Kirschenbaum, along with Sidney Simon, Joel Goodman, Margie Ingram, Jim Wilson, and Sam Barnett. Special thanks to Rod Napier from whom we gained much of our basic understanding of group and organizational development.

Our sincere gratitude goes to Sally Guskind and Theresa Dalla Riva, whose tireless attention to detail helped us greatly as we prepared the manuscript. Thanks also to Jill Mortensen for help with early drafts.

Above all, Ed would like to thank Nila, his wife of 22 years, for her encouragement, confidence, ideas, love, and patience in putting up with growing piles of notes, readings, and drafts on and under the dining room table. He thanks his children, Ari and Allison, whose amazement that we were working on yet one more draft desperately inspired him to finish this book so more normal family life could resume. He also thanks his brothers and sisters-in-law, Bob and Linda, John and Sharyn, David and Jackie, and friends of many years, Michael Madden, Vera Knapp, Dave and Joyce Turner, Bill and Renee Kennish, John Swisher, and Judy Vicary who have modeled balancing work, family, and fun in their lives.

Special appreciation goes to Ed's boss for the past eight years, Herb Conrad, President of Roche Pharmaceuticals, division of Hoffmann-La Roche Inc. as well as his numerous colleagues at Roche. As a mentor, coach, and model, Herb is truly respected as a professional and a person. He has provided opportunities to tackle assignments, expected and encouraged growth and development, reinforced Ed when he did something well, and identified areas where he needed to improve. Herb's spirit infuses this book.

Frederic is deeply indebted to his friend and colleague of 20 years, Sam Barnett, whose vision, creativity, confidence, and support have served as an abiding source of strength and inspiration. He thanks Ed Betof who conceived this book and shepherded it to completion. Bob Regazzi, Vice President of PAREXEL International, has modeled what it means to excel as a professional manager.

Frederic is grateful to his beloved, Brenda McRae, for her inspiration and wisdom as a businesswoman, her encouragement, laughter, and many ideas. Thanks to his sons John and Peter Harwood and to Derek Owens, to his brother John, and Earl McGovern for their support.

His advisor at the University of Minnesota, Stan Kegler, Temple

University's Paul Eberman, Sam Wehr, Tony Amato, Howard Blake, Bob Snyder, Bernie Miller, Rod Hilsinger, and Bob Walter, Angelita May, Irene Bender, Jay Miller of Hoffmann-La Roche, and Ned Joyce, now of Bristol-Myers Squibb, have given him support, confidence, and the opportunity to grow. To these, to his colleagues at Barnett International, and to the many others who have contributed to that growth, he is most grateful.

Edward Betof
Frederic Harwood

1
Introduction to Your First Year

Far and away the best prize that life offers is
the chance to work hard at work worth doing.
THEODORE ROOSEVELT

To successfully move up as a newly appointed manager you will need to:

- Establish yourself in your new assignment.
- Achieve an impact on your organization.
- Manage the impact of moving up on your family and personal life.

☆ ☆ ☆

In this chapter, there is useful information about:

- The three major *parts* of this book:
  1. Moving in: Establishing Yourself in Your New Assignment
  2. Achieving an Impact on the Organization
  3. Managing the Impact of Moving Up on Your Family and Personal Life
- Seven basic assumptions relating to moving up
- An overview of each chapter in the book

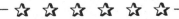

Just Promoted! An Introduction to Your First 12 Months as a Manager

Some people become managers with the grace of Baryshnikov and the coordination of an Olympic gold medal skater. Others, most, experience their first year of management as if they are tap dancing on marbles. There's a lot of energy and a lot happening, but very little that is certain, stable, or efficient.

During your first 12 months as a first-time manager, or as an experienced manager in a brand new position or company, you will often feel out of control. This is a common feeling, whether you are a group leader, department head, or plant manager. But you can take steps to lessen that feeling and to maximize your chances for success in your new job. We will alert you to career-damaging circumstances you should be aware of, and we will guide you through specific actions that you should be engaged in during your first days, weeks, and months on the job. Equally important, we will show you what to do to ensure that your life outside of work, your friends, your family, and your health don't get sacrificed to your new career responsibilities.

You will soon discover that moving into a new and important management position presents factors that are often simultaneously vexing and energizing. They lend much of the uniqueness to the process of moving up and are listed here. Each will be discussed in various chapters.

- Making the change from primarily individual contributor or first-line supervisor to manager and leader.

- For the first time, dealing more with people and organizational issues than with professional or technical issues.

- Dealing with the possibility that you will "lose your edge" or expertise when you enter management. Related to this is the criticism from some of your peers that you are "selling out" by becoming a manager.

- Realizing that you were promoted before you were actually trained to be a manager. You have distinguished yourself as a professional in your field, but not yet as a manager. Most managers end up learning on the job over many years aided by training courses. This is a tough way to get through your first year of managing people and a whole new set of issues.

- Figuring out a way to enter your new job in a way that is credible and makes a positive impression.

- Making the change from being a peer to being the boss.

- Determining how to become an advocate for your people while remaining objective to make improvements and plan for success. This is exacerbated during the first year, while everybody is watching your every move to try to find out your "real" agenda.

- Establishing a solid working relationship with subordinates, peers, and your boss. If this hasn't happened early in your management position, it likely will not happen later. A mutually supportive relationship with your boss must form in your first few months on the job. He or she wishes to excel, and you need to figure out how to help.

- Attaining, early on, a clear vision of your organization's future, and figuring out how to make it happen.

- During your first six months on the job, assessing the health and well-being of your organization.

- Selecting your immediate staff and building them into a well-honed management team. You will have to make tough decisions about people and will need to make your decisions stick. You may also need to terminate a person for the first time.

- Despite organizational resistance, building commitment and overcoming impediments to the success of your function. This is even more complicated during your first year, since there is added resistance to you because you were appointed and others were not.

- Setting personal goals and committing to expectations for your entire area of responsibility. Possibly for the first time, you will be judged on results that do not depend solely on your individual effort. Overall results of your organization now become paramount and will determine your individual success.

- Attending to other responsibilities to your family, yourself, and other areas of your life. You now have a major personal engineering and planning task at hand, because when you move up your life balance changes, sometimes dramatically. Achieving a desirable life balance begins with you. Managing the many pressures, the multiple pulls and tugs, is part of the process of moving up.

Trying to deal with all of these issues is, at best, difficult and tenuous. Because of the pace, number, and intensity of issues during the first year as a manager, people have described the period as one in which it is difficult to get your feet under you—as if you are tap dancing on marbles.

Seven Assumptions

This book, as well as the process of moving up as a manager and leader, is founded on seven basic assumptions for successful professional and personal growth as a manager and leader.

1. Previous job performance excellence is a prerequisite for moving up. People who move up have excelled in early assignments, regardless of how technical or detailed the task. Managers delegating responsibility are always on the lookout for those with the dedication, talent, and spirit to warrant promotion.

2. Success in moving up is determined by the quality of your problem-solving skills, the questions you ask, and the usefulness of the data or information you collect. We are confounded by the questions we didn't ask, the information we didn't have, and the answers we didn't pursue. Successfully moving up is directly related to your information base and how you use these data to identify, prevent, and solve problems.

3. Success in moving up is synonymous with your personal definition of life balance between career, relationships, family, and other personal life values. There is no one correct equation or formula. Many managers fail to achieve the balance they want and haven't yet found the key to their professional and personal success. This book is for those who are qualified to become strong leaders in the jobs they desire and wish to build greater quality into the other areas of their lives that are important to them.

4. It usually takes numerous professional qualifications and individual qualities to manage effectively the process of moving up, and the breakdown of even one can cause career derailment or family and personal distress. The *systems'* interplay within and between a newly appointed manager's work, health, and personal life is critical.

5. Balancing thoughts and feelings is key to successful transitions. Moving up requires clear thinking and planning as well as skilled and caring attention to our feelings and those of others during the process. Managers and leaders who are skilled problem solvers blend solid facts with "gut feelings" in almost everything they do.

6. Moving up is a job in itself and must be tended as if your future depends on it. You will need as much as a year to lay the foundation for long-term organizational results and personal satisfaction. This period must be managed well, for it is hard, if not impossible, to recoup time and progress lost.

7. Moving up will almost always disrupt the steadiness by which we work and live. The impetus can be abrupt or traumatic, such as a firing or

forced transfer. Other transitions begin more gradually, such as the desire for a promotion. In either case, the unrest caused by moving up dominates our lives until it is resolved. We struggle to manage professional change and increased responsibility while maintaining equilibrium in our personal lives. In the process, we are energized, revitalized, and discover strengths and abilities we never knew we had. Moving up can be troublesome and stressful, but it is self-renewing—the proving grounds for subsequent success.

We are surrounded by people promoted to more responsible, higher-paying jobs, people placed on the fast track, slow track, regular track, but promoted. Some seem to be on the way to the top so quickly that they do not stay in any one job long enough to fail. Some seem to be promoted just before the roof falls in. There are people who seem effortlessly to flow from one promotion to the next, one transition to the next, without much interruption and difficulty. Some seem to lead charmed lives. They seem to know exactly what to do on a new job, and do it successfully.

How do they do it? How can they move into a job, about which they may know very little, and perform like they know exactly what they need to do? What do they know that you don't know? And how can you learn it? This book probes these questions and proposes practical solutions to real problems. One of this book's primary goals is to help you achieve success at work, at home, and in your personal and professional lifestyle by setting your feet firmly under you during your first year of moving up.

Overview of the Book

This book is divided into three parts.

The Process of Moving Up

Part 1: Moving In: Establishing Yourself in Your New Assignment

Part 2: Achieving an Impact on the Organization

Part 3: Managing the Impact of Moving Up on Your Family and Personal Life

---

Part 1, "Establishing Yourself in Your New Assignment," considers how to move into your new position. Chapter 2, "Moving In," emphasizes making a good first impression, building empowering relationships, and challenging the organization for high motivation and high performance. At the same time, there is no relationship more important than that with your boss, and Chap. 3 discusses making that relationship firm, clear, and mutually supportive.

Part 2, "Achieving an Impact on the Organization," describes how to develop a vision that will result in organizational renewal and improvement. With the help of your organization, you'll need to begin crafting your vision (Chap. 4), understand the diagnostic or assessment process as you analyze your organization (Chap. 5), and develop the tools and techniques for assessing your organization's strengths and weaknesses (Chap. 6). Chapter 6 introduces the "Nine Target" model, which can be used as a diagnostic tool for assessing your organization's overall health. From this diagnosis, you can evolve a vision of what the organization could be like and where it should be headed.

With a sense of ownership and responsibility for the organization's health and growth, the vision that results from your early efforts should involve many members of your function and should be implemented by them. Thus, Chap. 7 describes how to select, build, train, and develop work teams that will be responsible for high performance and achievement of the objectives and vision. Chapter 8, "From Resistance to Renewal," describes how to build full commitment to that vision within the organization. Emphasis is on understanding, assessing, and managing your specific organizational politics, environment, and culture, including a customized activity titled "Your Political Inventory." Chapter 8 also examines the practical implications of group and organizational dynamics during your first year on the job. We examine forces resistant to change and principles of effective change, and we look at organizational change efforts that have failed.

Chapter 9, "Settling In," describes the period when the organization has absorbed change and is ready to seek equilibrium and a period of stability, including fine-tuning your leadership role. This chapter introduces SOARING, sharpening the way you think about your work and personal life.

Part 3 is titled "Managing the Impact of Moving Up on Your Family and Personal Life." Professional transitions inevitably result in personal transitions as well, and Chap. 10, "Up Close and Personal," discusses how your transition to management can affect your family, health, and time. It also discusses implications for dual-career marriages. Chapter 11 describes how to achieve a new life balance while making a management transition. To help you achieve that goal, it includes activities dealing with your real and ideal self, your personal time, and your personal plan of action.

This book is about professional and personal change. For managers, both are essential. Success in one area supports success in the other. We start with the professional dimension, looking at how to begin your new management position and enter the organization.

Quick Reminders to Keep
You on Track

- This book is about what happens in the 12 twelve months after you're promoted to a manager/leadership position.

- This is a period of professional and personal change unlike any other in your career. Your first year can, and likely will be, simultaneously vexing and energizing. You will certainly be challenged. You will need to draw upon your professional, interpersonal, and personal abilities and resources.

- You are no longer responsible solely for only your performance and the quality of your work; you now have to help others achieve the same level of skill, motivation, and knowledge that got you your position.

- When you are promoted to your first or subsequent management position, you are really making two transitions simultaneously: (1) the organizational/management elements of moving up and (2) a personal transition affecting you, possibly a spouse or partner, your family, and others with whom you are very close. Success in one major area of your life supports success in the other.

- *Just Promoted!* and the process of becoming a successful manager are founded on seven assumptions:

  1. Previously demonstrated high performance is an essential prerequisite for successfully becoming a manager.
  2. Success in moving up to management is greatly determined by the quality of your problem-solving skills, the questions you ask, and the usefulness of the information you collect.
  3. Success in moving up is synonymous with your personal definition of the balance you desire in life between career, relationships, family, and other important personal values.
  4. It usually takes numerous professional qualifications and individual qualities to become an effective manager; the breakdown of even one can cause career derailment or family and personal problems. The *systems* interplay within and between a newly appointed manager's work, health, and personal life is critical.
  5. Effectively balancing your thoughts and emotions is key to managing your career transitions successfully.
  6. Being promoted and moving up to an important management position is in itself a job and must be tended as if your future depends on it. Success generally won't come naturally or easily.
  7. Being promoted will almost always disrupt the steadiness by which you work and live. The first 12 months following your promotion

entail a process of transition management with all attendant pulls, tugs, and stresses on your professional and personal life.

- A primary goal of *Just Promoted!* is to help you achieve success at work, at home, and in your personal/professional life style during the first year after your appointment.

- There is a process for success during the 12 months after being promoted as a manager. This process corresponds with the organization of *Just Promoted!*

    Part I: Moving In: Establishing Yourself in Your New Assignment

    Part II: Achieving an Impact on the Organization

    Part III: Managing the Impact of Moving Up on Your Family and Personal Life

PART 1

Moving In: Establishing Yourself in Your New Assignment

2
Entering the Organization

You only make a first impression one time.
SOURCE UNKNOWN

I have climbed to the top of the greasy pole!
BENJAMIN DISRAELI

As you move in, a major objective in establishing yourself in your new assignment is to effectively enter the organization. You will need to:

- Meet all the people who work for you as well as new colleagues outside your function.
- Make good first impressions.
- Work very well with your boss.
- Begin figuring out what you are supposed to do in this job and what your job really is.
- Be an advocate for your people.
- Build expectations and hope.
- Begin to increase or sustain the confidence of your people through your style and approach.

In this chapter, there is useful information about:

- The First Meetings with Your Staff
- Establishing Ground Rules and Communication with Your Boss About the Transition Process
- Learning Your Job
- Becoming an Organizational Advocate
- Raising Expectations, Hopes, and Personal Empowerment
- Empowering Relationships: A Self-Concept Approach to Managing People

There are many ways that people become managers. Some have planned to become managers for years, and the opportunity finally presents itself. For others, becoming a manager happens suddenly and with no preparation or warning. There is usually a precipitating event that creates an open management position within the organization such as a promotion, resignation, termination, reorganization, or expansion of a business. Whatever the circumstances, a key opening needs to be filled.

Some people feel honored but decline the opportunity to move up into management. They are happy in their present job; they prefer to remain specialists in their chosen profession, such as research, law, finance, sales, or marketing. Bless these people; managers need people who love doing the work. Without a fair share of them, every manager would fail. But others compete feverishly for promotions, for the chance to show their ability to manage and lead people and an organization. This is where we begin the process of moving up. You have just been appointed, and you need to figure out how to begin and where to go from here.

Starting your job and entering the organization can be a treacherous time for a new manager. It's when the marbles are rolled out and the tap dancing begins. You will try to stay on a steady course, but it will not be easy. Whether in an old or a newly formed organization, you'll frequently run into expectations, resentments, and confusion. In almost all cases, change and management transition intensify people's feelings. In this chapter we will look at the six steps for effectively entering your new job and organization:

1. Make a good impression at your first meetings with your new staff. Immediately begin to connect with people on a personal level.

2. Establish the initial transitional ground rules with your boss, and negotiate his or her support.

3. Learn your job and the organization's work from your predecessor, your boss, and organizational sources of information and power.

4. Become an organizational advocate.

5. Begin to empower your organization and your people to achieve their hopes, goals, and objectives for the organization.

6. Build empowering relationships and a self-concept approach to managing people.

Manage these steps well, and you'll be off to a good start in your new job.

The First Meetings with Your Staff

Because the rumor mill develops quickly once you have been selected, the public announcement of your selection should be made as quickly as possible. A delayed announcement hurts the organization in two ways. Those in the running may continue expending energy in speculation and political maneuvering, affecting their own and others' productivity. In addition, the people in the department will be concerned with the impending change, their own futures, what changes you may make—all of which affects productivity. Moreover, performance often decreases in departments with lame-duck leadership. People may tend to let up; certainly they will be reluctant to make commitments that may not be supported later. A timely announcement will help lessen negative effects of the change.

You can predict many of the reactions to the announcement, so plan for them. If the search was competitive, competitors' reactions will range from disappointment to anger. If you were hired from the outside and are not known, there will be many questions about you and your agenda. If you were promoted from within, staff's reactions will range from disbelief that you were named (or someone else wasn't), to mild interest to genuine satisfaction that you were the best choice. Be aware and sensitive to these reactions, but never defend or feel that you must defend the decision to select you.

If there has been open competition for the job, your boss should personally inform the internal competitors. Because they will not hold onto this information once they know, the meeting should take place only an hour or so before the announcement. If you have been moved in from another in-house function, simultaneously meet with colleagues in your old department to share the news of your new job. Your previous boss should always be the first to know. Let people know in person. If a replacement for you is known, help make the transition for that person easier; it is an act of goodwill for your former department.

First Impressions: A Personal
Introduction to the Department

First impressions powerfully affect attitudes your new staff will form toward you. People believe what they want to believe, not necessarily what is factual. Therefore, you want to make a personable, effective first impression.

Your influence and power base within the department may initially be fragile. You will need to build your organization's support quickly. To do this, on a continuum of work orientation versus people orientation, concentrate your initial energies on the people side. Do this while your subordinates continue getting the day-to-day work done. Managing the work means, first and foremost, managing the people. This is where you should begin.

Plan on meeting with your department, including support staff, within the hour of the announcement if possible. A group meeting underscores your message that we are all part of one team where each person and the organization as a whole are what counts. This meeting should be followed as soon as possible with individual sessions, starting with key people, using the following guidelines.

Keep the department meeting short. People won't remember much of what you say. Your overall tone and style will make more of an impression than your specific message.

- Be positive. Project confidence, strength, and optimism.
- Be open, direct, and frank.
- It is a new beginning, for both you and your new staff.
  Be upbeat.

Briefly describe your background and qualifications. Be humble yet confident. Project the following:

- You are glad to be working with the department and to have this new challenge.
- The department has strengths we will build on, but every organization has problems, and we must strive for continuous improvement.
- The department's personnel are capable and committed. Be positive, and relay to them some of the complimentary things you learned about the department as a whole during the selection process.
- As a group, we will solve our problems; our whole is greater than the sum of our parts. Stress that everyone is interdependent, that you expect to rely on them and trust them just as they can rely on and trust you.

- We will succeed, improve, and grow individually and as a team.

From this first meeting, concentrate on building relationships with your staff, developing communication and personal access with each member of your work unit. Stress the people side of the job because

- You genuinely feel people are most important.
- You need staff support to get the work done.
- You need their assistance to solve the organization's problems.
- You need their assistance to plan and implement the future, the organization's renewal.
- You may not know enough about the work to make work changes yourself.

During this first meeting, mention that within a few weeks you will be asking the staff to participate in a comprehensive self-study of the organization's mission, goals, policies, practices, and procedures. Indicate that you are undertaking this effort so the department can better control its own future direction and prerogatives. Tell staff that as a group, we want to confirm our strengths and identify what we can do to become stronger—in other words, we want to adopt an organizational "fitness" program. Indicate that you will be meeting with the unit heads or management team to map out the self-study, and that there will be a role in the process for much of the organization.

People will want to know whether their jobs are secure. Assure them that no changes are imminent (if, in fact, that is the case). If you know or think that staff reductions will occur, be careful not to indicate that all is well, or your credibility is at risk. Focus on what can be done. In these initial days you need to learn the organization, and the work needs to continue. You must stress that *we*, as an organization, need to assess how good we are and where we need to improve.

Finally, indicate that you are here to listen and better understand where we are and how we need to grow. With the active help of everyone in the organization, we'll build a stronger, better organization.

Before adjourning, ask for questions, but keep answers succinct and general. Don't get into the details of the department self-study. Indicate that over the next few weeks, you will meet and talk with everyone. Thank staff for their warm welcome.

From *I* to *We* and *Our*

Your staff will have two fundamental concerns as you assume leadership: inclusion and control. By inclusion, employees wonder if they'll remain with their present jobs and maintain their primary work assignments. By control, they'll hope to have some say in what happens to them, and they'll wonder how much input they will have in what happens to the department or work unit.

Even at the first introductory meeting, you can address those concerns briefly. Although people may assume you will not announce any immediate changes, they need to be reassured that this is the case, at least in the short term. A more important purpose of this meeting is to encourage the group to think collegially. Shift the group's perception away from you—"What is *he* going to do?" Focus on them—"What are *we* going to do?" Minimize the word *I* in your talk, and emphasize *we* and *our: our* effort, *our* department, and *our* goals. Emphasize that *our* department will only be as strong as we work to make it strong; and that *we* will build on our individual, group, and organizational strengths. The sooner you can enlist your staff's support, the more success there will be for everyone.

The Unsuccessful Candidates

Meet individually with the defeated job candidates. They can affect your future performance. Start with those in your new organization who wanted the promotion for themselves. Some will take their failure personally and keenly feel disappointment, anger, and a sense of rejection or failure. Put yourself in their shoes. Acknowledge their feelings. At the same time, remember that they cannot let those feelings interfere with their responsibilities.

- Indicate that you will make every effort to use their expertise and experience. And mean it when you say it, because many of them are your most experienced and competent people. If they weren't good, they would not have been considered for the job.

- Acknowledge that some may be thinking about their future and their alternatives, but that this must not interfere with their responsibilities. Assure them that their future in this organization is their choice, and that the organization needs their energy and skills (assuming that is how you feel).

- Emphasize that their individual success is a credit to the organization; that they have grown in skills and knowledge is attributable, in large part, to the work they have done in the department. Assure them that you want to help them continue to be successful in their jobs and in their future with the company. You intend to become an advocate for the organization's members.

Personally Connecting with People

On this first day, try to talk to as many people as possible. Begin with those who report to you directly. Stop and introduce yourself to everyone you can, including secretaries, clerks, and professional staff. Going to meet them at their offices and work areas has a number of advantages:

- At first they may feel some natural distance, which may create reticence. You are not yet part of the group, and you are their new boss. Things are no longer quite the same, nor should you expect them to be. Going to their space is a way to indicate that you want to work with them and that you seek their active cooperation.

- By visiting them in their work area, you show that you value them.

- They will be more comfortable in their own surroundings.

- Visiting also establishes you as someone who will reach out, who wants to be accessible and hands-on, which is a good first impression to reinforce.

Keep your office calls informal, low key, and short. Get to know your staff by their first names; in pleasant conversation, find out how long they've been here, where they live, whether they have families. You'll find out who comes from your area, went to one of your schools, worked at a former company, shares an interest, or has something else in common with you. You'll begin building bridges.

Throughout this book we emphasize the importance of building and sustaining relationships throughout the organization. As much as any other single factor, trusting, empowering interpersonal behaviors determine success and failure. Be conscious of establishing solid relationships at all levels in the organization. Work at building trust and rapport with those who are under your supervision; with your boss and others at his or her level; and, importantly, with your peers and colleagues.

Make sure you begin spending meaningful time with your peers during your first two or three days. Think about others in the organization. Any secretary, for example, can help or hurt you depending on how he or she has been treated. Genuine concern and consideration for others, even small things like saying please and thank you, go a long way toward building strong relationships. Extend yourself and others will tend to do the same. Ask yourself the following:

- What can I do to build stronger relationships at all levels?
- Do I go out of my way for others?
- Do I ask for what I want, or do I demand things from others?

- What can I do to help people trust me?
- Am I straight with people? Do I minimize conflicts?
- Do I listen well to needs and feelings?
- Do I show warmth and concern and extend myself to others?
- Do I make people come to me, or do I reach out to them?

The First Week

During your first week on the job, you will be winding down your initial entry activities, working hard to learn your job, and preparing to begin the organizational self-study.

You have met with as many people as you can, either individually or in groups. You also met with the defeated candidates. You have circulated throughout the department and chatted with almost everyone. During this same period, you may need to tie up some loose ends and continue strengthening new alliances. You need to do the following:

- Meet with your old department.
- Meet or continue meeting with your predecessor to learn as much as you can about your new job.
- Meet with your boss.
- Continue meeting with each member of the department, individually and as a group.

Exiting Gracefully

Wrapping up unfinished business with your old responsibilities is an important part of the transition process. If you are an external candidate, your previous position will continue to be a source of friendships, connections, information, and possible employees. If you are an internal candidate, members of your former department can extend your personal influence within the organization. They can provide friendship, information, assistance, recommendations, and referrals to help with staffing.

A very classy transition was managed by the outgoing director of a city commission. At a news conference, she introduced her successor. She reviewed her past achievements, praised her successor's qualifications, and sketched out a bright future for the organization. She indicated that she would continue to cooperate with her successor and help as needed.

Her successor, in turn, praised her accomplishments, thanked her for her warm welcome, and assured her of his need for her help and consultation in the future. The transition process was carried out with mutual respect and good humor. Both parties were sincere. The stage was set for the incumbent to step aside gracefully, her good name intact. An outsider would never have suspected that she had been asked to step down from her job.

That the transition was later marred by the ousted director's continued and largely unwelcome intrusions into the commission's business highlights another truism of transition: Once you're out, you're out. This is true whether you are Steve Jobs, Ross Perot, or Henry Kissinger. You do not help yourself, or your departing organization, by continual meddling—even if your friends within the organization encourage that participation.

When you exit, consider the following:

- Help introduce your replacement in your former department if you know who it is. This ties your replacement's leadership to yours, emphasizes an orderly transition, and acknowledges your role in the transition. Even if you've been dismissed, exit with dignity. Even if you're angry, exit with grace.

- Offer your thanks to the entire department for their cooperation and assistance. Publicly thank people for special efforts, especially your secretary and those who have helped your career. Give credit where credit is due.

- Ask for your former department's support in your new job. You may need to call them for recommendations, favors, and information.

- Privately talk to as many people from your former department as necessary. Thank those who helped; make peace with those with whom you had differences.

- Privately update your successor on your goals, performance plan, and other important information. Help him or her sustain improvements you made. Let him or her know what you are working on that needs finishing. Warn your successor about the icebergs and the glaciers.

- Clear your desk, personal records, and your calendar. Call your network and your old clients and let them know of your new responsibilities.

Establishing Ground Rules and Communication with Your Boss About the Transition Process

Throughout the preemployment interviews and the hiring process, you should provide a broad overview of your process for getting started in your job. Review the process with your boss again when you actually begin work. Make sure you both understand and agree to the process and the timetable. Mutually establish your ground rules, such as the following:

- Your boss should expect no significant changes for a specified period (usually two to four months) while you are fact finding.

- Your boss should understand your change process. Explain thoroughly each step so your boss will support it and can handle inquiries or comments about the process. Good communication will stem your boss's impatience.

- Given an understanding of the process, your boss can more easily become a coach and consultant to you, advising you regarding the changes that may develop out of your data gathering or diagnostic efforts.

- Your boss should agree to meet regularly with you, to maintain strong lines of communication and information sharing. Questions or concerns should be aired immediately and not permitted to fester until your boss explodes in anger. Beware of a boss who is too quiet or nonevaluative. Whether or not your boss says anything, he or she is watching and thinking. Try to get your boss's views out in the open.

- You and your boss should agree on the type of reporting and decision making that will fit your boss's style. Agree on procedures for these.

Establish a schedule of events so both you and your boss will know the sequence of events and timeline for making your transition. You will lessen the pressure you feel to make something happen immediately if you plan the process in writing. A telecommunications manager felt that she received her promotion partly because she had worked closely with her new boss, which convinced her new boss that she knew what was wrong and how to fix it. Nevertheless, the manager negotiated a transition period of at least three months, during which she was allowed to assess the organization's resources, personnel, structure, and work flow. Even though her boss was impatient for some changes, the manager held her to her promise and kept her informed step by step of the diagnostic process. As the new manager developed a better understanding of the organization, her boss changed some of her own prescriptions and agreed to let the new manager do it her way.

Learning Your Job

Even if you were the assistant, heir apparent, and right hand of your predecessor, and even if you think you know everything about the job, take time to learn what is needed. Learning your job means learning from your predecessor, department members, and colleagues all the details you've ignored up to now. Begin as soon as you can to start learning important information from the right people.

Your Predecessor and Key Staff

If you can, debrief your predecessor, preferably before he or she leaves. Even if the person's been fired and angry, try to set a meeting.

There is much information that only your predecessor has. You can shorten your learning curve, sometimes considerably, by tapping into this wonderful resource. More importantly, you can improve your odds in the organization's political jockeying. Your predecessor will describe the organization's competitors, enemies, and allies and can tell you how to deal with each and where the land mines are.

Sometimes the meeting is a courtesy session. A manager who had been abruptly moved from a staff position in human resources to a line job in manufacturing confessed, "I was scared to death. I talked with the person I was replacing for about three hours. That is, mostly he talked. I tried to take some notes, but I didn't understand much of what he said. I felt like a real dummy."

This is a meeting that may or may not help you much. You may be overwhelmed by the amount of information, the terms, the technology, the politics. On the other hand, you may see why your predecessor is being moved; he or she may show a brilliant grasp of the job or a woeful absence of energy, commitment, and control of detail. You may be tempted to make this visit short, especially if your predecessor's tenure was not a success. You may feel you shouldn't have to ask these things— that you are supposed to know these things because, after all, that's why you were hired. You may feel embarrassed to ask the most elementary questions. This is a mistake. Strong people ask basic questions to get the information they need. They ask for help. Strong people even ask the questions when they think they know the answers.

You probably were not hired because you had the solutions immediately, but because someone was confident that you could identify the opportunities and problems, analyze them, and implement the solutions. The solutions are not on your back alone. You should not position yourself as *the* answer person. Rather, you are a catalyst for problem solving that, at times, can involve the entire organization.

Ask your predecessor's view of the mission, history, objectives, personalities, problems, and concerns of the department. Probe. Ask in-depth questions. Learn more about the budget. Since few others in the department will understand where the money comes from, ask what the constraints are and how the funds are allocated. Ask what never got into the budget that should have. Ask basic questions, even those that may have obvious answers. You may be surprised by what you hear.

In many organizations, these debriefings are standard operating procedure. In the U.S. Army, for example, they are part of the command transition. It is expected that the outgoing commander will thoroughly brief his or her successor before leaving command. In the military, where a change of command often occurs every 12 to 24 months, incoming commanders are less shy about conducting thorough debriefings.

Curiously, such briefings are less common in business. Perhaps because American business is so individualistic, new managers are supposed to get the job done on their own. In more age-sensitive cultures, including many European and Asian countries, the outgoing manager is more respected for his or her learning and wisdom and is treated with more deference and respect. In the United States, the younger generation can barely wait to push their elders and predecessors aside. American business could profit from such thorough briefings.

A checklist will help you focus the discussion. These topics can be used in your discussion with staff, which may give you even greater insights into the organization's health. The interview protocol is not very different from the one you will soon adopt to conduct the organizational fitness check, just a little more informal.

- *The Organizational Chart.* Ask about reporting relationships and "dotted-line" relationships. Trace the work flow on the organizational chart. Does your predecessor think the organizational chart is functional and reflects the actual work flow? How might the organizational structure and work flow be changed?

- *The Mission and Goals of the Organization.* What are the organization's mission and goals? What is your predecessor's assessment of how well the organization is reaching its goals? What does your predecessor feel are the strengths and weaknesses that affect how well the organization reaches its goals?

- *Your Predecessor's Evaluation of the Organization.* What is your predecessor's assessment of the organization's capabilities, achievements, strengths, and weaknesses? What have been his or her greatest disappointments? Greatest achievements? What has brought him or her the most satisfaction?

- *Your Predecessor's Judgment of Personnel.* What is your predecessor's assessment of department personnel? Who are the hard workers, high achievers, entrepreneurs, risk takers, and straight shooters? Where is the informal leadership? Who molds opinions? How does the grapevine work? Who pushes the limits, passes on stories, creates dissension? Who is temperamental? Who fudges time or information? Who would your predecessor like to get rid of? Who is in line for promotion? Who has earned it? Who expects it? Who can keep his or her mouth shut? Who can be trusted? Who is reliable?

- *The Most Urgent Needs.* What are the organization's most pressing needs to achieve its goals?

- *The Budget.* What is in the budget? How much of it is discretionary? What can be moved around? How much are fixed costs? When an unexpected requirement develops, where is the money usually taken from?

- *The Records.* What is in the files? Where are the personnel files? The confidential files?

- *The MIS.* What is your predecessor's management information system? How does it work, which files are available to others, and which are available only to your predecessor?

- *Prioritization of Your Responsibilities.* What are the major job responsibilities? What did your predecessor spend his or her time on? What responsibilities are most important to the organization? Contrast important responsibilities to how your predecessor actually spent time and energy.

- *The Committees.* What are the major committees? Is there an executive committee? Who is its spokesperson? How are decisions delegated and made? How supportive and helpful is the executive team? Where is your likely competition?

- *The Hidden Problems.* Where are the land mines, the submerged icebergs both within and outside the department? What are sources of unseen problems and danger to the department and to your own career? Your predecessor should be able to tell you pitfalls to avoid, your boss's hot buttons, and organizational areas that can cause problems for you.

It may not be a bad idea to set aside this information temporarily, using it only as a guide. You have gathered opinions and biases that may be different from your own, or from reality. You need to use this information carefully. Within days you will begin the formal organizational diagnosis; as this progresses, review your predecessor's comments, and compare them with your own perceptions. In some cases, your hunches will be confirmed, and you may get some insights into situations you have observed. And certainly you will get a running start that will ensure a smoother transition for you.

Other Sources of Information

A second source of information is organizational documentation. One manager spent many hours in his office reviewing documents during his first weeks on the job. The following documents should be reviewed:

- The department administrative or operations manual, which should include the organizational chart, descriptions of work-flow policies, department forms, standard operating procedures, job descriptions and grades, personnel policies, performance standards, and the system for performance management. You will learn how things are supposed to work, what policies do not seem to be in place, and what seems out of date, illogical, or wrong. You may discover, as one manager of a *Fortune* 500 company found, that there are no policies, the work flow is ad hoc, and there is no emphasis on quality and consistency.

- The secretarial manual for forms and flow of paperwork and information. A good secretarial manual should include important forms and describe the flow of important documents.

- Written monthly or periodic departmental and divisional highlights, which are usually good-news vehicles but may tell what's new and who is involved.

- The corporate and department mission statement. What is the department supposed to be doing? How does our mission fit into the corporate mission? When was it last updated and how?

- Internal reports, including committee minutes and reports of task forces. If task forces were formed or studies conducted to solve particular problems, read the report. Then ask whether any of the recommendations were implemented. One newly named manager, frustrated by what seemed to be the aimlessness of one committee, asked to see the committee's mission statement and its minutes. Surprised to learn that the mission statement was meaningful (to review departmental policies and policy decisions made by the leadership, and to assess leadership's performance), the manager suggested that the committee was not addressing its mission. Few on the committee knew its mandate, while others did not want to raise the potential issues and expend the effort that raising such issues would require. Committee minutes give an idea of issues people do not raise and may not be allowed to raise, and they may indicate how much people are willing to risk.

- Consultants' proposals generally describe problems serious enough to solicit proposals, as well as proposed solutions to those problems.

However, often these proposals or the recommendations they generate are not implemented.

■ Performance reviews will provide information on who has performance problems, the nature of those problems, and steps managers have taken to correct the problems. Reviews are a good source to find hidden minefields.

The difference between learning your job and diagnosing your organization is important. Diagnosis implies data collection, analysis, making judgments and assessments, and making decisions; it implies organizational change. Learning your job may be a part of that, but resist the temptation to push toward organizational change prematurely. For now, take time to learn what your organization does before deciding what is wrong and what should be changed.

A third source of information about your job may be the company's annual and 10K report. While it probably will not address your department's mission, it will describe the company's strategic direction, lines of business, branches, successes and failures, and the philosophies and values of officers and board members. An important consideration is the prospective role your department is to play in the coming years. For example, if you are in a research department and the company depends on a steady flow of new products, it is chilling to realize that the Board of Directors has decided to downsize all departments, including research.

Other similar sources of information include industry journals, trade publications, industry and trade organizations, and meetings of peers from other companies. For example, after the Drug Information Association's annual conference entitled "Global Pharmaceutical Development," the vice president of research in every pharmaceutical company recognized the need to conduct that research concurrently in the major countries where the company intended to sell the drug.

Over the past several years, many professional meetings have dealt with "imaging." Knowledge of this state-of-the-art information was limited even in the literature. But the observant manager would have identified from these meetings an important new technology. The journals and conference proceedings in a particular field are replete with information that a manager can turn into plans and decisions.

There is a tremendous amount of such information available to the manager. In just one industry (for example, pharmaceuticals), there are dozens of professional organizations, such as the Pharmaceutical Manufacturer's Association, Drug Information Association, American College of Clinical Pharmacology, American Association of Clinical Pharmacology and Therapeutics, Associates of Clinical Pharmacology, Regulatory Affairs Professional Society, Association of Clinical Trials, and the Food and Drug Law Institute. Attending meetings is a good way to gain expert information, network resources, ideas, and contacts. You'll find out what others in your job and in your field know, and what they are doing.

A fourth source of information about your job is your predecessor's secretary. He or she will know the whereabouts of vast stores of information—files, reports, and forms—and will offer a ground-level view of how the work gets done, and how well. That secretary probably has access to more confidential information than anyone else in the organization. Consider hiring this individual for yourself, if feasible.

As you mine these sources of information about your job, don't tire of asking the same questions over and over. When you accept a position and you think you know the answers, ask the questions anyway. Knowing the right questions to ask and hearing the range of responses will help you gather valuable information about your job in an efficient manner.

Early Resentment: Piranhas and Icebergs

We have already mentioned those defeated candidates who may be resentful and ready to criticize. Don't underestimate their resentment. One newly named hotel manager had been promoted from director of food service, a surprising and substantial promotion. More than a few staff members felt that she was unqualified; some suggested it was an affirmative action promotion. While some opponents resigned within her first month on the job, others who stayed were more passive-aggressive, withholding information, not communicating, offering lukewarm support for management decisions, and passing on critical comments as if they were informational.

Some employees will resent an insider's promotion. They are more familiar with an insider's strengths and weaknesses and may not feel that he or she was the strongest candidate. Some will welcome an outsider's fresh perspective. If business is bad, your chances of a warm welcome are better, no matter where you come from. In one company, an experienced sales director's energy and direction was greeted with relief, even by the piranhas.

Piranhas are those who would rather attack and criticize than support and fit into the new organization. Their behavior may be overt or subtle. There will be histories you probably won't know—for example, that a veteran was bypassed by your predecessor and is still resentful, or that another's conflict with a manager makes him a suspicious subordinate. The management team may not work well together because of jealousy or disagreements. Secretaries or managers may have morale problems.

You may be associated with a disliked senior manager. Your promotion may have been the outcome of a power struggle, and your appointment has already alienated a power block. Managers associated with a losing candidate may be uncooperative.

Happily, most situations are mixed. Some people will be pleased, others disappointed, but most will give you the benefit of the doubt. There are usually only a few certified piranhas.

Along with piranhas, watch out for submerged icebergs, which may be more numerous and can appear unexpectedly. They evolve from the politics, morale, jealousies, inefficiencies, and problems of an organization. Many will be political.

The new hotel manager could not have known that the often inept director of sales had once been secretary to the corporate financial vice president, or that the director of housekeeping was another corporate officer's mother. Nor could she have known that the hotel's advertising director was a make-work assignment for a favored but basically inept corporate manager. She could not have known that the parent corporation, which was not in the hotel business, viewed the hotel as a dumping ground for people they wanted to get rid of but didn't have the heart to fire.

New managers are frequently blindsided by networks they didn't know existed. Something you say about someone, some department, or some issue gets passed to people you didn't necessarily intend to hear it. Offhand and often innocent remarks come back to haunt us. The successful manager learns not to talk critically about people and personalities, not to comment on issues of no direct concern to him or her, and to describe decisions and issues in objective, problem-solving terms ("the program did not achieve its objective") rather than in the subjective vocabulary of personalities and people ("Robert failed").

An organization's economics contains its own icebergs. Until you see your budget, how it was spent, and how it was managed and what you have to work with, you won't fully appreciate your position. Where do the sales come from? Who are the buyers? Who are the clients? Who uses what your department does? What is the market? What do they buy from you?

Becoming an Organizational Advocate

You must become an advocate for your organization's people, resources, and mission. Working with your boss, you have to fight for what your new organization needs to do the job.

Being an advocate also means communicating your enthusiasm and optimism to your organization. Being positive about the organization raises the morale, energy, and confidence of the entire group. High performance is often a self-fulfilling prophecy. You tend to get what you expect. If you expect a lot, you often get a lot.

The president of Grey Advertising, the United States' second largest agency in 1987, felt that the agency's ads lacked creativity. (Their staple ad showed two middle-aged women in the grocery store chatting about the softness of toilet tissue or collars.) Without making personnel changes or organizational shakeups, Grey's president simply started selling the creative side of the business—he said that the organization's heroes were its creative people. He challenged and pushed their creativity. He believed in them; after all, they had gotten Grey to the number 2 spot in the industry.

He believed they had the capability, gave them the challenge, and, most importantly, supported them when they took risks with their account managers, their artists, and their clients. He acted as if they were creative; and in the process, in the eyes of the industry and clients alike, Grey's ads did become more creative. By 1991 they had grown to $4 billion in billings, but more importantly had added glamour accounts such as Dannon yogurt, Gerber baby foods, and the $60 million Domino's pizza account. For Grey, creativity became a self-fulfilling prophecy.[1]

Organizational advocacy means promoting your organization with insiders and outsiders alike. Fight to see that your people are awarded training slots, conference attendance, memberships on important committees and task forces, and that they get promotions. You will get as you give. If you are generous in your support for your people, they in turn will be generous in their time and energy. Their successes will reflect positively on your grasp of one of a manager's most important tasks: the ability to identify, nurture, and promote talent.

Similarly, if you are generous in your praise for people in your organization, they in turn will be loyal and generous in their praise for you. Hand out credit freely. Mention names of people who contributed to special accomplishments; give credit for ideas and suggestions, even if the help was only incidental to something you did. Above all, do not take credit for what your subordinates did.

One manager talked as though he was at the vortex of every decision, solution, or accomplishment in his department. In describing department activities, he spoke as if they were his ideas, or that he had been highly instrumental in planning and achieving them even when he had been only peripherally associated with an activity or had been only the coordinator. Asked to coordinate and facilitate communications between four different corporate subcommittees but given a decision-making or leadership role on none of them, he nonetheless talked about the subcommittees as if he were directing all four of them and all four were reporting to him, much to the chagrin of the committee chairs. He name-dropped shamelessly and had a way of dramatizing conversations with big names as if they were asking him for advice:

"Yesterday, Gabe called me to his office and he said to me, 'Jim, things aren't going very well over there, are they?' 'No,' I agreed, 'they're not.' 'Well Jim,' Gabe said, 'What would you do to fix it?'" (Notice that the dramatizations are inevitably on an insider, first-name basis.)

Eventually, this manager's people and coworkers shared less and less information with him and increasingly distrusted him, because they felt he would either intrude where he was not wanted or would take credit for what was not his. An organizational advocate supports when support is needed, stays out of where he or she is not needed, and lets those who earned the success get the credit.

Finally, an organization advocate supports the organization's goals and mission in a way that people become committed to the organization's success. A street sweeper at Disneyworld was asked about the tedium of the job; he replied that he was an entertainer, not a street sweeper. An advocate promotes the mission, the people, and the vision of his or her organization.

Raising Expectations, Hopes, and Personal Empowerment

There is no lever more forceful in your transition process than the notion that all members of an organization are personally empowered within their scope of responsibility. To feel empowered is to feel a sense of control, a sense that you have the power to affect the work and the organization. Rather than feeling helpless and on the dependent end of a parent-child relationship, empowerment gives employees a sense that they can exert control. By personal empowerment, leaders engender a feeling that

- People are part of the management, and they can improve the organization.
- Good ideas will be implemented.
- Suggestions will be appreciated and rewarded, even if not accepted.
- People can be trusted with responsibility.
- People are respected for their ideas and judgment.

Personal empowerment assumes that each employee has the ability and the will to do the job as well as he or she knows how. When the manager removes barriers to effective performance and creates a supportive climate, most employees will improve their performance, and some will achieve new levels of results.

The goal of personal empowerment is a sense of commitment and alignment, a feeling that members of the organization have an investment in, and can affect, the success of the organization. This sense of "psychological ownership" engenders feelings of responsibility, concern, and interest among the employees. We invest energy, commitment, and concern in things for which we feel ownership, in our children, spouses, homes, careers, jobs, and ideas.

When employees feel that the organization is not theirs, that it is not a part of them, they feel only minimum responsibility and often do the job only as it is given to them. The problems and difficulties are someone else's—whoever owns the organization and therefore the responsibility. If employees think the organization is yours (as the manager), they will believe that the problems are yours, challenges are yours, failures are yours, and successes are yours. They will act as if "you folks had better do something about this."

Some managers want to be the person who will get the glory, has the power, takes the responsibility, has all the answers, and knows all the details. A mayor of a large U.S. city, who did very little work to empower his staff, rarely deliberated with his aides or consulted with other politicians, city council members, or ward leaders. When asked questions, he rarely deferred answers to the people on the job. He personally cut every ribbon and made every important public appearance and every important announcement. He gained a reputation for shooting from the hip (and being wrong and often contradictory). He was seen as aloof and isolated from both those who worked for him and those who supported him. He increasingly viewed the job as his job, his city, his responsibilities, and he saw the city's problems as his problems.

As his top people sensed the erosion of their authority, their sense of ownership eroded. Some left the administration, others marked time. Responsibility for making things happen increasingly fell to the mayor, and he became personally less effective as his organization got weaker. He ended up with all the problems on his desk, without the organization to take them on and manage them effectively.

Empowerment must be genuine. To tell people they have power and responsibility, and then not empower them with responsibility, dissolves morale, lowers your leadership credibility, and creates hostility and opposition.

A common form of false empowerment is found in many public schools. Principals and teachers endlessly exhort students to "take care of the school—it's your school," which is anything but the truth in a place where kids sit silently in rows, listening, and doing what they're told. They follow teachers' rules, the principal's rules, custodians' rules, coaches' rules, lunch room rules, attendance rules, and hallway aides' rules. Go up the up staircases, down the down staircases, and one way in the one-way hallways. Take notes, finish an assignment, read a book, exit when you're told, do what you're told, and succeed and fail by someone else's standards. At no time in our lives will we be so strongly a part of an institution in which we are so powerless—unless we go to prison.

Nor do schools belong to parents, as can be verified by any parent who ever complained about a rule or a teacher, or made a suggestion to improve the school. Parents who are active are often snowed by public-relations-minded administrators, who relegate parent participation to deciding what to buy with the PTA treasury. Parents who want to get actively involved are asked to be teachers' aides. But administrators retain meaningful decision making for themselves and, when necessary, share it with the teachers' union. Then they complain that neither parents nor students care about the school. Why should they? They know the school is not theirs, that they are visitors in someone else's institution.

The famous battles of the 1950s and 1960s between the United Auto Workers (UAW) and the auto industry are another example of workers' lack of empowerment. Traditionally in American labor, management gave orders, and labor followed the orders. Labor felt that if management wanted the responsibility and power, it could have all the problems, too. With labor uninvolved in quality and productivity, quality fell. As management's control tightened, unions carved out work rules and job classifications to limit management's power; as the unions won work rules, both management and union increasingly went by the book.

By the 1970s, Ford Motor Company officials admitted that their cars were so bad that in Detroit many managers were ashamed to admit they worked for Ford. At the same time, Americans began to snap up Japanese imports. Ford and GM lost record billions, Chrysler was saved by a government loan, and American Motors was bought by Renault.

Ford Motor Company undertook three broad responses to the crisis. First, with a product engineer at the helm, they determined to produce autos designed according to customer preferences. Second, Ford adopted more efficient manufacturing procedures, such as just-in-time inventory. Third, in adopting their "Quality is Job 1" campaign, Ford instituted Quality Circles to solicit employees' suggestions and foster union-management cooperation.

Managers were trained to listen to and work with line workers. Through more active participation in the decision process, labor felt greater responsibility for the quality of the product and the company's productivity. Quality improved, and worker productivity increased for the first time in many years. By 1986, Ford profits outstripped GM's for the first time in 50 years, and by 1987–1988 only Ford, among the four American automakers, increased sales over the previous year.[2] Through 1991, only Ford maintained market share, as GM and Chrysler lost market share to the Japanese.

Ford improved its product, but GM thought they had, too. No American company committed itself to automation, robots, and technology like GM. But Ford was preeminently committed to empowering employees. They brought employee input into the manufacturing process, depended on their input for improving the product, and shared responsibility and credit for the product.

As we saw in the example of public schools, paying lip service to empowerment without adequate follow-through demoralizes the organization. Real empowerment can make dramatic improvements in productivity, quality, and job satisfaction. During your first months on the job, you will have great opportunities to help your people be a real part of the action.

Empowering Relationships: A Self-Concept Approach to Managing People

Key Concepts

A manager's ability to empower is an important element in facilitating successful employee job performance. Successful leaders and researchers point to the supervisor or manager's attentiveness, expectations, encouragement, attitudes, and evaluations as primary forces in influencing an employee's productivity.

Think about the following example: "After working at an entry-level position for two years, I wanted to challenge myself. I wanted to go back to school while looking for a higher-level job at the company where I worked. So I went to my boss to discuss it. My fear was that he would discourage me because I had only worked at an entry-level position. But he surprised me and said he was hoping that I would decide to do this. What a relief and a great feeling." An individual's self-concept and feeling of personal power can be influenced by his or her boss's support.

Feelings of personal power are linked to how one approaches the job and to actual success at work. What and how we think about who we are, and how we see ourselves in the eyes of others, often triggers a self-fulfilling prophecy. If we see ourselves as being effective, responsible, creative, and productive on the job, we generally will be. The high-achieving individual almost always feels his or her supervisor's support and encouragement.

Whether or not we perceive ourselves as high or low performers often depends on how we interpret reactions from important people in our work lives. Key to these perceptions are the behaviors and expectancies of our boss. These messages can be verbal or nonverbal, overt or subtle, strong or weak, supportive or destructive, but they are powerful. People will begin to sense how you feel about them in the first minute of your first meeting with them. Their emotional barometers will be fine-tuned, looking for clues about how you perceive them. They will be carefully assessing themselves through your communication with them.

Communication as an Empowering Experience

The process of empowering people to be productive depends on clear communication. Such communication can result in a subordinate feeling motivated to succeed or, conversely, in a feeling of apathy, anger, or depression. An empowering interaction between boss and employee can be potent. You can determine positive or negative self-fulfilling prophecies of those who work for you that will strongly affect job performance.

In a moment of reflection, a manager said, "My supervisor saw things in me that I didn't even see in myself. She kept challenging me with a variety of tasks and projects and truly expected that I would handle them well. She provided me with support when I needed it, and at other times left me alone to work. She seemed not at all surprised when I successfully met the challenges. Funny, it reminded me of when I was a kid and a neighbor asked if he could pay me to work on his lawn because I was doing such a good job on mine. I did an even better job on his."

How an Empowering Leader Views Others

A boss's style tends to be perceived as either personally empowering or personally diminishing. The impact that the empowering leader's behavior has on employees is great whether it is verbal or nonverbal, intended or not intended. People's needs to feel able, valuable, and responsible can have dramatic implications in the way they approach and perform their work. The manager may not be aware of the negative impact of skewed glances or "funny" putdowns, but nonetheless they have a very real effect. The empowering supervisor goes out of the way to challenge, coach, support, and reward.

There are psychological reasons for empowering approaches and the timing of your initial interactions with people. People's two basic needs are to feel worthwhile and to feel respected. People who work for empowering leaders typically describe themselves as feeling more able, valuable, and responsible. They feel that way because they are treated that way. By creating the right conditions, empowering others to succeed will act as a strong motivator for nine out of ten workers.

Empowering leaders have flexible styles. They adapt their approach to people's needs and to the situation. The empowering leader creates the best possible conditions for performance and career development. The message sounds like this: "I believe in you, your judgment, capabilities, and your potential. I expect you to be successful. I am here to aid you, to act as a catalyst for your success. My job is to create the conditions for your success; your job is to get it done. We will work on it together."

The psychological dynamics of this approach are both predictable and potent. It creates the Pygmalion effect, the self-fulfilling prophecy of success. Empowering leadership touches the core of our humanity, our self-concept. Nothing affects our behavior, our performance, and the achievement of our potential more than this vision of who we are.

To appreciate the potency of empowering leadership, you must understand the following principle: How we see ourselves on the job depends on how we interpret messages (verbal and nonverbal) from key individuals in our professional environment. One of these key people is our supervisor or manager. This is especially true as newly appointed managers assume their responsibilities. In new situations, people are often wary and inquisitive. Most want to look for opportunity and hope for a bright future. During your first few months, your empowering style can have an early and positive effect on an entire organization through your attitude, direct discussion, and behaviors.

Examples of Empowering and Diminishing Behaviors

There is a wide range of leadership behaviors that empower or diminish people and their performance.

Empowering	Diminishing
Shows approval	Resorts to name calling
Shows concern and empathy	Uses putdown statements
Shows interest	Embarrasses people
Facilitates learning	Has a sink-or-swim attitude
Reinforces	Blames; tends to look for the negative first
Respects	Gossips about shortcomings
Communicates and listens	Tells, directs
Sees the small and big picture	Picks on details
Trusts; tends to see the good as well as bad	Creates dependent relationships; primarily sees mistakes
Smiles	Is noncommittal; frowns
Is seen as supportive	Is seen as critical
Is assertive	Is aggressive
Creates cooperative and independent relationships	Creates competition and dependency
In conflict situations is balanced, sees others' viewpoints, and sees mutual solutions	Focuses on problems, not solutions
Usually uses an "I win, you win" style	In conflict looks for "I win, you lose" solutions

Creating the Conditions for Optimal Performance

Think of yourself as a catalyst striving for the best "chemistry" between you, your employees, and your work environment. Just as a farmer tends the soil, the empowering boss nurtures his or her people. There are six critical elements that will help you build a positive self-fulfilling prophecy that results in high performance:

1. Challenge and "stretch" people.
2. Give people choice in how to get the job done.
3. Show respect for others.
4. Relate to people in a mutually supportive way.
5. Practice self-monitoring.
6. Build on successful experiences.

Challenge.   From studies examining high-performing employees, we know that people tend to perform best when they need to "stretch" in their jobs. This usually means that people should be pushed (or preferably push themselves) to work just beyond their own view of what is comfortable. "Just out of reach, but not out of sight," is an excellent rule of thumb. Managers and employees should agree to performance and achievement standards that provide stretch and that enhance high-level performance. Here again, the self-fulfilling prophecy comes into play. People with low expectations usually work at that level. High expectations tend to result in high performance. Help your people set goals that will help them stretch.

Choice in How to Get the Job Done.   We tend to perform best when we are allowed to develop our own best way to meet established standards and expectations. We are energized when we bring our own knowledge, creativity, and resources to the solution of a problem. When General Schwartzkopf of Operation Desert Storm decided on a flanking movement to defeat Sadam Hussein, he required each division commander to develop the specific strategy for his division within the context of the larger plan. Auto workers in the door assembly section must feel that they have some control over the work flow, efficiency, and quality. Responsibility without control engenders resentment and defeat.

Respect.   People with healthy self-concepts generally feel that they are respected by their peers and managers alike. Agreement or disagreement—even conflict—especially with new bosses, subsides when people feel that their opinions and ideas are respected. Organizations need exchange of ideas. Better ideas are often forged from the white heat of disagreement. When we feel a foundation of mutual respect and support, we perform more confidently and use all our resources.

Mutually Supportive Relations. Empathy, the ability to relate to another's feelings and perceptions, is essential to empowerment. For years, psychologists have shown that the ability to "put ourselves in the shoes of the other" and understand another person's frame of reference is a critical factor in helping that person achieve his or her potential. Managers need to understand and respect the perspective of their employees, and employees need to understand and respect the perspective of the manager. There is no better time to begin working on your relationships than your first day and throughout your first year. Mutual respect is based on mutual understanding of needs and demands.

Self-Monitoring. Employees need feedback on how well they are doing, and supervisors need information on what employees are doing. Monitoring and feedback are essential in helping employees keep track of how well they are meeting the challenge. Employee choice in getting the work done requires self-monitoring and personal responsibility for quality and output. Periodic checks on progress, process, and quality, as well as coaching with reassessment and adjustment of work goals, help employees achieve their quality and quantity goals. Many managers also encourage peer monitoring, usually in team meetings where team members discuss goals and achievements and their contribution to the team's accomplishments. This approach is popular in self-directed teams.

Success Experiences. Success begets success! People who use their abilities in challenging situations are more consistently successful. They learn to use their capabilities, develop new skills and abilities, and learn what is required for success. Empowering leaders offer challenges which build on their people's successes and increase the chances for top performance under trying circumstances.

Empowering leaders help their people to be successful. They set up an environment that encourages a positive self-concept and a feeling that we are fulfilling constructive and valuable goals.

We have identified six things leaders can do to help ensure high employee performance. As a new manager, you have an excellent opportunity to affect your people in ways that can truly make a difference on the job. The process of "buying in" versus "dropping out" begins in the first days following your appointment. Employees often make the decision to be part of the solution rather than part of the problem within weeks, certainly a few months, of your arrival. Employees who feel empowered become positive and creatively committed to the organization's success.

Quick Reminders to Keep You on Track

- As you assume your new position and begin to meet people, you make a first impression only one time! Reach out, be personable, and make contact with everyone in your new function as only you can.

- As you begin your new management job, you'll frequently run into a wide range of expectations, including hope, resentment, confusion, and concern.

- There are six major steps to keep in mind as you enter your new management job and organization:

    1. Make a good first impression during your first meetings with your new staff. Immediately begin to connect with people on a personal level and build support.

        Expect a wide variety of feelings regarding your appointment, ranging from optimism and relief to concern, disappointment, resentment, and confusion.
        Initially, you will likely have a fragile base of influence and power that will need to be strengthened through credible work and positive relationships.
        Hold an initial, brief, but very upbeat meeting with your new organization.
        Spend a lot of one-on-one time with people.
        Begin to seed the idea that you will be asking people to help in an "organizational health check" program.
        Try to develop an inclusionary management style.
        Be careful of your vocabulary—emphasize *we*'s and *our*'s in your language.
        Meet individually with the unsuccessful candidates for your position if they are in your new function, and extend an invitation to fully utilize their skills and experience.
        You should plan to exit your previous position effectively. If possible, help with the transition of your replacement. This may go on simultaneously with your transition into your new job.

    2. Establish ground rules and communication with your boss about the transition process.

        Make sure you both understand and agree to the process and the timetable.
        Mutually establish these ground rules.

3. You need to learn your job.

   Use your predecessor and key staff as major sources of information.
   Review documents, files, organization charts, and many other
      available sources of information.
   Ask many people a wide variety of questions. Do perception checks.

4. Become an organizational advocate.

   Objectively promoting your organization, its people, and its re-
      sources with insiders and outsiders alike.

5. Accept the challenge of raising expectations, hopes, and personal
   empowerment of your people.

6. Build empowering relationships. Utilize a self-concept approach
   to managing people.

   Certain specific communication patterns and behaviors create the
      conditions for optimal employee performance. These build and
      strengthen employees' confidence and self-concept on the job.

Summary of Major Responsibilities (Chap. 2)

First Year by Month*

	Preappoint-ment	1	2	3	4	5	6	7	8	9	10	11	12

Moving in: Establishing Yourself in Your New Assignment
- Entering the Organization

*Times are approximate.

Legend
——— Primary period of emphasis
– – – Active but not a period of emphasis

Your Personal Plan of Action for Moving In:
Establishing Yourself in Your New Assignment—Entering the Organization (Chap. 2)

Activity	Suggested Timeframe	Perceived Barriers	Available Resources	Your Projected Timeframe	Completed (✓)

• Announcement of your appointment by your manager
• First meeting(s) with your staff
  — Positive first impressions
  — From "I" to "we" and "our"
  — Meeting with unsuccessful candidates
  — Personally connecting with people
• Exiting gracefully
	As soon after the decision to hire you as possible. Begins with day 1.				

• If appropriate, a meeting with your previous department	As soon after your appointment is announced on the first or second day.				
• Establishing and reviewing ground rules/communication with your boss about the transition (See Chap. 3 for details.)	Primarily pre-appointment through month 4.				

• If possible, learning as much about your job as possible from your predecessor and staff
  — Organization chart
  — Mission, goals, objectives
  — His/her assessment of organizational capabilities, achievements, strengths, and weaknesses
  — Assessment of department personnel
  — Identify organization's most pressing needs
  — Review of budget
  — Review of files
  — Understanding major job responsibilities of predecessor and staff
  — Understanding major committees
  — Understanding major dangers (obvious and hidden)
	Begins on day 1 with an emphasis on weeks 1 through 4.				

Activity	Suggested Timeframe	Perceived Barriers	Available Resources	Your Projected Timeframe	Completed (✓)
• Obtaining other sources of information — Review of many types of documents (e.g., departmental, corporate, consultant reports, minutes, industry journals.)	If possible, before the announcement of your appointment with an emphasis through months 1 and 2.				
• Discussions with predecessor's secretary	Beginning before the announcement of your appointment if possible.				
• Dealing with early resentment	Beginning with day 1 and then ongoing.				
• Becoming an organizational advocate	Beginning with day 1 and then ongoing.				
• Beginning to raise expectations, hopes, and personal empowerment (e.g., empowering vs. diminishing behaviors, creating conditions for optimal performance): — Challenge — Choice in how to get the job done — Respect — Effectively relating to employees — Encouraging employees to monitor themselves — Building successful experiences	Beginning with day 1 and then ongoing.				

41

3

Entering Your Boss's World

*With assertiveness training he confronted his
boss in a manner far from benign and
became the most assertive claimant on the
unemployment line.*

SOURCE UNKNOWN

An important aspect of establishing yourself is working effectively
with your new boss. You will need to:

- Clearly understand why you were hired.

- Do a perception check with your boss as you both make sure
  you agree on what your job is and what is expected of you.

- Act in the best interests of your boss and help him/her be successful.

- Understand the demands and expectations that others have of
  your boss.

In this chapter, there is useful information about:

- Why Were You Hired?

- Clarifying Your Role and Expectations: A Perception Check
  with Your Boss

- "Contracting" with Your Boss
- Helping Your Boss Be a "Star"
- Understanding Your Boss's Responsibilities and Preferences

In Chap. 2 we briefly examined the importance of establishing ground rules and clear communication with your boss regarding your transition strategy. This chapter pursues that relationship in greater detail.

Why Were You Hired?

In the heady moments surrounding your promotion, you'll feel proud of what you've achieved. It was the result of your hard work, ability, and commitment. You have a right to feel great satisfaction. But before you get too carried away, stop to think about the primary reason why you are where you are—your boss's need to have someone to count on for a major area of responsibility. When you succeed, your boss succeeds. Your selection and ability to perform is a direct reflection on your boss.

That you were hired to help someone else perform better means that you do not have a free hand to do and say as you wish. Rather, your decisions must fit into your boss's plans, goals, and style. You were hired to help your boss meet his or her goals.

William was hired to direct the mass transit authority in a large U.S. city. He pursued the job aggressively. He and his wife had attended school in that city and had personal ties to the region. He was the successful managing director of the mass transit authority in another large city, he was well qualified and experienced, and he seemed to be the ideal candidate for the job.

But within a week on the job he was embroiled in controversy. Within a month, the head of the Authority asked for William's resignation. The suburban representatives on the Authority voted "No Confidence." The Democratic big-city mayor and governor urged him to stay, and the Republican suburban head of the Authority urged him to resign. What happened? Certainly, party politics played a role, but they developed primarily after the situation had deteriorated. The opposing political factions on the Authority board—Democratic and largely urban, Republican and largely suburban—were quick to take sides and seize the political advantage. But what events triggered the crises?

During his first day on the job, William announced on television that fares were too high and he would like to reduce them. Within a week he had completely reversed himself, saying that finances were in terrible shape (which the Authority's chairman had been telling the public all along) and that he may have to seek a fare hike. That same week, he publicly disagreed with the chairman about resources, a statement that led to the chairman's first and then rapid subsequent public criticisms. In turn, William responded in public. The ensuing discourse, including the conditions and pricetag for a proposed contract buyout, were conducted for others to hear, usually reported by an enchanted media.

Of course, a number of mistakes were made. First, William was too public before he had taken time to assess the situation. In his premature diagnosis of the problems and choice of solutions, he caught himself in contradictions.

Second, as we will see in a later chapter, William acted before he had formed a leadership team that supported him. Essentially, when he made his statements he was speaking for himself, not for his leadership team. He had formed no management consensus. He had no support, no one to help him shape and defend his statements within his organization, with the board, and with the public.

Third (and more to the point of this chapter), William violated a cardinal rule of transitions: *He did not understand the reasons for which he was hired.* From his boss's point of view, several applicants could have done a good technical job. William was hired because his boss, the chairperson of the Authority's board, felt that William would do a good job for *him.* In doing a good job, William would make the Authority successful and make his boss appear more professional, capable, and effective. William did not adequately appreciate that doing a good job was linked to the mutual self-interest of both William and his boss, and that both wanted to be effective.

If you have any doubt about the importance of mutual self-interest, it should be put to rest when you consider what happens when it is destroyed. When it appeared that William was not serving his boss's self-interest, the situation deteriorated rapidly. Each side lost confidence in the other, and both suffered. The public increasingly perceived that the Authority was not well led and was riddled with politics. Similarly, the Authority's reputation for being well managed suffered. William seemed ineffective. Democratic politicians called for the chairman's resignation; the area's major newspaper editorialized about the politicizing of the Authority's management; one editorial called the Authority "the laughing stock of the nation." The Chamber of Commerce publicly said that the Authority's ability to manage itself was in question. How different would these perceptions have been had the rift not occurred, had William abided by a primary law of successful transition and served his boss's self-interest while determining how to perform well in his job.

Clarifying Your Role and Expectations: A Perception Check with Your Boss

Given the differing sets of expectations for you, things can become very confusing. Your own expectations can be both your greatest source of strength and your greatest problem. You should have conducted careful, two-way discussions with your boss before you were hired so you understand his or her expectations.

Ted felt he had a clear reading of his mission. His boss, who was Director of Training, wanted new programs, "the ones written about in the training journals," including some internal consulting, organizational diagnosis, and executive team building. That's what Ted thought he was told, and soon after he was hired he was well on his way. He conducted needs assessments with first-line supervisors and mid-managers, and organized problem-solving teams. He instituted mid- and upper-level management development programs, planned and facilitated a retreat for top management, and developed a succession plan. He was confidently moving ahead with what he had been told to do, and he thought that he was regularly staying in touch with and tuned into his boss. He was fired after about six months by a boss who felt that Ted was too pushy, had disrupted the organization, and upset the people he was supposed to help.

In getting the programs started, Ted had become more aggressive and prominent than his boss had anticipated. Ted was becoming a star. Even worse, he took credit for accomplishments. He acted as spokesperson and leader for his programs. Few of the figurehead or spokesperson roles were given to his boss, and his boss got little of the credit for the new programs. In brief, Ted had not met an important part of his boss's expectations: that his boss's standing would be enhanced by Ted's activities. Rather, Ted was building his own reputation and role, and little of the activity was benefiting his boss. In making himself look good, Ted had failed to make his boss look good and, in fact, was viewed as a threat.

Another common difficulty is a boss who hires you to implement his or her solutions rather than solve a problem. You cannot be sure the solution addresses the problem, or even that there is a problem.

Sally, an internal consultant, was asked to plan a one-day problem-solving conference in which the department would come together for the day to identify solutions for some organizational problems. Her boss had decided that a workshop was the best way to identify the organization's problems and identify solutions. Sally spent three days interviewing people, identifying the critical problems, and planning the workshop. But in a one-day workshop, the group of 35 did not get beyond defining the problem or identifying possible solutions. Her boss, disappointed with the group's progress, blamed her. In retrospect, Sally doubted all along that the goal could be accomplished in one day, and she wished she had used better approaches. She should have re-thought the solution to the problem instead of accepting her boss's solution at face value.

Diane is the marketing director for a financial organization in a large city. Her manager contracted with an advertising firm to design the annual promotional campaign. The agency designed a $385,000 program that included image ads in a local business magazine, the local mass audience magazine, the daily newspaper, and some mailings. Fortunately, the large budget gave both Diane and her boss pause to reanalyze the problem. When they did, they came up with a different solution, including more direct sales, a larger sales force, and more face-to-face contact with qualified customers. The ad campaign was scrapped, and the new program worked, for about one-fourth of the cost. Diane was lucky—the shock of the large budget gave her and her boss cause to refocus on the problem. But even while changing direction, Diane was careful not to outdistance her boss or to make her boss' original decision seem like a bad one.

Pay attention to your boss's expectations about the role you will play and what you will accomplish. But don't assume that you have his or her mandate to do what you're doing. Nor should you assume that what you are handed is exactly what you have to do without discussion and negotiation.

Another of your boss's expectations regards the pace of your work. You may feel lots of pressure to make something happen, to be decisive. As part of your hiring discussions, you should have agreed on how your transition will progress, with a rough timeline. In the continuing discussions, you need to remind your boss of those agreements and to keep your commitment about regularly discussing your progress. Reiterate that the first major part of the transition will take about six months, that your boss should not expect to see changes of any consequence for at least one to three months, and that your completed diagnosis is going to precede any big decisions. Even though you negotiated those conditions with your boss when you were hired, you need continually to provide updates on that plan, with reminders that you are sticking to it.

Review what stage of the plan you are at. Review your progress and the steps you have taken, and indicate your next steps. Be sure your boss is fully briefed and has the chance to voice and work through any reservations or concerns about your progress. Don't assume that just because your boss hasn't said anything, he or she isn't interested or worried. Keep your boss informed and up to date. Your boss's silence is often an expression of concern. Suffered quietly, this can explode on you with surprising force. Be aware that your boss is under pressure, just as you are. Your boss's supervisor, and other influentials, expect that when your boss hired you, he or she hired the right person.

Other sources of expectations can also make you doubt yourself. Those who work for you will have their own expectations that you will be decisive, "hands on" or "hands off," innovative, experimental, cautious, or participatory. Some will feel that they know what the organization needs, and in both subtle and direct ways make these needs known to you. You'll feel the pressure.

You may feel expectations from many other sources, including upper management, your peers in other departments, the department's informal leadership, customers, consultants and contractors with whom you have contracts, friends, even your spouse. All their expectations will affect how you approach the job and the pace of the transition. If your spouse is anxious about your success, you could begin to resent the trip home to face the same inquiries, the same disappointment, the same impatient (or exasperated) tone of voice, the same advice about being more decisive. You may have the same feelings from friends. You will feel people's expectations and pressure from many directions at once.

That is why you need a transitional plan. When you are secure in the knowledge that you are on schedule, moving ahead, and the goal is in sight, you will be able to parry the pressures by placing expectations in context. You will feel more secure knowing that at the appropriate time, expectations, including your own, will be met.

"Contracting" with Your Boss

A "contract," the specific agreements with your boss governing the transition, is very important. Even if it is not a written, signed document between you, your contract is a clear understanding of the terms of your transition into the job.

The explicit contract or agreement between you and your boss should support an evolving transition process. The contract should include the following points:

- That you will describe each step in the process and the milestones to your boss, preferably in writing; that you and your boss will agree on the schedule and the milestones.

- That you will update your boss regularly on where you are in the process, including what you have accomplished, what you have learned, and your next steps in the process.

- That before the next steps are undertaken, you will review the process with your boss and listen to and, whenever possible, implement his or

her advice. Advice you do not implement you will discuss with your
boss candidly.

- That communications between you and your boss, especially disagreements, will remain private and privileged, between the two of you.
- That your boss will not pressure you to make premature changes to
  the transition plan, and that he or she will allow you to stay on the
  schedule you negotiated together.

Decide how success will be defined, first in terms of process and then
as measurable results. Early success should be defined by how well you
conceive, organize, and manage the transition process, and it should include at least the following:

- The effectiveness with which you develop a leadership and management team to make policy decisions and help manage the diagnosis
- The success with which your leadership team identifies and confronts
  the organization's problems
- The effectiveness with which you schedule the organizational diagnosis, keep it on schedule, and troubleshoot
- The effectiveness with which you build and maintain your organization's support for the diagnosis, and communicate the process so it is
  understandable to the organization, including parts outside your
  immediate functional area
- The success with which you delegate and manage the problem-solving process, implement changes, and maintain the things that do not
  need fixing
- The effectiveness with which you communicate the process and your
  decisions with your superiors, and communicate decisions to your
  peers in departments affected by any changes

The bottom line is the effect of the decisions you make and implement on organizational productivity and effectiveness—in short, the
real results. The bottom line depends on your situation and may include
goals such as increased profitability, more empowering leadership from
your top managers, higher morale among those asked to participate in
decisions, better work flow as bottlenecks and inefficiencies are eliminated, and/or better quality or service as suggestions are implemented.
It may be a change in the financial picture, a measure of productivity, a
measure of staff morale or stability, or a change in the way work gets
done.

Define the bottom line with your boss. What is his or her measure of your success? Put it in writing, in as measurable or observable terms as possible. Make sure you know and have both agreed on these goals.

Helping Your Boss Be a "Star"

To discuss why you were hired is to discuss how to help your boss be a star. There is little difference between the two. A primary goal of your promotion or appointment is to make sure your boss looks good. When William, head of the transit authority, inadvertently made his boss look bad, he diminished his own, his boss's, and ultimately his agency's real and perceived effectiveness.

Lu, on the other hand was much more careful. She carefully negotiated with Marsha (her boss) the scope of her authority and the scope of decision making she would have. Even though she negotiated the power to make key decisions, she discussed each decision with Marsha before it was implemented. When Marsha seemed ambivalent, Lu backed off making the decision until they had discussed it more and Marsha seemed more positive. They began to work as a team, Lu discussing organizational problems and needed changes with Marsha, Marsha delegating to Lu many of the decisions agreed on. Thus, the first rule Lu followed was to discuss organizational issues with her boss and to agree on the decisions. The second was to follow through on those decisions her boss supported and to back off or continue to "sell" where Marsha seemed unsure or ambivalent.

The third rule Lu followed was to keep disagreements with her boss private. As far as the rest of the organization was concerned, Lu and Marsha understood each other and were a perfectly synchronized team. This made the organization's top management seem well oiled and well organized, and it enhanced the organization's managerial reputation.

The least-known element of their partnership was that Lu made sure that Marsha was the star. Even though Lu had written most of the business plan, Marsha presented it to the Board of Directors. When sales dramatically increased, Lu deflected much of the credit to Marsha, even though Marsha and the management team attributed much of the credit for the sales increases to Lu's marketing efforts. When a national magazine contacted Lu for a feature about women managers, she suggested they do the piece on Marsha instead.

In the process, Marsha appreciated Lu's essential contribution toward her success. Within the executive team, Marsha publicly credited Lu for helping with the company's turnaround and promoted her to group head. But as far as the Board of Directors and the outside world was concerned, Marsha was and is the star. Lu's loyalty enhanced both her own and her boss's careers.

Understanding Your Boss's Responsibilities and Preferences

Your boss can't always give you what you want. Monies you need may be committed for other purposes; people you don't want may be politically connected; capital improvements you want to make may be slated for other departments. The needed purchasing program may only be acquired in the next fiscal year, and you have to wait your turn.

Nonetheless, you can help your boss to help you. As you help make your boss a star, he or she should also help you succeed. But your boss's attention will be pulled in many directions. Thus, for your boss to help you, you may have to ask.

First, be part of your boss's "mental in-basket." Have a set time every week when you meet. Choose a time that's relatively unpressured, like early morning for coffee, Friday afternoon, or maybe even after 5:00, when much of the work force has gone home and you both are beginning to unwind. Your boss may be more relaxed and in a frame of mind to listen and think with you. It is critical that you get your boss's dedicated time.

Many a transition has gone sour because, in the absence of regular communication, the new manager thought he had a mandate, thought he was doing what he had been hired to do, and thought his boss was pleased with what was happening.

Nancy is an independent, self-reliant person. She was a field representative for the home office, a job that afforded her a great deal of personal independence and authority. She liked making her own decisions, doing things her own way. When she represented the company in the field, she was generally the final authority. Even though her independence could make her difficult to work with, she was quite effective. The field force generally felt that she made things better for them.

However, Nancy's effectiveness in-house was tempered by her difficulty in being a team player. She felt that she was competent and should be allowed to do her job as she felt best, and she resented her boss's oversight. Accordingly, she often made decisions without checking them out; she sent reports, directions, and analyses that her boss had not reviewed; she made commitments her boss had not approved; and at one point she used her boss's initials on a proposal that they had discussed in concept but that he had not seen. Her boss learned about too many decisions after the fact, and saw reports after they had been sent and analyses after they were bound.

At heart, Nancy may have felt that she was more competent than her boss. Certainly her expressed need was to "hire me to do the job and I'll do it," a style in contrast to her boss's. He had worked hard to develop the product line, worked hard to develop the clients, and was very fastidious about what was done with clients. He expected to review materials before they were sent to clients and expected to be told of client decisions before the fact. In defending her need for authority, Nancy avoided interactions with her boss because she felt they might lead to control, a short-term strategy that was to defeat her in the long run. The promotion to department head went to someone less experienced and younger, but who the boss felt would work better with the clients and keep him better informed.

Nancy did not adequately discern the limits of her authority. She did not appreciate that her boss felt proprietary about the work in the department, and that Nancy's decisions and performance directly affected her boss—the amount of business, the clients he had developed, and the product lines he had developed. She did not adequately appreciate that authority is delegated by one's superior and that her performance directly affected her boss's performance.

You need to work *through* your boss. Meet regularly. Keep the meetings brief and to the point. Make sure you come prepared, with an agenda. List the milestones achieved, things you are working on, pending decisions and choices, and problems and recommendations. Solicit your boss's feedback and advice, and really listen. Don't agree and then not follow through. Involve your boss, especially in the parts of your job that will make him or her shine or would otherwise be areas of vulnerability.

Determine to build your career through your boss. When appropriate, ask to be included at lunch with his or her peers or with influential others. Ask your boss to nominate you for corporate committees or for special assignments and task forces where you can gain some corporate visibility. Joe built his reputation in the company through his boss, Mattie. Mattie had him appointed to important corporate committees, important accounts, important products, and significant new product development efforts. Mattie always felt she could rely on Joe to represent her interests, to keep her informed, to follow her counsel. But as Joe matured, developed his own network and his own corporate constituency, he became less and less part of Mattie's "in-basket" and depended less on Mattie for help and direction. When Joe finally took an independent stand on an important policy issue that was directly contradictory to Mattie's, the relationship was damaged and Mattie's support receded. Joe now had to be strong enough to stand on his own, as

Mattie's peer, or to seek a new employer. He was no longer a part of Mattie's world, and that part of his career had ended. Within a few months Joe had joined a competitor. As long as you are dependent on your boss, you must stay close to his or her thinking. When you show independence, you had better be prepared to stand on your own.

In this chapter, we stressed the importance of working well with your boss and helping your boss be a success. Pay attention to these points throughout your first year, especially in the first two months after you begin your new position. It is then that you have the opportunity to start off smoothly and build the impression of your value to the organization. In Chap. 4 we turn our attention to one of the first elements necessary for having an impact on the organization—beginning to craft your vision and direction.

Quick Reminders to Keep You on Track

- Most likely, the primary reason you were promoted was your boss's need to have someone to count on for a major area of responsibility. When you succeed, your boss succeeds.

- You won't be completely free to do as you wish; your decisions must fit into your boss's plans, goals, and style.

- Take time to assess each situation and evaluate your choice of solutions. A premature assessment or diagnosis of your situation may cause you to contradict yourself later, or may result in embarrassment to you and your boss.

- Recall the example of William, the newly appointed director of a large transit authority. Your self-interest is linked to your boss's self-interest. Remember the reason you were hired.

- In your careful, two-way discussions with your boss before you were hired, you should have clarified your role and your boss's expectations of you. Understanding your role is critical to your success.

- Even though you think you understand your boss's expectations in general, don't assume that you have his/her mandate to take a particular action.

- Remember that you and your boss agreed about the pace of your work during your transition period. Provide your boss with updates on your progress as a reminder that you are achieving your mutually agreed upon goals.

- Make sure you have defined the "bottom line" with your boss. What is his/her measure of success?

- As we saw in one example, Lu helped Marsha be a star by discussing organizational issues with her and agreeing on decisions, by following through on the decisions that her boss supported and "reselling" those of which her boss was unsure, and by keeping disagreements with her boss private.

- You can help your boss help you by being a part of your boss's mental in-basket, meeting regularly, and soliciting your boss's feedback and paying attention to it.

- Determine to build your career through your boss. Always remember why you were hired.

Summary of Major Responsibilities—Year 1 (Chap. 3)

First Year by Month*

	Preappoint-ment	1	2	3	4	5	6	7	8	9	10	11	12

Moving in: Establishing Yourself in Your New Assignment
- Entering the Organization
- Entering Your Boss's World

*Times are approximate.

Legend
— Primary period of emphasis
--- Active but not a period of emphasis

Your Personal Plan of Action for Entering Your Boss's World (Chap. 3)

Activity	Suggested Timeframe	Perceived Barriers	Available Resources	Your Projected Timeframe	Completed (✓)
• Understanding why you were hired	Begins during the selection process and confirmed during months 1 and 2.				
• Clarifying your role and expectations—a perception check with your boss	Begins during the selection process and confirmed during months 1 and 2.				
• "Contracting" with your boss	Begins during the selection process and confirmed during months 1 and 2.				
• Helping your boss be a star	Begins during the selection process and ongoing thereafter.				

55

PART 2

Achieving an Impact on the Organization

4

Beginning to Craft Your Vision and Direction

If you have an important point to make, don't try to be subtle or clever. Use a pile driver. Hit the point once. Then come back and hit it again. Then hit it a third time—a tremendous whack.

WINSTON CHURCHILL

Creating a "fire in your belly" mental picture of what your organization is capable of becoming is essential for you and your people. You will need to:

- Understand and help others understand the concept of vision.
- Develop your vision of the organization.
- Skillfully involve others in either helping you create the organization's vision and/or carrying it out.
- Be able to communicate enthusiastically your vision and its major points.
- Become a role model of your vision through consistent and reinforcing actions.

In this chapter, there is useful information about:

- The Concept of Organizational Vision
- Seeding Your Vision in Your Organization
- The Importance of the Group's Quest for Vision
- Key Planks in Your Platform
- Acting Consistently: Developing Good Public Relations for Your Positions
- Questions to Consider

Caterpillars and Spotlights: The Concept of Organizational Vision

Processionary Caterpillars feed upon pine needles. They move through the trees in long procession, one leading and the others following—each with his eyes half closed and his head snugly fitted against the rear extremity of his predecessor.

Jean-Henri Fabre, the great French naturalist, patiently experimenting with a group of the caterpillars, finally enticed them to the rim of a large flower pot, where he succeeded in getting the first one connected up with the last one, thus forming a complete circle, which started moving around in a procession which had neither beginning nor end.

The naturalist expected that after a while they would catch on to the joke, get tired of their useless march, and start off in some new direction. But not so.

Through sheer force of habit, the living, creeping circle kept moving around the rim of the pot—around and around, keeping the same relentless pace for seven days and seven nights—and would doubtlessly have continued longer had it not been for sheer exhaustion and ultimate starvation.

Incidentally, an ample supply of food was close at hand and plainly visible, but it was outside the range of the circle so they continued along the beaten path.

They were following instinct ... habit ... custom ... tradition ... past experience ... "standard practice" ... or whatever you may choose to call it, but they were following blindly.

They mistook activity for accomplishment. They meant well, but they got no place.[1]

Like processionary caterpillars, many organizations seem to go in circles; they lack purpose, meaning, and a true sense of their mission and

future. These organizations rarely innovate and are almost always follow-
ers in their industries.

The caterpillar analogy can help us understand aspects of individual
behavior at work, too. Under conditions where direction, common work
values, goals, and accountability are lacking, employees generally will do
what they must to get by. A type of "group think" characterized by a "we
versus they" and "we've always done it that way" mediocrity takes over.
Like processionary caterpillars, habit and standard practice becomes a
way of life. Energy is low, and creativity and cooperation are lacking.

Vision results when people squint their eyes to look outside themselves, put aside individual interests, and capture what they want their
organization to achieve and be like. An organizational vision should
make a real difference. When committed leadership with a strong vision
of the future makes itself felt, great things can begin to happen. People
quickly develop a clear understanding of what is most important to the
organization. Commitment to vision is an industrial-strength fervor to
act on the core values of the organization.

A vision works like spotlights on a runway. It points in a direction and
can guide people to a desired endpoint. Through word and deed,
strong leaders model what is important, obtain needed resources, hold
people accountable, and recognize people frequently and reward them
appropriately. Importantly, they enlist the help and support of employees at all levels in the organization. Employees realize that they are part
of the action; that what is good for the organization can be good for
them as well.

Those working with visionary leaders begin to share a similar notion
of where the organization is heading and what success means for themselves and others. They tie their success to that of the organization.
While individual responsibilities and accountabilities exist, the language of work becomes spiced with the words *we* and *our* as described in
Chap. 2. People begin to "own" problems and work together for excellent solutions.

Most importantly, employees feel that what they do matters and that
their efforts contribute to something worthwhile and valuable. They
feel that they can affect the course of events and take responsibility to
see that the right things happen. Employees find that they enjoy sharing
in a coordinated, aligned work effort with common purpose. The feeling is similar to an orchestra playing in beautiful harmony or an athletic
team executing their plays as they were designed. Shared purpose—a
vision of what an organization is capable of becoming—can be a powerful and positive force. Some employees have trouble describing what a
vision is, but they all know when it's there.

Healthy, high-achieving organizations have their heart and soul in
their vision. Used in this sense, the term *organizational vision* has been

an important part of management lexicon in the 1980s and 1990s. While the term is relatively new, the importance of pulling together for a deeply felt common purpose and sense of the future has been around for many years. In this century, the vision of victory over Germany and Japan in World War II galvanized nearly every citizen in the United States and other countries under siege. It was also the impetus that welded a tight coalition of diverse countries known as the Allied Powers.

It is *power*—the power of people who feel important and involved, of people and organizations being all that they can be—that makes visionary leaders so valuable. In areas as different as business, education, politics, and sports, visionary leaders have demonstrated an ability to unify and drive their organizations to greater heights by unleashing the energy and drive of their people. Visionary leadership is a common link between great industrial leaders such as Watson when he helped build IBM, Iacocca during the Chrysler crisis, and Job's early work at Apple. The accomplishments of these and other greats of business and industry can be compared to Roosevelt's and Churchill's efforts to preserve freedom in the 1940s and Martin Luther King's vision of civil rights during the 1950s and 1960s. Sports dynasties were established in New York, Boston, and San Francisco by McGraw, Stengle, Aurbach, and Walsh, who practiced visionary leadership. Their successes were due in large part to the motivation, potency, and coordination of people working together to achieve great goals.

As we move through the 1990s, an increasing number of organizations of all kinds strive to identify and achieve their vision and core values. Here are some examples:

- In part, Bell Atlantic's vision is of a commercially successful fiber optic intelligent network transmitting audio, video, and data signals. Building on its traditional roots and proud history, CEO Raymond Smith has introduced the "Bell Atlantic Way" with an "Obligation of Leadership" at its foundation. To achieve their business goals and vision, Bell Atlantic's employees have the opportunity to take initiative, to know what is important, and to understand where the company is going. They are part of a change process that values employee empowerment.

- Once nimble and quick, Hewlett-Packard was described as slow and bureaucratic during the 1980s. Today, John A. Young, H-P's CEO, has dissolved dozens of committees, flattened the organization, developed specialized sales and marketing teams, and is cultivating a number of key executives to recapture the innovativeness and quick time-to-market that H-P experienced during its peak growth years.[2]

- Dedicated to achieving a new vision of effective, equal, high-quality, world-class education, states such as Kentucky and New Jersey are in the process of designing and implementing major reforms of their public education systems.

- International travelers between Europe and the United States seem to gravitate to certain airlines because of their outstanding records for service, safety, and security. Frequent travelers of Swiss Air or KLM, for example, are confident that their plane will leave on time, that they will have fine food and be treated courteously. These qualities are part of the value system of each employee of these companies, reflected in the way they've been hired, trained, and rewarded.

- Lufthansa calls it a "Passion for Perfection." In a popular advertisement appearing in many magazines, Lufthansa highlights its attention to detail while preparing an airplane for flight. It presents the following description of one of its mechanics: "He's tough, unforgiving, obsessive, totally inflexible and not very tolerant. Perfect."

- Apple Computer Co. has staked much of its future on its vision of making teaching and learning come alive in classrooms through exciting, highly interactive, computer-based learning. Apple's vision of the Learning Society is described in a speech by Dr. Bernard Gifford, Apple's Vice President: "As a way of beginning, let me say that most educators seem to know that Apple's deepest roots are in education, and that we've always been the leader in computer technology for education. What's less well known is the amount and intensity of internal conversation we have about teaching and learning, because this just isn't a business for us. It's a passion!"[3]

- Many companies, such as Colgate-Palmolive, have implemented Self-Directed Teams (SDTs) to empower their work force as part of a major effort to achieve the production and quality goals so essential to their corporate success. These companies believe that their futures depend on the ability of their people to learn continuously, cooperate, innovate, and take responsibility for their success.[4]

- The Corning Corporation has brought new meaning to the vision of a profitable family company in a family town. Over the past decade, its CEO Jamie Houghton has "renewed" the corporation by redefining the way it does business. He has used family, company, and community as a special competitive advantage. Bold in approach, he has both sold and purchased units of Corning. The company has six growth strategies on which its profitability and future are based: Focus on Quality; Forming Alliances; Sharing Technology; Cooperating with Labor; Promoting Diversity; and Improving the Community.[5]

- One major health-care company summarized its vision by striving to become the "gold standard" of its industry in terms of people, policies, products, and profits. Another corporation's vision was powerful in its simplicity: "We will always provide service, the best service for all our customers."

- One NFL coach simply says that everything he does has one and one purpose only: "winning the superbowl." No players, assistant coaches, members of the press, or fans have any doubt about what is important to the team. Yes, an organization's heart and soul is in its vision.

Seeding Your Vision in Your Organization

Even during your first day's remarks, you started to seed your vision, your view of what the organization is capable of becoming. You talked about working as a team, shifting emphasis from *I* to *we,* the upcoming organizational self-diagnosis, and the goals of shared self-improvement. Seeding and beginning to establish your vision for the organization is a major objective during your first six months in your new position.

As you got to know your staff and conducted the early familiarization interviews and discussions, you asked individuals to share with you how they'd improve or contribute to a higher-performing organization. You shared with them your determination to improve the organization through mutual team effort.

At subsequent executive team meetings, department meetings, sub-group meetings, and informal conversations with individual department members, continue to establish a vision of what the department or function can become. Talk about problem-solving task forces, and begin to seek opportunities for growth and improvement. Ask people how they might solve particular problems or identify business opportunities. Invite their participation in the process. Invite others to share, broaden, or further develop your vision. Ask people to work with you in shaping thoughts and hope into a dynamic view of the future.

Ask your staff to help make it happen. Share the responsibility for ensuring the department's success. Share your excitement, and ask people to volunteer their ideas with you and others. Affirm that these ideas will help create a highly motivating and inspiring view of the future. The process of visioning should become a deeply felt, strongly valued sense of purpose in which all of the organization can participate.

This sense of purpose is characterized by ideas and beliefs that bind people's efforts and energies. You must generate commitment to a vision. Because ongoing work must get done, the process of identifying or working toward a vision will make extra demands on the organization's time and energy.

Three principles will help mold the organization's commitment to the process:

1. *People must believe that their commitment will simultaneously result in benefits to the organization and to themselves.* People must be able to identify themselves with a different, better, possibly broader view of the future. The vision can be generated by you or can evolve out of a group's work. Employees must believe that working together is genuine and that their efforts will make a difference between today's reality and tomorrow's growth or improvements. For others to own the process, they must believe that they are real and empowered participants.

Know in advance that you will encounter resistance from some people. For example, Coreen's often-expressed doubts had by now become tiresome to her colleagues—"But how will I get my regular work done; but do we really have the expertise to be doing this ourselves; but are we really committed to following through on the project; but do we have top management's approval to make some changes?" It is difficult to tell whether Coreen's concerns are her way of saying "I want some attention, I want to be consulted," or "there are some real problems here," or "I'm not going to let this work."

Alan, who felt he should have received your promotion, is passive-aggressive. He will go along, verbally agree, but not actively participate. Instead of contributions at meetings, he makes ironic asides. Asked his opinion, he will pass or make a humorous comment to deflect a serious response. His participation is only halfhearted, with no real sense of commitment or purpose.

You may want to reduce Alan's visibility because he puts a damper on the organization's commitment to your values of shared process and goals. You'd like to isolate him from power and control so you can ignore him. That solution is like a belch at the dinner table—everyone heard it, but no one says anything about it.

More forceful action is sometimes warranted. Coreen's boss met with her privately, gave her some descriptive feedback about her negative behavior, described how it annoyed him, described its effects on others, and described for her the more positive behaviors he'd like to see. He gave her some time to think about it, and he scheduled a follow-up meeting in about four weeks. The result was a change in her behavior. She showed her boss she really wanted to be a part of the group, and the future. Alan's case remained troublesome; he became increasingly isolated, and the problem ended only after he left the firm.

The point is do not move ahead with the process until there is adequate commitment from the key opinion makers and leaders under you. Especially important is the support of your management team. Describe for them the steps in the organizational growth process. Collaborate with them on the design of the process, and ask them to assume leadership in developing various task forces and problem-solving groups. Do not move without them. But neither should you wait until you have total commitment, for this could be a long time in coming. Rather, focus your efforts primarily on those who are with you. Deal with the laggards as necessary. Always encourage people to be positive, to say "I wonder," "I wish," "I hope," "If I could," and then help them to make things happen.

2. *You must keep driving toward achievement of the vision.* You must model real "fire in the belly" dedication. Your role is architect and crew chief of a process and a view of the future that touches people in a way they can embrace. But the heartfelt purpose around which people pull together is often intangible. Thus, the power of a committed vision is likely to include important principles or values, such as quality, excellence, or high levels of consistency or service. While potentially uplifting, the vision must be grounded in reality so it can be understood and achieved with hard work. But it must also target new and greater individual and group performance. The process is participatory; the organization shares its dreams, its resources, and the responsibility to act as one. Words will never be enough. Action and behaviors convince people.

3. *Keep top management commitment visible.* As long as people believe top management is interested, supportive, and participating themselves, they will maintain energy and commitment. Ask your boss to sit in on a few of your meetings, to address the total group periodically, to provide words of encouragement and appreciation. In short, keep your boss informed and visible in supporting your vision, goals, and values.

The Importance of the Group's Quest for Vision

Keep your vision focused on the group's power to accomplish great things. Individual team members' contributions are not additive. Together, they create a powerful synergy. Two working together have the potency of three or four working individually. Whole organizations have almost limitless potential and energy. The dynamics of working together result in insights, creative ideas, leaps of logic, and associations that one often cannot attain working alone. New ideas are generated from people building on each other's ideas, constructively criticizing each other, competing, joking, and thinking together. People from different backgrounds, with different perspectives and viewpoints, will often strengthen the vision and positively alter it, much as plant biologists strengthen genetics through hybridizing. Trust the strength, power, and ability of the group. Trust your process and others will follow your lead.

Key Planks in Your Platform

You need to decide early on your key values, the keystones of your vision. When Bruce was appointed Vice President of Finance and Administrative Services, he immediately faced a number of major challenges. His new areas had not been managed effectively. Even before he had an opportunity to delve into the functions, several problems were apparent. Several core financial and computer systems were at least 5 to 10 years behind the times. There had been several cases of illegal practices and kickbacks in the two previous years. Lack of effective management and leadership was apparent throughout his division. There was much to be done.

From the beginning, Bruce had a clear vision of his functions and the role of his people. Three major themes became the foundation of his early leadership platform. From the beginning, Bruce insisted on and involved his organization in (1) the simultaneous value of individual initiative and intergroup teamwork, (2) establishing sound standard operating procedures, and (3) building state-of-the-art computer systems. Bruce felt that these issues were the foundation of his leadership platform and the seeds of the vision to be achieved.

Bruce realized that words alone would not be enough to emphasize his points, so he combined his written and spoken words with symbolic actions to communicate his priorities. Within a few weeks, there was no question in anyone's mind about what Bruce felt was important and what issues would be emphasized before others. He spent a lot of time with people, individually and in groups, not only asking questions but stressing his main themes. His personnel decisions, including the way he organized people in projects and how he assigned work, all conveyed his early priorities. In particular, Bruce effectively utilized an approach that we call "managing vocabulary." He used several key words and consciously repeated them to emphasize the major points in his leadership platform. Words such as *initiative, teamwork, systems, integrity, ours,* and *we* became the symbolic lexicon of the division. This repetition of key themes was a valuable tool in Bruce's efforts to build alignment in the organization. During this early period, people began to adopt Bruce's thinking and direction. The early period is a time for molding and setting important precedents and for visionary leadership. It is a time when your key values must become part of the organization's vocabulary.

Acting Consistently: Developing Good Public Relations for Your Positions

As your direction and priorities become clearer, how you communicate and how you act as a leader become increasingly important. Seemingly well-conceived platforms and great visions have failed not because of their content but because of the way they are communicated. Effect should match intent. People have a desire and a right to expect consistency between word and deed. A governor of a western state was recently elected based on a well-articulated vision of that state's future, but within weeks of his election a firestorm of opposition arose because public remarks during his early days in office seemed inconsistent with his election platform. People felt betrayed.

People look for and trust consistency between what is done and what is said. If your vision includes the desire to share organizational power and control in the interest of the overall good, your actions must match the vision. A recent *Fortune* magazine poll found a 25 percent gap between what top managers said about quality and how their employees saw those words in terms of action and commitment.[6] Inevitably, employees will become cynical if words and actions are not consistent.

On the other hand, John F. Kennedy's inspired challenge, "Ask not what your country can do for you, but what you can do for your country" developed an expectation that leadership would invite citizen involvement and greater empowerment in a vision of America's "New Frontier." Kennedy started highly visible, idealistic programs such as the Peace Corps and VISTA to help realize this vision, and such actions made him appear consistent, believable, and able to energize the loyalty and commitment of millions of people.

Questions to Consider

Consider the following questions as you plan your vision and direction. Writing your answers will help you incorporate them into your overall first-year plan of action. This written information might help you complete your personal plan of action (at the end of this chapter).

- In organizations you've worked for, did the leader establish priorities early? How? What was the effect? If he or she did not, what was it like to work there? Did you and others know what was important?

- Describe effective symbolic behaviors and signs you have seen. What are some of the things you can do to symbolize your vision or expectations?

- What are at least three ways that you, as a newly appointed executive, can help influence and organize your unit's early mindset regarding your key priorities?

- In groups, certain people are the high influencers. During the first few weeks in a new position, how might you "influence the influencers" in the organization?

- Are there work assignments, special projects, and task forces that you can organize around a key issue that can further strengthen the direction of your unit?

- How might you use your ability to recognize and reward efforts during your first few months in a new leadership position?

- How might you facilitate setting team, group, and individual goals in a way that promotes perceived consistency between your intentions and actions? How can you use recognition and reward in a similar fashion?

- How can you ensure that you are consistent in what you say and do?

- Over the next several months, can you pick people for special responsibilities, assignments, and promotions based on their willingness and ability to work within your platform and vision? Remember to act so others in your organization see the relationship between your selection of people and your commitment to certain goals and directions for your organization.

- How can you make the people around you feel like winners? What can you do to continue this feeling? If they don't feel like winners, why not? Together, how can you turn this feeling around?

- As a means of building consistency, some leaders have periodically updated a top-priority "to do" list. For example, twice a year one director mobilizes people around those key problems and opportunities that are viewed as gateways to success. How might you apply this approach? What are its possible uses for concentrating people's attention on what is really important? What methods can ensure that all individuals in the organization are problem solvers, solution makers, and identifiers of opportunities? (Consider the incredible power of secretaries! Try unleashing their potency on several important problems.)

- Are there work assignments, special projects, and task forces that can be organized around your goals and can further strengthen the direction of your unit?

- How can you make sure that you are effectively communicating your early priorities downward, upward, and across the organization?

The lesson is clear. Acting consistently on your stated positions, priorities, and values is a prerequisite for establishing acceptance of you and your vision.

Quick Reminders to Keep You on Track

- Vision and direction is what results when, together, people look outside themselves, put aside individual interests, and capture a common notion of what they want their organization to achieve.

- A committed vision should drive the organization; people in high achieving organizations have their heart and soul in their vision.

- A key to success is involving your people in developing ways to achieve the vision you are seeding.

- There are important ways to seed your personal vision in the organization; they include the use of the following three principles:

  1. People must believe that their commitment to building a strong organization will simultaneously result in benefits to the organization and to themselves.
  2. You must keep driving toward the initial identification and subsequent achievement of the vision.
  3. Keep top management commitment visible.

- Be a catalyst, a facilitator, and a model; orchestrate the group's quest for vision.

- Clearly identify, model, and manage the key planks in your leadership platform. Use symbolic behavior and language ("imaging vocabulary") to communicate your vision clearly.

- Acting consistently—having your actions match your intent and words—is the key to developing good public relations for your positions.

Summary of Major Responsibilities—Year 1 (Chap. 4)

First Year by Month*

	Preappoint-ment	1	2	3	4	5	6	7	8	9	10	11	12

Moving in: Establishing Yourself in Your New Assignment
- Entering the Organization
- Entering Your Boss's World

Achieving an Impact on the Organization
- Beginning to Craft Your Vision and Direction

*Times are approximate.

Legend
——— Primary period of emphasis
– – – Active but not a period of emphasis

Your Personal Plan of Action for Beginning to Craft Your Vision and Direction (Chap. 4)

Activity	Suggested Timeframe	Perceived Barriers	Available Resources	Your Projected Timeframe	Completed (✓)
• Seeding your vision in your organization	Major emphasis in months 1 to 6 with continued attention over the next few years.				
• The importance of the group's quest for vision	Major emphasis in months 1 to 6 with continued attention over the next few years.				
• Confirming key planks in your platform	Major emphasis in months 1 to 6 with continued attention over the next few years.				
• Acting consistently: Developing good public relations for your positions	Beginning on day 1 and continous thereafter.				
• Planning and assessing your activities in the area of organizational vision and direction using the "issues" to consider section in Chap. 4	Major emphasis in months 1 to 6 with continued attention over the next few years.				

5

The Diagnostic Process: The Importance of Good Organizational Information

The major causes of problems are bad assumptions and solutions.

SOURCE UNKNOWN

To be successful in transforming your organization with the goal of achieving your vision, you must have an accurate picture of your organization's strengths, weaknesses and other vital information within your first five or six months. You will need to:

- Ensure that your people understand the importance of accurate information in order to strengthen their organization and achieve its vision.

- Explain what an organizational diagnosis/assessment is.

73

- Involve many people in completing the organizational diagnosis while they continue their regular work.

- Facilitate a logical diagnostic process with a sense of urgency.

- Complete the diagnosis and prepare to act on its recommendations in six months or less.

☆ ☆ ☆

In this chapter, there is useful information about:

- Positioning the Diagnosis Within the Overall Problem-Solving and Transition Management Process

- The Diagnostic Process

- The Hazards of the Process

Positioning the Diagnosis Within the Overall Problem-Solving and Transition Management Process

The diagnosis allows the organization to assess itself for the purpose of strengthening what is good, improving what is problematic, and correcting what is wrong. Conducting a successful organizational "health check" is a key step in the organization's process of achieving its vision. This check usually takes from several weeks to half a year.

As a general rule, by the end of your sixth month in the job, the data collection phase should have been completed, solutions to problems and growth opportunities identified, and implementation of your plans begun. You need to move fairly rapidly. You have an agreement or "contract" with your boss, who expects that you are going to make improvements. You've asked your staff to participate in self-renewal, and they will expect that once completed, the diagnosis and recommendations they've made are going to be implemented. You've set up expectations that you have taken charge of the process, and it will be time to move ahead.

The diagnostic process *must* go on while regular work proceeds. You will hear complaints that both cannot be done together. They can be, but it takes considerable work and committed effort. It is amazing what people can do when they are motivated to make things better. Performing high-quality work and completing the diagnostic process requires people to believe in what you are doing. A diagnostic phase as part of a transition management process is equally applicable for start-up organizations, in which there is generally less "history" to overcome but the challenges remain great to establish a strong, sustainable organization.

The Diagnostic Process

An effective diagnosis can be conducted in a number of ways. We will describe a step-by-step process that we have found to be very useful. Precise steps and timeframes vary by organization and circumstances. While we emphasize a process involving many people from your organi-

Sample Steps and Timeframes		
A.	Appoint a steering committee representing different levels and functions within your organization.	Weeks 2, 3, or 4
B.	Designate the support and consultative resources, if applicable.	Same as above
C.	Issue the steering committee's mission and scope of authority.	Same as above
D.	Develop a timeline and activity schedule for the process.	Same as above
E.	Steering committee identifies critical issues to be studied.	Weeks 4, 5, or 6
F.	Delegate critical issues to task forces, designating leaders from the steering committee, selecting representative task force members from across the department or organization to complete task force membership. (As a rule, steering committee members will serve on no more than one task force.)	Weeks 4, 5, or 6

G.	Task forces develop and implement a timeline and critical events schedule, within steering committee deadlines.
	
	Task forces should complete three primary functions:
	• Identify and collect data on the issues. For example,
	  – Develop knowledge from within the task force.
	  – Develop interview data from others outside the task force who have information (often done by you and/or consultants).
	  – Identify case studies and events that show the organization's strengths and weakness.
	• Analyze data and organize findings, conclusions, and recommendations.
	• Develop draft of a "Critical Issues" paper, submitted to the steering committee for discussion.
		Weeks 4, 5, 6 through weeks 12 to 16

H.	Steering committee reviews task force "Critical Issues" papers and develops overall findings, conclusions, and recommendations.	Weeks 12 to 18 depending on timing of preceding steps
I.	Steering committee issues final report.	Weeks 18, 19, or 20

zation, we cannot emphasize enough the importance of your involvement as a diagnostician. You are as good as the information you get. Use your people as we suggest. But talk to people, dozens of people, in and out of your new function. We call it 360° feedback. Ask dozens of people dozens of questions if necessary to build your information base.

Appointing a Steering Committee

To gain influence, you must give influence and empower those around you. Appointing a steering committee is an effective way to gain power by sharing power. The steering committee will oversee the organizational diagnosis. It will coordinate and drive the diagnosis forward and develop and help implement the solutions. The steering committee is critical to the success of the project.

Appointing a steering committee helps accomplish many of the goals of the diagnosis. A steering committee encourages participation in the diagnostic process, building organizational buy-in and commitment. It focuses energy on renewal, communicates a sense of "we-ness," and fosters the belief that everyone can help make things better.

The steering committee membership should represent the part of the organization's structure that reports to you, functional reporting lines, levels of responsibility, and experience. But it should not be so large that decision making becomes unwieldy. Depending on the size of your organization, a group of 6 to 10 is an ideal representation and concentration of power. The larger the group, the more difficult it is to arrive at a consensus, and the more vulnerable the group becomes to the will of a strong chairperson, who tends to be the one with the most information.

Steering committee membership should also represent the department's formal and informal power. Appoint primarily those in designated roles of authority, most of whom will be members of your management team. Appoint people who are respected and can represent others. That they have earned a leadership role or are viewed as influential means not only that they are generally knowledgeable, but because of their power and influence they are key to implementing the committee's recommendations.

It is important to appoint key informal leaders at all levels in the organization, including those not necessarily in officially designated leadership positions but who department members respect and listen to. Some of these people may be low on the organizational chart, but they will communicate with and create an informal constituency. These people can be expected to make strong recommendations and explain steering committee decisions to their constituencies. They will be able to build support for recommendations in which they participate. In some organizations, these people may represent labor, supervisors, or clerical and secretarial supervisors.

While the selection of steering committee members should be thoughtful, it should not be manipulative. Choose people on their merits as energetic problem solvers. The recommendations that the committee generates and implements will affect the entire department and must speak for the department. People must feel that the committee was fairly selected and represents all viewpoints and constituencies, not just those the established leaders may favor. Beware of stacking the deck.

Diversity of opinion will generate a better solution as long as the group listens. President John F. Kennedy felt that the Bay of Pigs disaster suffered from the limitations imposed by a small group of like-minded planners too insular in their thinking. When he faced the Cuban Missile Crisis, he composed a large, diverse group of experts from government, industry, and academia. The successful strategy they devised was quite different from the strategies that the President's inner circle proposed, and it was the product of lengthy and sometimes heated discussions. A superior consensus was achieved by a diverse group of problem solvers intent on an excellent solution.

Union members can be a particular concern if they are more concerned with defending the contract and work rules than with improving the organization. Fortunately, labor-management tension has generally subsided, as each recognizes its mutual dependency. Labor representatives generally are prepared to help strengthen the organization and thus help ensure their jobs within a viable organization.

You might discuss your preliminary selections with a few key associates and department members, partly to get some feedback and advice and partly to bring them into the process of managing the diagnosis. They can help you select committee members who will bring talent, energy, and effective representation.

Next have a series of brief individual or small-group meetings with those selected, describing the process, their responsibilities, and time commitments, and making sure they want to serve. At the same time, select and begin to brief the committee chair on his or her responsibilities and charter.

Depending on the organization, elections may be a way to select the steering committee chair. In the public sector, elections are the norm and unions seem to prefer them. In the private sector, people seem more accustomed to appointments and faster decisions. The organizational polarization and conflict engendered by the win-lose of elections is anathema to most businesses, which prefer win-win solutions or situations where losers are not subjected to the public conflict of an election.

The steering committee chair should be someone with both formal and informal authority. He or she must have the respect of the department's most experienced and expert personnel, must be able to work with the most demanding and difficult people, and must be capable of moving the individual members toward consensus and implementation. It is a demanding and time-consuming task. The chair must also be someone with whom you can work, who can help keep the process on schedule, help committee task groups that are floundering, and move the process toward completion.

Since the organization will usually defer to your leadership, there will generally be little resistance to an appointment if the person has the organization's respect. People recognize that the committee chair will have to speak to you, negotiate with you, and represent you.

The steering committee oversees the five primary steps of the organizational diagnosis in close collaboration with you:

1. Develop a statement of objectives or goals.
   - State the objectives of the diagnosis. The objective of the diagnosis is generally to strengthen the function.
   - Describe activities and timelines.
   - Describe the expected outcomes and benefits.
   - Identify resources needed.

2. Develop areas of study.
   - Determine specific subtopics to be studied.
   - Identify critical issues to resolve or examine.
   - Specify the objectives, activities, and timelines for task forces.
   - Indicate potential sources of data.

3. Receive, review, and analyze task force findings and recommendations.
   - Receive task force findings and recommendations.
   - Analyze and prioritize findings and recommendations.

4. Make final recommendations and design implementation.
   - Review, approve, reject, or modify and prioritize recommendations.
   - Plan implementation resources, activities, and timelines.

5. Monitor and evaluate implementation.
   - Oversee implementation activities; ensure implementation (in doing this, the steering committee works closely with you and your management team).
   - Troubleshoot implementation.
   - Fine-tune implementation to ensure it achieves project goals and objectives.

- Assess whether outcomes and benefits are achieved; adapt as necessary.

As the steering committee monitors and oversees the overall process, so should you monitor and oversee the work of the steering committee, consulting with the chair on managing the committee and with the committee on managing the diagnostic process.

Your role is not to control the steering committee's conclusions and recommendations. However, you need to be comfortable with its direction and goals. Candid discussions with the steering committee can ensure your support or communicate your discomfort with particular initiatives or goals. These discussions should begin as soon as possible.

You should know the diagnostic process as well as anyone on the steering committee (excluding internal or external consultants who may be involved). Use your knowledge and your commitment to the process.

You know that participation should be broad and should represent different subgroups and the diversity of skills and experience in the organization. You also know the limitations of the diagnosis, if there are issues that cannot be touched (these should be very few, if any), and what the resource limitations are. These can often be identified early in the process and should be defined as the limits and boundaries of the organizational improvement process.

By selecting the steering committee and insisting on the "we-ness" of the effort, you can help ensure fair representation as the process continues. Through pronouncement and example, you can ensure that the problem-solving process is applied to all areas under you, that the *real* organization is accurately described, and that the task forces rethink and analyze the organization's functions and processes in a creative problem-solving mode. Similarly, the *ideal* organization, represented by the steering committee's recommendations, must be objectively considered looking at both alternatives and consequences. Get the groups started and give them plenty of room to operate. Intervene only when necessary.

Your primary role is to coach the steering committee. Much of your coaching will be done in private, with the steering committee chair and task force heads. Attend some, but not all, steering committee meetings. At steering committee meetings, ask questions. If meetings are problematic, redirect the group to stay on the agenda, to consider multiple approaches, to resolve its conflicts, and to develop consensus. Your more active input should be one-on-one with the chair, away from steering committee meetings so you don't undermine the chair's authority.

Develop a contract with the steering committee chair that describes his or her prerogatives and yours. Agree that if either of you feel the agreement is being violated, you may call "time out" before the problem festers. Project your own confidence and a strong sense that you understand the process. You should not be all-knowing of the "right" answers. Avoid giving the impression that you have been hired because you are the immediate expert and have all the answers. Project your commitment and strength by stating that you need and value all the help and input you can get. Demonstrate that you expect success, through your approach and your ability to ask the right questions. You will build confidence by making tough decisions whenever needed.

The diagnostic process intentionally gives the impression of order. But it may create discomfort, some dissonance, and tension. There's a lot going on at once in addition to the organization's regular work. Reassure people. Build on each other's hopes for a stronger organization. Listen to what people are saying, to their concerns. Encourage your people. Give them your time. Remind them that the process works.

Designating Support and Consultative Resources

Consider the type, if any, of support services the steering committee or the various task forces may require. Consultants, internal to the company or from outside, can provide three types of key assistance: (1) help with the design of the diagnostic process, (2) help with technical aspects of the organization's work, and (3) help with conducting aspects of the diagnosis and implementation.

Consultants can provide assistance with the design of the diagnostic process itself. One of the steering committee chair's critical roles in the diagnostic process is facilitation. The chair's primary concern as a facilitator is to ensure that the diagnostic process is well organized, functions smoothly, and stays on schedule. A process or facilitative consultant can be assigned the following tasks in conjunction with either you or the chair:

- Help ensure that the steering committee, and each task force, develops a reasonable approach and schedule and adheres to schedule.

- Assist task forces and ensure that each member's input gets a fair and reasonable hearing.

- Help the steering committee and task forces resolve conflicts and develop consensus.

- Help ensure that the steering committee and task forces adhere to a problem-solving model, that alternatives are fairly considered, that solutions evolve from reasonably considered alternatives, and that recommendations fit the conclusions.

- Act as a source of ideas for creative problem solving and innovative directions.

The steering committee chair will perform the role of leader and process facilitator and function as a group member on issues where he or she has a strong opinion or input. Some people wear all three hats more easily than others. When the chair's process and facilitator skills are not strong, group members may feel railroaded, inadequately consulted, and forced to go along with things they do not support. A facilitator from outside, however, can safeguard the process by projecting an outsider's detachment and objectivity. The outside facilitator can coach the chair and help him or her stay in touch with the group's feelings and direction. A skilled facilitator will also be able to intervene in the group's deliberations, to reorient the group or draw attention to and help solve a developing process problem.

A second purpose of outside consultants is to provide needed expert information. For example, a steering committee or task force considering reorganization will profit from information on how other similar organizations are structured. Often, a consultant familiar with the industry has worked in a number of companies within the field and can describe different kinds of organizations as well as strengths and weaknesses of different structures and work-flow patterns. Consultants experienced in the field provide a broad spectrum of how the work is done in similar organizations and how you might improve your own.

A third role for outside consultants is to conduct parts of the diagnosis itself for the steering committee. Management studies by outside consultants are common because they provide an objective, independent viewpoint. One newly installed manager, for example, used outside consultants because he did not feel internal resources would look critically enough at an organization long accustomed to doing things the same way.

In another case, the consultant became the surrogate for a steering committee that had too little time to pursue all the sources of data required. In this case, the diagnosis was organized into subparts that were assigned to different consultants: One analyzed results of a questionnaire distributed among employees; a second conducted diagnostic interviews with all top managers and a sample of the first-line work force; a third conducted interviews with people who had left the organization or declined offers to join it. The steering committee synthesized the three different elements of the diagnosis and directed the review and consolidation of consultant reports into a comprehensive "Critical

Issues" paper, which included the final recommendations. The biggest disadvantage of such an approach is that it significantly reduces the involvement of the organization itself in the self-analysis. In turn, this may reduce the ownership of the data and solutions. Consultants must ensure that they do not end up owning the process, the findings, and the recommendations. They must help the organization take responsibility for itself. Consultants who own the process end up getting the blame from organization members who do not support their recommendations.

Issuing the Steering Committee's Mission and Scope of Authority

The steering committee must receive its charge from you, the organization's leader, for you control the committee's mandate, scope of authority, and resources.

At the committee's organizing meeting, announce the committee chair. Describe the role of the chair, steering committee members, anticipated task forces, other department and organization members, and yourself.

Describe how you envision the diagnostic process. Broadly describe the data collection, analysis, and problem resolution process you expect the steering committee and each task force to follow. Be flexible and encourage variations and new ideas. Describe the role of committee members, and outline the can-do behaviors each group member is expected to follow.

Stress that the analysis should position the organization to build on its strengths. On the other hand, few if any, topics or issues should be off limits. The committee should analyze the organization's weaknesses, without defensiveness, to identify areas that need strengthening. Focusing solely on what's wrong simply builds defensiveness; rather, identify where the organization can improve while building on its inherent strengths.

Insist that the steering committee and its task forces address critical issues and growth opportunities facing the organization, including the sensitive issues. For example, include business projections not achieved; perceptions that staff work assignments are unequal, reporting relationships are confusing or contradictory, project deadlines are not adhered to, lines of communication are not open, training is weak, people's skills are stagnant, and procedures are inefficient and inconsistent.

Stress that no steering committee or task force issue is to be presented without a recommendation. This is the key. No one is to pass the buck. Findings, conclusions, and recommendations are to be issued in a "Final Report" paper.

Task force "Critical Issues" papers are to be submitted to the steering committee. These are then consolidated as the steering committee's final report, which is submitted to you. This will become a vital guide and tool for you. Review it in detail with your boss and later summarize it for your organization as a whole. This last point is important because you will be seeking to mobilize the organization to implement the steering committee's recommendations.

Developing the Timeline and Critical Events Calendar

The steering committee's timeline and deadlines are largely governed by your expectations and by the time required by constituent task forces. Typically, a task force will require about six weeks to four months to organize, collect, and analyze its data and draft its conclusions and recommendations. Add two weeks for organization and another four weeks for the steering committee to review task force "critical issues" papers and develop final conclusions, recommendations, and a plan for implementation. The timepoints depend on the size and scope of the study and the organization as well as the time available to members, who are also doing their regular work.

A critical events schedule marks activities that should be completed if the diagnosis is to be done on a timely basis:

- Whom to interview inside the department with what deadline
- Whom to interview among clients, customers, and vendors and contractors with deadlines
- Documents and products to be reviewed, with deadlines

Identifying Critical Issues

The diagnostic targets described in this chapter and more fully in Chap. 6 can define the task forces that will be required. There may be obvious problems or growth opportunities around which task forces can form. Take advantage of existing information and reports.

The task forces may be involved in the nine broad-based target areas described in Chap. 6, such as organizational mission and objectives, leadership, delegation, and culture. On the other hand, the steering committee may narrow the analysis to specific issues. One organization's task forces, each led by someone on the steering committee, were as follows:

- Evaluating the new product development portfolio

- Improving computer systems
- Reviewing a consultant's report on how the department's functions were managed in 14 different companies, and identifying recommendations for our company
- Making recommendations for training and employee development
- Considering workload distribution

Another organization's steering committee organized five task forces:

- Improving communications and procedures with the department from whom we receive our work, with particular emphasis on role definition
- Working on coordination between the home office and branch offices
- Improving computer systems and management information systems
- Identifying career development opportunities for plateaued employees
- Improving the training and employee development program and improving performance review and appraisal

A third company identified three broad task forces: the planning process, doing the work, and data management. Yet another company organized functionally, with a task force examining each business unit (product line). A broad array of potential targets is described in Chap. 6. With your coaching of the chair and direct involvement (as necessary), the steering committee identifies the scope of the diagnosis and the task force issues to be analyzed.

Organizing Task Forces

Task forces should be organized around growth opportunities and critical issues. As noted earlier, the diagnostic targets are identified by the steering committee. We have seen task forces include no steering committee members, although this is rare. It is preferable that each task force be represented on the steering committee and often led by a steering committee member. Task forces should include a variety of viewpoints among knowledgeable people. As with the steering committee, be sure to include formal and informal leaders in the area of the task force's domain, so recommendations will have organizational support. Task force members can include any employee from any job position. They predominantly come from mid-management and first-line supervisors, supported by individual contributors in the work force.

Task forces commonly consider how the work gets done, and should be comprised of people closest to the work.

Task forces should use a problem-solving process, including issues identification, data collection, data analysis, consideration of alternatives and consequences, and selection of a solution. Task force deadlines and critical events should fit the steering committee's schedules and deadlines and should result in a "Critical Issues" report containing findings, conclusions, and a clear recommendation for each finding.

Like the steering committee, the task forces should draw input from multiple resources:

- A properly constituted task force will represent considerable information from within its membership, including individual contributors and first-line supervisors. Much data is available simply through discussions within the task force.

- Task force members may draw from consultants, who may work with other task forces or the steering committee, or from individual employees whose input helps shape the findings and recommendations. As mentioned previously, consultants may be retained to assist with or conduct the diagnosis for sensitive issues. If the steering committee retains a process consultant, he or she should sit in on task forces as needed, and possibly randomly, to ensure that the task force is functioning in an open and participatory manner.

- Task force members should draw on information not only from inside but outside the organization, including clients, customers, those who provide the organization with input or products, those who use the organization's output, and others who observe or interact with the organization.

Each task force should develop its own "Critical Issues" paper, describing methodology, findings, conclusions, and recommendations that will make the organization stronger. These will be consolidated or summarized in a final report of the steering committee, which is presented to you.

Developing Roles for the Functional Members of the Department

Broad participation in data collection is a way to gain support from across the department or function, and to profit from that work unit's diversity of knowledge and viewpoints. At the same time, it builds interest in the organizational improvement process and increases its visibility. As a rule, when management and employees participate in the process, they develop ownership for both the process and the outcome. The broader the participation, the greater the sense that people have been included, that they have gained recognition and status, and that their concerns were heard.

Some will serve on the steering committee. There are roles for others on one of the task forces, which usually have from three to six members each. Others will be interviewed by task force members as sources of information that can help the effort.

As with the steering committee, smaller task forces may collect data more quickly and possibly develop a consensus more efficiently. Larger groups, on the other hand, will be more representative and tend to have a greater richness of ideas.

Each task force should include a member of the steering committee. Steering committee members may volunteer to head particular task forces, even though the task force leader should be chosen by you and the steering committee chair. Select a leader who knows the task area. Also consider a person's interest in the area. A top manager would be most familiar with broader issues of mission, policies, goals, and objectives. His or her ideal task force members might be predominantly upper- and mid-management people who are familiar with looking at the organization from a broad, wide-angle view.

On the other hand, task forces that look at work-flow and work-force issues should include people at an operational level: mid-level and first-line supervisors and experienced workers, who are more familiar with the day-to-day operations.

In general, the most experienced people will make the strongest contribution to task forces. They know the culture, history, how things got that way, intervening factors, and the solutions. More importantly, they know how to get answers and have the organizational resources to defend and implement solutions. A bright, less experienced person may add much because of his or her initiative and fresh perspective. A word of caution, however: Overly frank newcomers, whose advice and observations are not always welcome by veterans, can get in trouble for being too direct. Participation on task forces can be a career maker or breaker for young people, depending on how they handle themselves. A little precoaching can save young people from a lot of trouble.

What about your critics? By excluding them from the problem-solving task forces, you can deny them influence and power. In most information- and knowledge-based industries, information is a source of power. People without information are left out of decision making, and they lose power. But denying your critics access to decision-making authority can also harm you. Excluding them lessens your chance of bringing critics on board, giving them some stake, and turning negative critics into positive forces that can help both you and the department.

We have seen it both ways—critics who came on board and were won to the renewal process, and critics who, primarily because they were angry, psychologically withdrew from the discussions or were difficult to cope with. It's a tough call. We generally suggest including a few known critics but choosing people who see things in different ways, not people with a personal ax to grind. You need diverse opinions, not negative attitudes. At the very least, convey a willingness to hear a true diversity of opinion. *No one* should ever be criticized or punished for their candor during a formal diagnostic process that you sponsor. Not only is it unfair, but your credibility could be damaged permanently.

A salesperson with six months of experience with a company was given the opportunity to brainstorm and problem solve the organization's training and development program. She stated that the program was very weak in her division, that she was spending almost no time in the field, was left alone in the office too often, and saw the sales director and other experienced salespeople taking two- and three-hour lunches. It took only a few hours for her sales director's friends to relay what his new employee had said about him. After the closed-door meetings, department meetings, explanations, and memos, the new employee was transferred to a different site, fortunate that she still had a job.

Broad-based participation can foster team building and the development of cohesion within the function. Two recently merged organizations used problem-solving task forces to get people from the different merged units talking to each other, sharing perceptions, experiences, and knowledge, and building trust and commitment with each other. Another organization used creative problem-solving approaches to help four group leaders learn to work together. In the process, they shared definitions, perceptions, experiences, and objectives. They developed better working relationships as they shared mutual problems and carved out shared solutions.

The Hazards of the Process

Broad participation and group problem solving do not automatically strengthen your organization's renewal process. There are a number of hazards that can undermine the broad-based support you are trying to build.

One major difficulty is that of heightened expectations. Inevitably, someone's ideas will not be solicited, solicited but not heard, heard but not heeded, or heeded but assigned a low priority. People will make suggestions that are not adopted. Hopes that pet ideas or suggestions will be adopted are dashed as decision-making committees sift through all the ideas and recommendations.

Unrequited expectations can defeat the process. If people begin to feel that they are not heard, or if they feel the process is a ploy to build support but that you'll do what you want anyway, your staff will feel used and manipulated and lose enthusiasm for the project, and the process and you will lose credibility quickly.

Endless task force meetings without decisions or a feeling of closure also sap energy. People begin to question why they are meeting. Participation becomes a burden. Task force meetings must have deadlines, milestones, and be conducted with purpose and an end in mind. They should give everyone time to be heard and to develop a consensus.

Another related cause of failure is the leader's overemphasis on process, to the detriment of results. To overemphasize process is to meet, participate, and deliberate without coming to conclusions and action. It is talk without action, participation without closure, deliberation without decisions. It is problem solving without solutions, without action. Nothing ever goes anywhere, nothing ever gets done.

Leadership is the ability to set in place a change process for the group and to give employees an overall direction and vision without prescribing all the details. Leadership is setting deadlines, upholding your standard and expectations, and insisting on well-conceived results. It is being willing to confront or criticize when the outcome is not up to standards or is seriously flawed. It is also being willing to accept good ideas with which you disagree for the overall good of the organization. In Chap. 6 we will explore these issues in greater detail as we introduce the nine-target model for assessing organizational health.

Quick Reminders to Keep You on Track

- Conducting a successful organizational health check, a diagnosis, is a key step in the organization's achieving its vision.

- The purpose of the diagnosis is for the organization to strengthen what is good, identify what is problematic, and correct what is wrong.

- As a general rule, by the end of your sixth month in the job, the data collection phase of the organizational diagnosis should have been completed, solutions to problems and growth opportunities identified, and implementation of your plan begun.

- This diagnostic effort is part of the agreement, or "contract," with your boss that you have discussed and negotiated.

- You will want to involve your immediate staff and others, as appropriate, in the organizational self-renewal effort.

- Once completed, your employees will look to you to lead the charge in implementing the recommendations identified in the organizational improvement process. Your personal credibility and reputation are on the line if you do not.

- The diagnostic process goes on while regular work proceeds. Some will complain that it is too much to do. Keep the "open for business" sign out while you initiate the diagnostic process.

- An effective diagnosis can be conducted in a number of ways. Regardless of approach, it always includes your active involvement as the prime orchestrator.

- You will need to ask many questions of many people in order to build your base of information (360° organizational feedback) and to check how different people view issues and problems.

- We recommend an approach that utilizes a wide representation of people from your function usually organized into task forces and a small steering committee to guide the effort.

Summary of Major Responsibilities—Year 1 (Chap. 5)

First Year by Month*

| Preappointment | 1 | 2 | 3 | 4 | 5 | 6 | 7 | 8 | 9 | 10 | 11 | 12 |

Moving in: Establishing Yourself in Your New Assignment
- Entering the Organization
- Entering Your Boss's World

Achieving an Impact on the Organization
- Beginning to Craft Your Vision and Direction
- The Diagnostic Process: The Importance of Good Organizational Information

*Times are approximate.

Legend
—— Primary period of emphasis
- - - Active but not a period of emphasis

Your Personal Plan of Action for Your Diagnostic Process: The Importance of Good Organizational Information (Chap. 5)

Activity	Suggested Timeframe	Perceived Barriers	Available Resources	Your Projected Timeframe	Completed (✓)
• Positioning the diagnosis within the overall problem solving/transition management model	Begins during week 1 with the entire diagnosis completed and ready to be implemented in four to six months as a *maximum*.				
Sample Diagnostic Process (Precise steps and timeframes vary by organization and circumstances.) • Timely appointment of a steering committee representing different levels and functions within your area of responsibility	Weeks 2, 3, or 4.				
• Designation of the support/consultative resources, if applicable	Weeks 2, 3, or 4.				
• Issuance of the steering committee's mission, scope, and authority	Weeks 2, 3, or 4.				
• Confirm a timeline and activity schedule for the process	Weeks 2, 3, or 4.				
• Steering committee identification of critical issues to be studied	Week 4, 5, or 6.				
• Delegation of critical issues to task forces, designation of leaders from the steering committees, selection of representative task force members from across the department/organization	Week 4, 5, or 6.				

Your Personal Plan of Action for Your Diagnostic Process:
The Importance of Good Organizational Information (Chap. 5) (*Continued*)

Activity	Suggested Timeframe	Perceived Barriers	Available Resources	Your Projected Timeframe	Completed (✔)
• Task forces develop and implement timeline and critical events schedule, within steering committee deadlines. Task forces: Identify the issues: — Knowledge within the task force — Interview data from outside the task force (often done by you and/or consultants) — Case studies and events indicative of the organization's strengths and weaknesses — Analyze data, and organize findings, conclusions, and recommendations — Develop draft critical issue paper, submit it to steering committee for discussion	Beginning in weeks 4, 5, or 6 through weeks 12-16.				
• Steering committee reviews task force critical issues papers, develops overall findings, conclusions, and recommendations	Weeks 12-18 depending upon timing of above steps.				
• Steering committee issues critical issue report to you	Week 18, 19, or 20.				

6
Assessing Your Organization's Health

There's a certain amount of disorder that has to be reorganized.
WILLIAM S. PALEY, upon his return as CBS chairman after his retirement

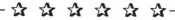

To complete your organizational assessment, you have to know what to look for and what your targets are. You will need to:

- Use the nine-target model to complete the organizational diagnosis/assessment.

☆ ☆ ☆

In this chapter, there is useful information about:

- *The Nine-Target Model*—the organizational indicators of vision, that are used in diagnosing (assessing) your organization.
    1. Mission Statement, Planning, Goals, Objectives, Policies
    2. Leadership, Delegation, Accountability, Control
    3. Politics, Power, Culture
    4. Recognition, Rewards, Incentives

5. Relationships, Communication, Teamwork
6. Competency, Training, Performance Management, Recruitment, Staffing Levels, Retention
7. Resources including Financing and Capital, Equipment and
   Supplies, Data Management
8. Enabling Mechanisms—Work-Flow Systems, Procedures,
   Work Locations
9. External Factors—Laws, Regulations, Community, Social
   and Economic Conditions

- Findings, Conclusions, and Recommendations

The Nine-Target Model:
The Indicators of Vision

There are a number of fundamental concerns an organizational diagnosis should consider. Whether the diagnosis is concerned with a single
function or with all organizational functions that may be under your
direction, you and the steering committee should consider which target
should be selected. There are nine primary organizational targets that
determine the health of your organization. Once assessed, the present
status of these nine areas should provide a clear picture of the overall
well-being of your function. We call these targets *indicators of vision*
because they are your starting point for what you want the organization
to become. They indicate the number and nature of the organizational
issues needed to achieve your vision.

Target 1: Mission statement, planning, goals, objectives, policies

Target 2: Leadership, delegation, accountability, control

Target 3: Politics, power, culture

Target 4: Recognition, rewards, incentives

Target 5: Relationships, communications, teamwork

Target 6: Competency, training, performance management, recruitment, staffing levels, retention

Target 7: Resources (Financing and Capital), equipment and supplies,
data management

Target 8: Enabling mechanisms—work-flow systems, procedures, work
locations

Target 9: External factors—laws, regulations, community, social and
economic conditions

Target 1: The Mission Statement, Planning, Goals, Objectives, Policies

The mission statement is a succinct statement of corporate or functional purpose. It states why the organization is in business—what it is trying to achieve. The mission statement provides purpose to employee efforts beyond just making money. It provides a philosophical touchstone to guide management and staff in determining the business they are in and how they conduct business.

Sperry Corporation's (now Unisys) Customer Education had a simple mission statement. When one division began a program to make the corporation (traditionally an engineering-oriented company) more customer oriented, the program's leaders built the program rationale around the mission statement formulated a generation earlier: "The needs of the customer are always foremost in importance. When the concerns of our customers are no longer our concern, we have lost our reason for existence."

IBM, legendary for its service, professionalism, and product quality, is guided by this mission statement: Respect the individual, commit to service, commit to excellence. Ford Motor company says, "Quality is job one." As Tom Peters has repeatedly stated, successful companies are shaped by their corporate philosophies.

Mission statements can take different formats. Russell Conwell, founder of Temple University in Philadelphia, was a nationally known nineteenth-century orator. More than 1500 times during his lifetime, he delivered a single speech entitled "Acres of Diamonds." In booklet form, more than 1,000,000 copies of the speech have been issued, and it is still in print today. The speech reflects the belief that America's genius is in the intellectual and social resources of all its people, including the poor and the immigrant; that our immigrant cities hold acres of these diamonds, who, given the chance to gain an education and given the opportunity of America, will shine like diamonds. The speech grew out of a mission Conwell gave his university, a mission that guides Temple administrators and faculty today, over 100 years after its founding.

The mission statement should help shape what the company does and how people do their jobs. It should be reflected in how work is done at the department level. Reviewing it and thinking about how it affects the department's priorities and activities should be an important part of the diagnostic process. How should the mission affect what we do? What's not happening that should be happening; what are we presently doing that is not in line with the mission statement? Conversely, as a key indicator of your organization's vision, the mission statement should be reexamined periodically to determine if any changes are warranted. Changes in a mission statement should not be made lightly, as they are fundamental in describing an organization's reason for being.

Another important point of this first diagnostic target is that of planning, including long-term goals and short-term objectives. Review the corporate or functional five-year plan. Does long- or even short-term planning exist? Is there contingency planning in which provisions are made for the unexpected or for emergencies? In your judgment, will these plans hold up under the pressure of a crisis?

Compare emerging markets and product lines for synergy. Do they match? For example, one large mainframe computer company sees no long-term future for personal computers (PCs); another mainframe manufacturer sees the PC as virtually its only future. One pharmaceutical company sees great growth in fighting infections and central nervous system diseases; another is committed to biological approaches to cancer and diseases of the immune system. One hospital's goal is to increase profits by testing drugs; another company emphasizes efficiency; a third stays small to increase doctor-patient loyalty.

How does your department fit into the company's long-term goals? Make sure your long-term goals help achieve the corporate goals. Similarly, make sure your department's short-term and yearly objectives are specific, concrete, and measurable. Identify the signposts that measure how well they are achieved. Make sure the department objectives are related to the corporate objectives.

Comparing objectives is a spiral process. Departmental objectives should develop from divisional and corporate goals and strategies; work-group objectives should evolve from departmental objectives; individual leader objectives should be related to work-group objectives; and subordinate objectives should be related to leader and work-group objectives. Goals and objectives from the most operational level upward should help achieve corporate objectives and longer-term goals.

Policies

Review corporate and departmental policies. Make sure departmental and work-unit policies are in line with corporate policy. Policy states how organizational leadership wants work to be done. Effective policy should reflect quality, efficiency, and effectiveness and should be followed by the people carrying it out. It is policy to date-stamp documents as they arrive in the department; it is policy to complete internal review of documents within 48 hours; it is policy to enter data on the database before it is validated; it is policy for data editors (not researchers) to correct and verify the database. It is also policy that smoking is not permitted in the workplace and that the company does not allow compensatory time for weekend or evening travel.

Many policies evolve over time and become habits. All policies should be reviewed periodically. Some need to be revised. Some simply add bureaucracy and may have no useful purpose. Other policies may reflect legal requirements. The diagnosis should first review critical policies and preserve the ones with most impact on productivity and morale. Others should be eliminated whenever possible. For example,

- All research conducted internationally is to follow the corporate standard so findings can be used equally by all countries worldwide.

- Handling of hazardous materials must follow all local, state, and federal laws.

- Management must communicate information to employees about divisional and departmental performance, sales, productivity, and profitability if the work force is to take responsibility for problems and their solutions.

- We will acquire or license only those products that fit our strategic long-term objectives.

- Individual development plans (IDPs) are to be developed jointly by the employee and supervisor on the basis of a performance review. Plans are to be reviewed by, discussed with, and approved by the supervisor. The supervisor is to review progress every three months, in writing.

Target 2: Leadership, Delegation, Accountability, Control

A diagnosis should review departmental leadership. We have stressed the leader's importance as a diagnostician, problem solver, and manager of people, resources, and processes. Because of its sensitivity, this is one area that may not be the responsibility of the steering committee or task forces. It is an area that you may have to assess alone or with consultant help as part of the diagnostic process.

Analyzing leadership includes issues such as the group's expectations of leadership, the quality of the leadership, leadership's expectations of employees and the organization as a whole, the informal or earned power of your management team, and the efficiency of the reporting structure. How does the group expect leadership to behave? In the smokestack culture of 25 to 50 years ago, for example, workers expected management to be directive, arbitrary, and demanding, which led to divisive union-management relationships.

In today's U.S. Army, some senior commanders are still directive and authoritarian, while others delegate authority and expect individual initiative. Some junior officers chafe under one style; some resent the other. What is the organization's expectation? Examine the needs of the work group. Consider the situational requirements of leadership. A young, inexperienced, relatively immature group may require close directive supervision. On the other hand, a skilled, experienced, and mature work force may resent close supervision and is often more productive in an atmosphere in which responsibility is more fully delegated. Assess the leadership expectations and needs of the group to ensure that the style fits the needs of the group.

Leadership Quality

You must also assess your own direct reports, the departmental leadership. You must delegate to them the management of the work and, to a large extent, control of the day-to-day operations. You must be comfortable that you have the leadership in place to whom you can delegate with confidence. If you cannot delegate to them with confidence, you will soon be overwhelmed with work—your own and theirs.

A manager for a large information organization had not sufficiently delegated responsibility to his direct reports, partly because he lacked confidence in them and partly out of his own compulsion to check everything and know all the answers. So he edged toward the 70-hour work week (that's seven 10-hour days). He pressured himself with the three O's: to be omniscient, omnipresent, and omnipotent. He felt he had to know everything, be everywhere, and do everything. In the process, he created tremendous backlogs in the work. Deadlines were missed, customers upset. His own work force became demoralized and angry as they found their own work scrutinized and often redone by their boss with little apparent improvement. This led to continued conflict between the employees and the manager; ultimately he needed to leave the organization to keep the peace.

Your diagnosis should assess your mid-managers' ability to demonstrate leadership and manage managers and work groups. Do they supervise capable people to whom they can confidently delegate responsibility? Review with your managers their direct reports, and encourage them to train or closely manage the performance of those about whom they have reservations. Transitions are a good time to make tough decisions, including termination of people who have been low performers but to whom your predecessor felt personal loyalty.

In this case, coach your direct reports on how to handle counseling sessions with the problematic or low-performing employees. Sometimes you may need to counsel the employee yourself. But do take straightforward, short-term steps either to redress the weakness through training or supervision, or develop careful performance improvement plans that could lead to terminations. Your total management team will be little stronger than the weakest link.

Also assess the key department tasks and who is accountable for each. In many organizations, people look puzzled or point in multiple directions when asked, "Who is accountable for a certain job or task?" Lack of clear accountability is a sure sign of trouble. Does the accountable person exert sufficient control over the task to be sure that performance meets standards? Efficient organizations are disciplined to work quickly, profitably, efficiently, productively, or by whatever criterion you set or approve for performance. You may feel that present managers lack adequate control over the work; that financial, supervisory, workflow, or planning matters are undisciplined. Conversely, and depending on the type of organization, you may feel that things are overcontrolled in a way damaging to morale, productivity, and creativity and that individuals and teams aren't given the chance to assert themselves.

The Informal Power of Your Leaders

Check the difference between informal and formal leadership. A manager of a document center had earned her position on the basis of diligence and hard work. She was the best document filer in the group. Unfortunately, she was not very friendly or outgoing and had earned neither the friendship nor the respect of her colleagues. After her promotion, the group grudgingly followed her lead. Most of the time they simply ignored her. Before promoting her, her boss should have seen that she was not the group's informal leader. She had no informal power and no informal authority with the group. The manager would have been better off promoting the group's natural leader or going outside the department.

An Efficient Reporting Structure

Also check the organizational chart. The reporting structure should help people work efficiently. Structure should be simple and reflect the work flow and the way people really work together. Make sure the organization chart reflects how people really need to interact and encourages efficient work flow that maintains the standard for quality. As we move through the 1990s, the rule of thumb is to keep organizations as flat as possible, which can reduce bureaucratic organizational gridlock. "Flat" organizations minimize reporting levels; many report to one; hierarchy is "flattened," i.e., reduced.

Target 3: Politics, Power, Culture

When assessing the politics of your new organization, look for centers of power. Where is the informal and formal power? Who has networks of influence and can get things done, and who doesn't? Look at your organization's climate and culture and its values and beliefs. Make sure they are in agreement with your own beliefs and the corporate culture necessary to achieve the mission and ultimate vision of the organization.

Formal and Informal Influence

One of the most difficult diagnostic problems is assessing the power of those who do not initially support you. Because they may have been in the department a long time, you may feel that they have more political allies than you. That may be true. But because they have more allies does not mean they have more power. While they have informal power, you have the formal power, and, depending on how you build your vision and develop support and influence, you should be able to develop very strong informal power and influence as well. The issue of power and allegiance to you is part of *your* diagnostic responsibility *and should not be delegated to a diagnostic task force.*

John was named to head the Video Production department of a large information technology company. His first job out of high school was as a technician in the department, and he assumed greater responsibility as the department grew to more than 25 people.

Even though John was clearly the department's top performer and deserved a promotion, he had some liabilities. He was independent and strong-willed. He often kept to himself, and was not comfortable with the give and take of group problem solving. His people were not sure he heard their concerns or even cared about them. In time, two of the earliest employees developed grievances about decisions that John had made. They decided to informally organize themselves to force John to face all the group's complaints and to share decision making with a "management board," which they felt they could numerically dominate.

John was willing to listen to the grievances and attempt mutual problem solving, but was unwilling to share decision making with a management board. Having firmly decided that, his disgruntled employees had few options. They could disrupt the work, which they were partially able to do. But the ambivalence of other employees toward the disruptions, and the general weariness of the employees caused by scheming, secret meetings, and gossip took its toll. The group's spirit and commitment to this quiet revolt soon soured. Within six months, the employees who led the disruption decided to leave John's group.

Formal power is the right to hire and fire, transfer, demote or promote, and reward. Informal power is the ability to persuade, influence, and be listened to. Formal power is bestowed; informal power is earned through competence and relationships. In a showdown, formal leadership holds the money and power. It's difficult for "Turks" to beat them.

Analyze the political climate of your department. Do those with formal power also have informal power? Who has earned informal power, and how do they choose to use it? Do they help or hinder your efforts? Do they help or hurt the organization's progress?

Where are the power groups? If they are aligned along functional lines, such as cohesive work groups, your organization may be stronger for it. But if the political structure conflicts with the organizational structure, the conflict within work groups may affect productivity, cohesion, and organizational effectiveness.

A marketing manager brought into a family-owned oil distributorship to increase sales, suggested to the president (who was the founder's son-in-law) that his wife (the founder's daughter, who had worked there since she was a girl) was not organized and in fact disrupted office effectiveness. The marketing manager also suggested that one of the salesmen, who was the founder's son, was not productive and should be fired. He suggested that the company had hired too many friends and neighbors, and that some should be let go because they were not productive. His observations were correct, but nonetheless within three months it was the marketing manager who was fired. He had missed the informal politics (the wife and son's real power) and, perhaps, misunderstood the culture (hire family and friends, help people we like, work with people we trust). The owners didn't really want to get big or efficient; they just wanted to be a little more profitable, a little bigger, and hire a few more friends.

Climate and Culture

Are the department goals in sync with the organizational climate and culture, and is the department's culture aligned with the customer's? For example, a bottom-line-oriented hospital management corporation decided to conduct research for pharmaceutical companies. However, when it comes to drug research, cost is not the highest concern for most pharmaceutical companies. Given the government regulations, the company's sense of ethics, the impact that negative publicity can have on a company's reputation, and the cost of product liability, most pharmaceutical companies value quality and speed far above cost. In general, they believe that researchers concerned about the bottom line will cut corners and eventually get the companies into trouble. The obvious clash between the hospital company's cost-conscious culture and the quality goals of pharmaceutical executives is based on the cultures and values of each. What does each value? What is important to each? And can the two work well together?

Cultures differ in other ways. Financial institutions are often bureaucratic and tend to be conservative. Direct mail insurance companies tend to be very entrepreneurial, marketing oriented, and aggressive. When one buys out the other, there is bound to be a clash of values and culture complete with whining, complaining, and general disagreement. Cultures have to be shaped and cultivated; this is a process requiring hard work, dedication, and time.

Values and Beliefs

Look at the corporate values. What is really important to this company? Does your organization's culture conflict with corporate culture? Even in radically different organizations (e.g., basic research and marketing), there should be a core of common cultural beliefs. For example, if a company's mission statement is "respect for the individual, commitment to service, and commitment to excellence," it should permeate the beliefs and values of those throughout the organization, including those in different departments, such as marketing and research.

There are some beliefs you may question—that talent should be home grown; that everything we sell should be invented here (the NIH, or not invented here syndrome); that we should never use subcontractors or outside consultants; that we should only maintain products that support a certain return on investment; that we should always take the lowest qualified bid. You may question the organizational climate—the climate for risk taking, for marketing, for growth, for developing new products, for realizing better quality, better timelines, or the climate for managing and developing human resources.

Since you are in the diagnostic phase, see if individuals or the organization hold certain values for a good reason. Certain clashes of values by different individuals or departments may raise new issues, lead to reconsideration of purpose, and be ultimately helpful. Other features will conflict with top management. Before you decide that culture or values need adjusting, make sure you understand their role in the organization and the source of their support. We will take a much closer look at culture and politics and how you can use them to your advantage in Chap. 8.

Target 4: Recognition, Rewards, Incentives

The use of rewards and incentives is an important issue that a task force should address. It is usually a target for which people have a lot of energy. How are people recognized and rewarded? Are they rewarded for performance, or do they get an automatic raise based on longevity or contacts? Does your organization have performance standards and goals, and do managers use the standards and goals when appraising performances and making financial rewards? Are performance goals specific and observable? Employees should not just be told to "do your best."

Check incentive programs. Are top performers rewarded not only financially but with attendance at meetings and conferences, special projects, corporate committee assignments, awards, bonuses, public recognition, or internal promotions? Do incentives help build a sense of pride and accomplishment, or are they withheld and used to intimidate?

Are incentives used appropriately and creatively? An important area to look at is the basis for incentives. One large corporation rewards research and development vice presidents on the basis of the number of new products brought to the market, not on the basis of product success, which may take much longer to assess. Think of the message this goal creates for managers:

- Emphasis on short-term accomplishments, with pressure to produce before the yearly deadline.

- A tendency to focus on quantity before quality, to look for products that quickly get to market.

- A tendency to push aside marketability questions and market research in the rush to produce new products.

- Little attention to a product's profitability or return on investment. Because of the reward for total numbers of new products, the research vice president fights just as hard for a product with a small market or low margin as for the home runs.

- A tendency to focus on products that are easy to develop because the technology is known (often by competitors as well) rather than focus on breakthroughs, which take more time and are more expensive to develop but often produce greater profits.

What are people rewarded for? Quantity? Quality? Loyalty? Longevity? Performance? Profitability? Teamwork? Knowing the incentive system can tell you a lot about individual and group performance. The ultimate question is, Does the design of the reward and recognition system place the organization in the best position to achieve its vision of the future?

Target 5: Relationships, Communication, Teamwork

A task force can effectively analyze communication and teamwork. How well do people get along? Do they cooperate to complete a project? Do they informally share information? Are there regularly scheduled meetings to share information? What is the trust level? Will people disclose important information to others who need to know?

One of the key teamwork variables is feedback. When things go wrong, how do people express their feelings? Do they attack, or do they attempt to describe the problem and describe their feelings? Can they express anger and yet maintain trust, communication, and mutual respect? Can they use crisis to increase communication about behavior and feelings?

What is done to increase group cohesion? Are there shared events, like parties, teams, and recreational activities? How do internal committees work to increase group cohesion?

Turnover hurts communication and cooperation. The time it takes a new person to become an informal member of the group, which can be three months or longer, is a time of reduced communication and information sharing between the new person and the rest of the group. Excessive turnover affects the performance and productivity of work teams and the overall organization.

Japanese management approaches point to the slow promotion and lifetime employment in Japanese companies as a way to increase internal communication and problem solving. Long-time employees build up networks of contacts within the company that enable them to get things done quickly and efficiently, albeit informally. There is no better example of this than the U.S. Army, where a first sergeant, with 10 to 20 years experience, can get just about anything accomplished through a personal network of sergeants in supplies, administration, the motor pool, communications, planning, the mess hall, building maintenance, and housing. Conversely, when the sergeant doesn't want to do something, he or she will go by the book and cite regulations. It is a smart captain who tells the first sergeant to "get it done." A good officer knows better than to tell a good sergeant how to do his or her job. "It will be done," the motto of the U.S. Fifth Army Corps, is no empty slogan for an army that runs on the savvy of its sergeants.

Target 6: Competency, Training, Performance Management, Recruitment, Staffing Levels, Retention

An organization's human resource management practices entail a wide range of activities, including recruitment, selection and hiring, maintaining staffing levels, training and development, and competency assessment. A task force can make an excellent appraisal of the effectiveness of an organization's strengths and weaknesses in these important business-related people issues. In addition, your personal observations and interviews of staff, individuals outside of your function, and customers and clients, will provide valuable information.

Competency of Your Managers and Work Force

The competency of the work force is the strongest single determinant of your ultimate success as a manager. To the extent that you and your direct reports successfully manage and motivate your human resources, you will increase your chances of achieving your goals. Your most important job is to lead and manage to ensure that the work gets done. This begins with assessing your immediate staff and the overall competency of your work force. Whenever possible, use the insights and experience of a task force to provide input, compare approaches to building competence with functions and competitors, and recommend new programs and services.

Your direct reports should, in turn, appraise the competency of their staff. Ask for a thumbnail description of each subordinate, including his or her strengths and weaknesses, training, experience, and history with the company. It is too early to make personnel decisions based on a single reading, but as you gather data and gain perspectives on the competency of staff, these thumbnail sketches will expand and help you decide how best to use critical staff. When assessing your staff, include their technical knowledge (about the work) and their ability to manage subordinates. Once you have done your homework, give your top people your impression about the quality of their key people after they have shared their assessments with you.

Read your organization's goals, yearly objectives, structure, job descriptions, and performance standards, if they exist. They will describe what the department is supposed to accomplish, its individual roles and responsibilities, the reporting relationships, and the chain of authority. These can help you make judgments about what people are supposed to do and their expected and actual levels of competence.

Performance Management

Performance management practices help ensure that personnel do what is needed in the way it should be done. In too few companies are performance management practices used effectively. Often they are not taken seriously. Performance appraisas are generally considered a yearly ordeal that employees and managers alike endure. But if properly managed, performance management will point to performance discrepancies, help set career development goals, and help the employee set interim and yearly goals that will help the department achieve its work. Contemporary management points to the need for situational uses of performance management. Experienced workers probably need less focus on the actual job skills (which they should be reasonably expert at) and more on project achievement and maintenance. They should be more goal oriented and help the department achieve its goals. Feedback, coaching, and counseling on how the job is done and on goal achievement should be the hallmarks of a performance management program.

Performance standards should be customized to the job and should provide information on the tasks and the standards of accomplishments for individual performers. As such, they are more helpful than job descriptions alone.

Reviewing the yearly performance plans of people in your new department gives a sense of their capabilities. What does their supervisor think they are capable of? Performance goals indicate which high-priority department tasks must be accomplished within the year. Update these tasks with your direct reports. Are projects on schedule; will project members accomplish their goals; is the project still worth doing? *Where confidential personnel information is involved, you or your managers should have the only access to employee information of this kind.* The task force working in this area should provide you with a candid evaluation of how the performance management practices throughout your organization are working and what can be improved.

Recruitment and Staffing Levels

Check the recruitment and selection process. How are staff recruited? Are there selection standards? Is the recruitment and selection program set up to recruit qualified people? If not, why? What is the real cost of hiring unqualified people (i.e., in mistakes they make and in lost productivity to supervisors and trainee alike)?

Is there a training program? One company figured the cost of not formally training a new employee at between $12,000 and $15,000 in terms of downtime, inefficiencies, and the time experienced professionals and supervisors needed to review and redo work.

Is there a human resource staffing plan? Does the human resource plan fit the organization's long-term plan? Does it anticipate the types of skills the organization will need to help the company meet its long-term plans? Are personnel being recruited to help achieve the long-term plan? In a small consulting firm, two-thirds of the business consisted of training programs and materials. But the firm's probable future strategic direction consisted of management development and data-based management information systems. Who should the company be hiring—people for the old business, who could help with the present heavy work load, or people for the future business, for whom there was not yet a full work load? Should the company's top people be developing the new product line, or should they continue to lend the old line their strength and experience to keep it healthy and profitable while others develop the new products? What is the best use of resources? It is the fortunate organization that has a work force and leadership for both.

Another question is whether the department has analyzed its human resource needs. Are people working overtime, taking work home, and missing deadlines? Do they joke or complain about the work load? Perhaps people don't want to admit that they can't keep up, afraid of giving the impression that they don't have what it takes. How many new projects are coming on line in the next six to eight months, and is the organization properly staffed with enough of the right people? Worse, there may be no new projects scheduled in the near future. Are supervisors or managers who would normally delegate the work doing it themselves to justify their time and salaries? Are other people fighting over the little there is left? One manager, told he should delegate the training of new employees in his unit, said, "But then what would *I* do?" Maybe people are not busy enough. Is there dead wood? When was the last analysis of human resource needs conducted? What has changed since that analysis?

Retention

Finally, look at retention. Does the department hold onto its talent and experience, or is there constant turnover, the constant need to recruit, train, and the accompanying costs of lost productivity to supervisors and new staff alike? Talk to some who have left. Why the turnover? One company found that it was the lowest paying large firm in the industry; another, which hired mostly nurses, assigned them to travel 70 to 80 percent of the time, which many, especially those who had children, soon grew tired of. A third company's work force consisted of an all-male executive team and an all-female mid- and first-line management staff. It was the women who left.

Target 7: Resources (Including Financing and Capital), Equipment and Supplies, Data Management

Look at the department's resources. Is there money to do the job? Analyze the adequacy of the budget, the line of credit in a company where cash flow may be uneven, and financial management and reporting systems. Also review equipment and supplies available, and balance the need for technology with the need for efficiency. GM has learned that in its most technologically advanced plant, the cost of purchasing and maintaining the technology makes producing a car more expensive than at Honda's much less automated but more efficient plant in Tennessee. On the other hand, a research-based firm without automation can be seriously inefficient.

Eastman Kodak has placed word processors in executive offices, with generally favorable results from managers who can now compose correspondence and reports directly onto their screens. Many Bristol Myers Squibb executives use Xerox work stations to track projects, budgets, and the work load. As companies increasingly identify and quantify the timeliness, resources, and quality of the work, managers will require automated information systems. A task force to assess present resources, equipment, and supplies may be supported by a group to analyze the need and opportunities for automation.

Target 8: Enabling Mechanisms—Work-Flow Systems, Procedures, Work Locations

Work-flow systems analyses describe how the work gets done. They are important to help ensure consistency and quality among those responsible for the major departmental tasks.

Examine written procedures. Are they up to date? Do they reflect departmental policy? Are they consistently followed? Do they seem efficient, and do they make sense? Does the work get done efficiently in spite of or because written procedures exist? Is the informal way of communicating procedures, from experienced people to inexperienced, adequate for getting the job done, or are there inconsistencies and inefficiencies? Are people confused about what they are supposed to do and how management wants it done?

Analyze the work flow. Trace a sample of work through the system. Follow the process. Does the work flow follow well-documented procedures? Is it efficient and on schedule? Are resources available when needed, and are they up to quality? Is output of the required quality and is it on time?

What is the effect of breakdowns on quality, efficiency, and costs? What are the causes of breakdowns? Are people in the right place at the right time? Does the equipment function as it should? What are the downtime and delays? Are parts, supplies, and other inventory available when needed? What types of inventory controls are in place?

Is the work up to quality standards? Is raw material (input) of specified quality? What percentage does not meet specifications? Does the process make sense and result in the expected quality? Do individual procedures make sense? Is the work force trained, and do workers follow procedures?

Do procedures result in the specified quality? What is the quality of the product or output? Where are the quality breakdowns? What problems are uncovered by quality control? What problems come back from the clients? What kinds of problems do long-term users have? What is the reliability record compared to other similar projects or products, or according to client expectations?

As part of the organizational diagnosis, consider three approaches to collecting data about work systems: interviews, observation, and data analysis. These three approaches can be useful for you and for the work of the task force assigned to look at this target. Through interviews with supervisors and, especially, with those who perform the job day to day, you can describe the work-flow functions and the tasks that comprise each function. You can also inquire about real and ideal timelines for task performance and determine the real and ideal quality standards. This information can be compared with industry standards or regulatory requirements.

Then try to reconstruct on paper the entire work flow, from start to finish, using documents such as reports and sign-offs from an ongoing or completed project. Compare actual dates for performance tasks against a theoretically ideal project management timeline to determine how long tasks actually take with how long they should take. Examine related documentation, such as correspondence, that would indicate start and stop dates and problems; check memos and other internal communications; review committee actions. Compare work flow at different periods of time or for similar projects. Compare successful projects with problematic ones or failures. What are the patterns? Where are the problems? Hire a consultatnt to compare your operation against the competition or industry baselines.

Then observe the work flow yourself to the extent possible. For a production process, observe the different tasks and compare task performance to what you know should be happening from the expert interviews and document review.

Intellectual tasks are more difficult to observe, although you can attend committee meetings and review current documents and reports. You can attend and observe key activities—team meetings, project management activities, sales calls, field visits. Review and analyze meetings, and compare what is happening against what should be happening.

Work location is a part of work-flow analysis. Are the right tasks being done in the right place? For example, what are the consequences of validating or correcting field data at corporate headquarters rather than in the field? Should elements be completed off site by a subcontractor? Should tasks be consolidated at a single site?

Target 9: External Factors—Laws, Regulations, Community, Social or Economic Conditions

Many industries, including pharmaceuticals, chemicals, food processing, insurance, banking, transportation, and manufacturing, are regulated by government agencies and laws. As regulations change, they affect the way business is done. To analyze the present regulatory climate and how your organization responds is a part of the diagnosis. For example, as health care insurance, food labeling, and production become increasingly regulated, the laws will affect the way managers conduct both research and development and marketing.

Legal judgments strongly affect future performance. Up to 50 percent of the cost of many products (e.g., lawn mowers and all-terrain vehicles) pays for product liability insurance to protect the manufacturer from lawsuits brought by misuse of the product. Similarly, the United States has only one remaining manufacturer of small pox vaccine, primarily because there is a small but real chance (less than one in a million) that children inoculated will contract the disease from the vaccination itself, with possibly fatal consequences. So even though the vaccine is of great benefit and required by local and state public health officials, the damages recovered by parents of those few children who died from the inoculation have forced the majority of pharmaceutical companies to abandon vaccine manufacturing. Recent changes in legislation to protect manufacturers from such suits may encourage more manufacturers to produce these vaccines.

The change in government regulations for approving the marketing of new drugs has, among other things, permitted drug companies to use foreign medical data to prove that their drugs work. As a result, many companies are conducting more foreign research and requiring that research be conducted abroad so data can be included with U.S.

data. A change in government regulations, then, has led to changes (and possibly opportunities) in how business is conducted outside and inside the United States. In addition to your work and that of an assigned task force, internal audits and regulatory inspection reports provide a wealth of data about your organization's compliance with laws and regulations.

Local, state, or federal regulations can create tremendous burdens that make a business's survival more difficult. For example, many states have regulated pricing for insurance and transportation. Environmental regulations, while necessary and well intended, increase the complexity of doing business and may close down some natural resources firms. The smart and effective companies not only deal successfully with today's reality but invest heavily to predict trends and patterns. They adjust today and plan for the future. They are more fluid than stagnant and more flexible than rigid in their ability to adapt to changes around them.

Community standards can also affect a business. Concerns about safety have affected the tobacco, liquor, and auto industries. Concerns about achievement affect the organization and management of schools.

Review economic and social conditions as well. The population is getting older. People are more aware of health and fitness. The population is more highly educated. Diagnose the economic and demographic trends that will affect your new department. What will increasing consolidation mean in industries as diverse as airlines, communications, and banking? What will increased international cooperation and joint ventures mean in industries such as manufacturing, advertising, and construction? What will increased emphasis on licensing mean in pharmaceuticals, novelties and toys, and the apparel industry? What will be the effect of technology on companies that are stretching the capabilities of their present hardware rather than replacing it every four years? What does a cheaper dollar mean for an American service industry? How can a service company do business abroad?

Findings, Conclusions, and Recommendations

The steering committee ultimately receives findings, conclusions, and recommendations from each task force and consolidates this input into its overall conclusions and recommendations.

In our example, in about the twelfth to eighteenth weeks of the process, the steering committee should start to develop preliminary findings. First, the steering committee should review the task force reports for adequacy and completeness. Was the diagnosis adequate?

Did it address the right questions; was data collection adequate; were the proper people interviewed; was consultation with outside experts appropriate and sufficient; were adequate documents examined; were the customers, clients, and other outsiders interviewed significant to the work?

There are other common problems involved in the development of findings, conclusions, and recommendations. Review for issues such as the following: Do the findings seem reasonable? Balanced? Without bias? Do the findings and conclusions match your perception and the information you have collected in many private discussions and interviews? Do the findings reflect all data sources? Whenever possible, findings should be represented in objective and quantitative terms, in terms of percentage or proportions of those interviewed and using datelines or milestones described in documents.

Individual comments are significant primarily as they illustrate a perception or observation made by a significant percentage of those interviewed, or a significant percentage of documents analyzed. But individual comments that are unrepresentative of the group consensus are not balanced and sometimes unfair. Be careful, however, not to discard individual comments indiscriminately. Sometimes an individual might provide valuable insight or, at the least, contrasting ideas that can be helpful for comparisons.

The steering committee should discuss each task force's report in detail with the task force chair. If the chair is a member of the steering committee, also include at least one other member of the task force. To undergird the morale of the task force, to underscore the value of wide participation, and to ensure that task force members are heard, they must have an opportunity to appear before the steering committee and discuss their report. Steering committee members should have read the report and be prepared to discuss it. Discussion of the report should be the meeting's focus. The presentation by task force members should be limited, for example, to a 10- or 15-minute synopsis of findings, conclusions, and recommendations, followed by a discussion period.

Moreover, as deliberations continue, the steering committee should keep the task force periodically advised of its thinking and status. It is easy for task force members to confuse extended deliberations or unforeseen delays with lack of interest or rejection of their findings and recommendations. For one agency, whose work is to evaluate the quality of products to be sold to the public, product evaluations were conducted by highly educated reviewers. Their recommendations to approve or disapprove marketing of the product passed through three successive levels of management review. While the overwhelming bulk of the work was done by the first-level reviewers, who often invested hundreds of hours in their reviews, but once the review was passed onto the next level of management, the original reviewers remained uninformed about whether their recommendations were supported or not, and which of their analyses were rejected or accepted by next-level reviewers. It was as if the product of their hundreds of hours of work disappeared into a black hole. It was demoralizing to them and contributed to successively less rigorous reviews. The first-level reviewers would have preferred rejection to ignorance. Negative feedback was preferable to no feedback. For the participatory process to be credible, people must feel that their input was heard, even if it was ultimately rejected. To feel ignored is worse than being turned down.

Summary

The nine-target model involves many possible areas of study. Some include the leadership capabilities of your direct reports and are assessments you will have to make with the help of your boss. These are limited primarily to targets 2 and 3, which concern power, leadership, and organizational beliefs and values.

Other areas, including target 1 and targets 4 through 9, can be reviewed by the steering committee or by task forces organized under the steering committee. Eventually, you will review their recommendations and be involved at the decision level, but in most areas you can get considerable help.

Even in the largest organizations, it's unreasonable to study all functional areas. Doing so will overwhelm your organization's ability to collect and analyze information and to absorb and implement recommendations. With the help of your steering committee, you will ultimately derive conclusions regarding the areas of study, and develop a plan of action that will build on your organization's strengths and correct its problems.

Quick Reminders to Keep You on Track

- In Chap. 5, we described the rationale and organization of the diagnostic process. In Chap. 6, we outlined the nine-target model for focusing your diagnostic efforts.

- The nine targets are the organizational indicators of vision and direction. Your data collection efforts will be keyed to describing the relative health of these target areas within your organization.

- The nine target areas are:

  1. Mission statement, planning, goals, objectives, policies
  2. Leadership, delegation, accountability, control

3. Politics, power, culture
4. Recognition, rewards, incentives
5. Relationships, communication, teamwork
6. Competency, training, performance management, recruitment, staffing levels, retention
7. Resources including financing and capital, equipment and supplies, data management
8. Enabling mechanisms—work flow systems, procedures, work locations
9. External factors—laws, regulations, community, social and economic conditions

- With the help of many people in your organization, you will draw a number of conclusions and begin to develop a plan of action that will build on your organization's strengths and remedy its problems.

Summary of Major Responsibilities—Year 1 (Chap. 6)

First Year by Month*

	Preappoint-ment	1	2	3	4	5	6	7	8	9	10	11	12

Moving in: Establishing Yourself in Your New Assignment

- Entering the Organization
- Entering Your Boss's World

Achieving an Impact on the Organization

- Beginning to Craft Your Vision and Direction

- The Diagnostic Process: The Importance of Good Organizational Information

- Assessing Your Organization's Health
  — The Nine-Target Model

*Times are approximate.

Legend
— Primary period of emphasis
- - - Active but not a period of emphasis

Your Personal Plan of Action for Assessing Your Organization's Health (Chap. 6)

Activity	Suggested Timeframe	Perceived Barriers	Available Resources	Your Projected Timeframe	Completed (✔)
• Through diagnostic procedures described in Chap. 5, the following nine targets need to be studied and assessed. — Target 1: Mission, plans, goals, objectives, policies — Target 2: Leadership, delegation, accountability, control — Target 3: Politics, power, culture — Target 4: Recognition, rewards, incentives — Target 5: Relationships, communication, teamwork — Target 6: Competency, training, performance management, recruitment, staffing retention — Target 7: Resources (including budget), operational equipment and supplies, data management — Target 8: Enabling mechanisms such as work flow systems, procedures, work locations — Target 9: External factors such as laws, regulations, community, social or economics conditions	The entire diagnostic/assessment process should not take over four to six months. Implementation of recommendations should follow as close to the conclusion of the diagnostic/assessment process as possible.				

7

Selecting, Building, and Developing Your Work Team

If you want one year of prosperity, grow grain. If you want ten years of prosperity, grow trees. If you want one hundred years of prosperity, grow people.

CHINESE PROVERB

The only way to make a business live up to its potential is to get tough. . . . Nobody admits to promoting people on longevity. Most companies do and get organizational hardening of the arteries. Keep raising standards. Keep rooting out the lesser performers.[1]

ANDRALL E. PEARSON, Professor at Harvard Business School and former CEO, Pepsico

The most important decision that you will make during your first year is selecting your management team, building teamwork, and making sure your team and organization are effectively trained and developed. You will need to:

- Skillfully use a selection process and make good choices in establishing your work team.

- Make sensitive decisions about people, but be honest.

- Decide if certain people must be redeployed or terminated.

117

- Implement a strong team building process.
- Train, coach, and develop your people.

In this chapter, there is useful information about:

- A Conceptual Model for Selecting Your Management Work Team
- Deciding Whether to Keep Everyone
- Building a Strong Work Team and Strong Teamwork
- Training and Developing Your Work Team

Your most important responsibility during the 12 months following your appointment includes selecting your leadership staff, molding this group into a productive and confident management force, and ensuring the best possible training and development for your people. This is a process that begins in the first weeks after your appointment and continues thereafter. Accomplishing this is sometimes easy—if the organization already has good people, good direction, and good results. Unfortunately, when moving up to your new leadership role, the situation is usually neither that simple nor that clear. The following scenarios illustrate this point.

Four Team-Building Scenarios

Scenario A

Claudia has been named general counsel for a large financial services corporation. The opening resulted from the retirement of a highly respected veteran, who announced his retirement 12 months in advance of the effective date. The incumbent weakly recommended two of the three associate general counsels as his successors. Claudia was selected from a major competitor, where she was second in command of the law department. She is bright, experienced, and highly qualified. As Claudia assumes her new responsibility, she has little information about the commitment and competence of the staff she has inherited.

- What should Claudia be thinking about?
- What type of plan should she develop in regard to her staff?
- What, how, and when should she communicate with her department?

Scenario B

Phyllis has been appointed dean of a college, one of five deans at a large, private university. Selected from within, she was just about everyone's obvious choice—she had an excellent intellectual and research record, was a fine administrator, and was well liked and respected. Her peers considered her a "safe choice." Phyllis's major dilemma is that she is not confident that the existing department heads can lead the college in achieving her vision for it. She has been a long-time friend and a close colleague of the tenured staff, which now reports to her. While professional and social ties are close, she realizes that about half the tenured faculty have become stagnant and overly comfortable. She faces many of the predictable problems of those selected to move up from among their professional peers. In a rather conservative and traditional environment, Phyllis has a different vision for the college than those with whom she has worked for many years.

- How would you handle this situation if you were Phyllis?
- What are some of her alternatives and likely consequences of these potential choices?
- What timeframe would you establish for progress in achieving her vision?

Scenario C

Ron is a true entrepreneur. At 32, he is well to do, confident, experienced, and about to start his own company. He has identified a niche in the communications industry and is preparing to exploit it commercially. Ron's strengths are accounting and marketing. He needs help in new product development, sales, and in day-to-day operations. His plan is to form a new company within 12 months. Financial backing exists; he has many contacts in the financial and marketing community. Ron is unsure how to proceed in selecting his top management team.

- What should Ron be thinking about?
- What type of expertise should he be seeking—what criteria should he establish for making his selections?
- What type of help is available to him in making these important choices?

Scenario D

Len has just been appointed CEO of a medium-sized health-care company. The company's sales and profits have waned over a five-year period. There are a half dozen major competitors, with several others gaining market share. Len's predecessor retired, but the rumor is that he was forced out.

Len was appointed from within the corporation. He had two other serious internal challengers for the position, both of whom are experienced and possess valuable skills and experience. The three worked in a wide variety of management positions in the company. They have been with the company for periods ranging from 15 (Len) to 22 years. The competition for the top spot was spirited; each of the three felt uniquely qualified. As Len took over the CEO position, he was not sure how many scars remained; he was not sure of the residual politics resulting from his selection.

- How should Len proceed in selecting and building his management team?

- What factors should be most important? Least important?

- What timeframe should he give himself?

- How can he best learn from the experiences of others?

A Conceptual Model for Selecting Your Management Work Team

The approach you use to select and establish your team will be based on a number of factors:

- Your organization's mission and the ultimate vision you hope to achieve. You need people with the skills and attitudes needed to carry out the mission and your vision.

- The work. Are the managers knowledgeable about the present and future work of the organization?

- The management talent that presently exists. Does the management group get the present job done effectively? How well do they manage for present as well as future results? Is there talent you can rely on?

- How well the present staff works together. Is this a group of individuals or a team with synergy? Do they have the potential for working cooperatively and creatively as your team?

- The talent outside your organization that could fill gaps or strengthen your team. Who is available to bring knowledge, skills, and experiences to strengthen your management team?

- The extent to which the staff will align themselves with you as you assume leadership. Do they want to be on your team?

- Your prediction of which managers and staff members will choose to leave on their own during the next year. Anticipate some inevitable fallout whenever there is a formal shift of power. Whom might you need to replace in the short term? Remember, you may also need to force personnel changes.

- The organization's ability to attract talent based on its prestige, compensation, or opportunity. Will you need to take exceptional action to attract the talent that's needed? You may need to structure a job to be especially appealing or custom design compensation packages—signing bonuses, benefits, or relocation arrangements to get the talent you need.

Once these points have been considered, you can assess the organization's needs and begin to determine whether to retain or select new individuals for your management team. In assessing and selecting talent, first define the job and then determine whether the candidate measures up.

Defining the Job

Defining the job requires identifying four job elements:

1. Tasks performed on the job and the technical and management abilities needed to do the job

2. Attitudes, feelings, and other affective elements needed to be effective

3. Expected performance level

4. Performance conditions

Tasks Performed on the Job.   First review the technical and managerial tasks performed on the job under review. Reviewing these tasks will give you a sense of the type of training, background, and experience a good candidate will need. In general, a position will have between 6 and 12 primary tasks, including management and supervision tasks and technical and professional tasks.

Directly related to the tasks performed on the job are competencies needed to complete the tasks. Competencies are the skills, abilities, or talents required to perform the job tasks successfully. In what areas must the candidate demonstrate competence in the technical and professional skills needed to do the work as well as the necessary supervisory and management abilities (including self-management).

Examples of technical competencies include

- Ability to perform a particular task
- Ability to apply government regulations
- Ability to run a particular piece of equipment for a specific outcome
- Ability to analyze and evaluate technical material of a particular field
- Ability to describe, analyze, and improve the work procedures
- Ability to perform a particular computer application

Examples of management competencies include

- Ability to set organizational goals
- Ability to create a strategic or operational plan to achieve goals
- Ability to negotiate
- Ability to lead and manage diverse personnel
- Ability to make an effective management presentation

Affective Competencies.   Affective competencies include those attitudes, beliefs, and feelings needed for effective performance. You must determine what the job demands and what you require in terms of the following:

- Initiative or independent action. Does the job require a self-starter who likes working on his or her own, or someone who prefers close communication and supervision?
- Motivation. Does the job require a highly motivated professional, or can the job be adequately performed by a less directed employee?
- Teamwork. What are the requirements for teamwork, cooperativeness, and the ability to work with others?
- Desire to learn new areas and take on increased levels of responsibilities. Does the job require someone who can maintain the system as it is, or someone who can grow and expand his or her responsibility?
- Willingness to communicate openly. Do you require a close working relationship for this position, or do you prefer arms-length delegation?
- Willingness to align oneself with the values and culture of the organization. Does the position require someone who will fit in closely, or

can it (and you) tolerate independence from the organization's values and culture?

- Willingness and ability to work well with leadership and with colleagues, including diverse personalities. Does the job require an adaptable, flexible personality with good people skills?

Expected Performance Level. For each necessary knowledge or skill competency, analyze the level of competence required for the position you are assessing. Levels may range from awareness to partial performance to full, "mature" performance.

Describe the level of performance in concrete terms. For example, an accountant will require detailed, extensive knowledge of financial management systems, with many financial subskills. An operations manager may only require an overview of financial systems, along with specific skills needed to manage his or her budget. A technician may only need to be aware that the finances get managed according to a budget, which determines the resources and equipment he or she gets.

Some managers may need to set organizational goals; others should be able to develop a clear and specific implementation plan to achieve those goals. Some operations employees should be aware of implementation plans and goals, and others should be able to perform the skills needed to implement the plan. Your challenge as leader is to ensure that the people you select have, or are capable of developing, the level of skill required for the expected performance level.

Performance Conditions. Performance conditions include the environmental conditions affecting the job. These may include factors such as:

- *Travel:* Does the job require travel, including overnight stays? What percentage of time?

- *Workplace location:* Is the position at corporate headquarters, or is it at a manufacturing or research center? Is it a local assignment or one requiring relocation?

- *Working alone or on a team:* Does the job require team work or autonomy? To what degree?

- *Working independently or under supervision:* Does the job require delegation and independence, or close coordination and cooperation with you?

In summary, by analyzing each job to define all the aforementioned job factors, you can begin to determine whether you have the leadership necessary to achieve your vision. Almost all organizations have professionals trained in human resource management who can perform a detailed job analysis. This analysis can help you select leadership but will also serve as a basis for assessing training needs and managing your employees.

Determining What the Individual Brings to the Position and Management Team

Having determined the technical, managerial, and affective competencies required for each job, as well as the expected level of performance and conditions under which a person will perform, you now can assess each person's ability to meet those requirements. (See Fig. 7.1.)

The best predictor of future job performance is past performance. Even though experiences may not be identical, the core competencies needed for success in one situation can be highly predictive of success in other positions. Some managers feel that the core management competencies are of sufficient value and that a technical knowledge of the work is not essential to manage effectively. Others, supported by research in effective management, argue that a manager who knows the

Candidates' Abilities

J O B		1. Candidates' demonstrated technical and management skill and knowledge	2. Candidates' demonstrated affective competencies, e.g., attitudes, feelings	3. Candidates' demonstrated ability to work at designated levels of performance	4. Candidates' demonstrated ability to work under designated conditions of performance
R E Q U I R E M E N T S	A. The job's managerial technical and managerial task and competencies				
	B. Affective competencies needed, e.g., attitudes, values, feelings				
	C. Required levels of performance				
	D. Required conditions of performance				

Figure 7.1. Selection Model: Determining what the individual brings to the position and management team candidates' abilities.

basic work, the related technology, and procedures is better equipped for the job, gets up to speed more quickly, provides more decisive leadership, and makes better decisions. Either way, past performance is an excellent predictor of future performance.

Use multiple approaches to evaluate the present and potential members of your management team.

1. Use interviews to assess their competencies, skills, and attitudes. With the managers already in place, use a variety of settings. Conduct a formal individual interview in your office; discuss an issue briefly in their office or the hallway; or take an informal coffee break or lunch together. Attend a meeting, or travel together. Get to know how the individual thinks and works.

    When possible, also talk with your managers in groups to compare their knowledge of issues, the quality of their thought, their group problem-solving abilities, and interpersonal skills.

    The following sample questions will help you assess an individual's qualifications and attributes:

    -   What unique knowledge or skill does this person have that contributes to the strength of our management team?
    -   How has this person been utilized? What initiatives has he or she demonstrated in the present or previous positions?
    -   In what environment or assignments did this person thrive or not do so well?
    -   Of this person's top achievements, which ones relate to what we need? To our future needs?
    -   How does this person like to work? What is his or her work style? Does this person fit in with our culture and with my style?
    -   What are the strengths, weaknesses, and areas that this person is presently developing?
    -   How do this person's personal goals, desires, and aspirations match what we need?
    -   In summary, what does this person bring to the job and to our management team?

2. Observe performance on the job. See who gets the job done and who misses deadlines or has to redo work. Review documents the candidate has authored and programs he or she has developed. Observe internal candidates at staff meetings; watch them work with their staff at meetings and informally in the department. As you discuss work with the candidate's subordinates, be alert to suggestions of problems or strengths, and follow up on them.

3. Ask people you trust to refer candidates to you. Attend professional meetings and talk to people with their own networks of strong candidates. Your colleagues and contacts outside the company have

seen potential candidates in a variety of settings over a period of time. Ask for counsel and advice. Also ask people in your department to make recommendations. If you use this approach, be cautious in your discussions, particularly as they relate to incumbents. It is easy to start unnecessary rumors and create uneasiness in your organization.

When the requirements of the job match the employee's qualifications, you have a strong candidate. This is true when you select managers and professional and support personnel. As mentioned earlier, take particular care in choosing your secretary. He or she should become one of your most important and probably the closest member of your management team. Where gaps exist, assess a person's present and future ability to perform the job. Knowing the gaps allows for custom designing training and development for employees with potential, and helps determine where you may need to go outside for help, or where you can make internal adjustments in work and managerial assignments.

Deciding Whether to Keep Everyone

On occasion, an incumbent does not rate well over an extended period of time and after thorough appraisals. If you are contemplating termination of an employee, seek the advice of legal counsel with expertise in personnel and labor law and, if available, your organization's specialist in human resources and employee relations.

Today's laws can be complicated and laden with difficulties. However, you must not let your understandable reluctance to get involved in the legal and personal complications of a termination deter you from selecting, building, and developing the best management team possible. Do not keep marginal people because of sympathy or false hope. If you have a substantial doubt about an individual, mutually work on a performance improvement plan over a reasonable period of time. This plan could include a different work assignment that more closely matches a person's abilities. But it may be necessary to terminate individuals. Marginal performers will ultimately affect your own performance and your organization's success.

Sound ethics and good business practice should guide your treatment of employees who are barely holding on or those who should be terminated. Make every effort to see that the company helps them reestablish their careers elsewhere (including severance packages and out-placement counseling). They should be assisted in preserving their personal integrity, psychological well-being and, within reason, their financial stability. Professional out-placement services and your human resources department can provide excellent guidance in structuring support services and equitable severance packages for terminated employees.

Building a Strong Work Team and Strong Teamwork

As you decide whom you want on your management work team, you should also be thinking about how to shape them into a cohesive unit. Building a strong and committed work team is fundamental to the success of the newly appointed leader.

Generally, the leader struggles to transform the independent, and sometimes disjointed, efforts of professionals and managers into a well-oiled, dedicated, and directed work team. More than any other period, the first nine months of new leadership prove to be the most opportune period for individuals to come together and mesh into an effective work team. This window of opportunity is critical for you. This is the time when new expectations can best be instilled and new habits formed. The challenge is to aid the group in identifying and strengthening the fundamentals necessary to achieve a motivated, focused, and dedicated team. If this transformation is not well under way early in your transition, and if not in place after approximately nine months, it becomes increasingly difficult and sometimes impossible to effect. If a strong management team has not been formed by the end of your first year, your supervisors may take steps themselves that may affect your career directly. Let's look at what can be done during this early period.

A Winning Team

How do you know when you have a well-functioning work team? Take a moment to list 5 to 10 characteristics or attributes of the best work teams of which you have been a part.

1. _____
2. _____
3. _____
4. _____
5. _____
6. _____

7. _____

8. _____

9. _____

10. _____

The teams that have consciously worked on making themselves strong tend to be the backbone of their organization. They exhibit positive characteristics and become the framework to build high achievement. They consistently outperform less focused, less energized work teams.

Common Characteristics of Well-Functioning Work Teams

An effective leader fosters a well-functioning work team. Characteristics include the following:

1. The team understands and supports the organization's vision and goals.

2. The team shares a small, focused, well-understood set of beliefs or values about quality and service.

3. The team is aware of, and works to improve, its process or how it operates. This includes issues such as how decisions are made (generally by consensus), communication (open, direct), leadership styles (collaborative, situational), membership (flexible), and norms (shared).

4. Members listen well to each other and pull for each other.

5. People openly express feelings and ideas. Conflicts are managed constructively rather than stifled. Win-win conflict resolution is a norm, and both sides can accept the outcome.

6. Group decisions are often made through consensus, as opposed to a majority vote or minority power plays. As necessary, those with authority make tough decisions when consensus is not possible or a decision needs to be made *now!*

7. Assignments and responsibilities are clear and accepted by members.

8. The team effectively manages influences from external forces such as policies, regulations, procedures, politics, and constituents or customers.

9. The team gets *results:* high-quality products, in the shortest time frame possible, requiring fewer resources. High-performing work teams focus on results. Results are their constant target.

Team-Building Experiences

The purpose of team building is *to become a more effective work team* to achieve the organization's vision and defined goals. In his practical book *Working in Teams,* James Shonk identifies five factors that influence team effectiveness:[2]

1. *Environmental influence: The impact of influence outside of the team.* This includes

   Policies and procedures: corporate, client, government regulations
   Systems: rewards and communications
   Organizational structure: the hierarchy
   Outside demands: customers and government

2. *Goals: What the team is to accomplish.* This includes

   Clarity of goals
   Ownership and agreement of goals
   Specific and measurable goals
   Sharing of goals among team members
   No conflicts regarding purpose and goals

3. *Roles: Who does what.* This includes

   Understanding and need for clarity of roles
   Agreement and ownership of roles and responsibilities

4. *Processes: The way in which the team accomplishes work.* This includes

   Collaborative, win-win decision making
   Seeking consensus
   Open communications
   Efficient, effective meetings
   Collaborative, situational style of leadership

5. *Relationships: Quality of interaction.* This includes

   Expression and acceptance of feelings, attitudes, and emotions
   Open airing of interpersonal issues

Shonk's model is helpful for understanding the key factors in team effectiveness and is useful for building organizations. You must act in ways that assure strength in your team, and you must set up means to continuously evaluate your team's health and effectiveness.

Team-building efforts take many forms, from a short, manager-led discussion about important team issues to a consultant-facilitated series of meetings or offsite "retreats." The goal is always the same—to become a more effective work team in order to achieve desired results and the ultimate vision of your organization. Leadership teams that work on improving themselves increase both their diagnostic and problem-solving abilities. The team's ability to analyze and improve its process is heightened. Team members are conscious of their behavior in groups and are striving to improve their group performance.

Situations in which Team Building Is Most Useful

Team building is most effective in the following situations:

1. Formation of a new team, such as
   - New department, or a new district or region.
   - New offshoot function of an established department.

2. New people joining an existing group, such as
   - New director who wants to establish new work standards moves to an existing function and inherits a staff.
   - New team members join the organization, possibly with an existing leader in place.
   - Corporate reorganization results in new members or a reorganization of roles and responsibilities.
   - Staff expansion for a growing organization.
   - Staff reduction results in a new management team.

3. Revitalization of a stagnant staff or a staff in trouble, such as
   - Corporate team with no growth in market share. Group is defensive, balky, unhappy.
   - Staff attempting to build new procedures and practices into the organization.
   - Rebuilding a staff that has performed inadequately or has not competed successfully.
   - Seeking to become more effective while under constraints of budget and potential staff reductions.

4. Building greater strength into an existing healthy team, such as
   - Twice yearly periodic "preventive health" team building to identify and remedy small problems.
   - Creative problem-solving training designed to strengthen teamwork within the organization.
   - Interdisciplinary work team meetings for three days off site to plan progress and to build teamwork.
   - Annual retreat for your leadership team to decompress, keep each other informed, and to plan and problem solve.

5. Building strong teamwork between two or more functions, such as
   - Increasing collaboration between a marketing organization and the sales and research organizations.

- Building a stronger working relationship between your organization and a contractor or vendor responsible for fulfilling contract specifications.
- Building trust and teamwork between a home office executive staff and management in a regional branch office.
- Creating teamwork between U.S. and international management teams that are competitive and need to manage in a multicultural setting.

Guidelines for Team Development

You can learn much from other managers' team development successes and failures. Here are some guidelines for success.

1. *Have a clear, simple goal for the team building.* Be clear about what your leadership team is to accomplish—its *task*. Task objectives identify changes in what the organization does. The leadership team should be clear on what to develop, such as a new set of organizational goals, new products, a new organizational structure, a new set of standard operating procedures, a new image or ad campaign, a new technology, or a more efficient work flow. A leadership team of an insurance company recently worked on its accountability for key tasks as a way to improve how it develops new products.

2. *Solicit involvement and input before beginning.* Participation builds commitment. Get team members involved in planning the sessions. Get individual and group input on membership, where to get information, issues to address, communication, and decision making. Make sure you have developed a climate of support for the process itself and how the process is to proceed. Do not start without the support of key opinion leaders.

3. *Create conditions for candid discussion, honesty, and objective feedback.* Model constructive behaviors that help establish a successful team. Those positive behaviors focus on behavior and performance, not judgments and opinions. Be descriptive rather than judgmental. Describe the *effects* that behavior and practices are having on the organization rather than their motivation or rightness or wrongness. Keep things objective, based on observed performance and effects, not labels.

4. *Stay work oriented; use solid data.* Team building, because it requires analysis and feedback, is often seen as risky. People may get angry or hurt. They may let out their emotions. Whenever possible, use projects and responsibilities as the basis for team building rather than having the team analyze only communication and dynamics. People are more willing to try new approaches and behaviors within the context of work.

While focusing on work, the astute group leader can help the group members build awareness of their individual behavior and performance to strengthen their effectiveness.

5. *Don't expect changes overnight, but do expect changes.* Most of our organizational and personal behavior is ingrained. For most of us, change is difficult, even when we want it. Team building should be thought of as an ongoing process, not a single event. Your constant attention to the process of team building, modeling helpful behaviors, providing feedback to team members on their successes and failures, and maintaining positive expectations that teamwork will improve, will help team members unlearn dysfunctional ways and foster improved teamwork.

6. *Do not raise expectations that cannot be met.* Credibility and trust, gained through a positive team-building process, are difficult to earn but easy to lose. Be careful of promises that are not directly under your control. Organizational and political constraints frequently are limiting.

Gary, an experienced manager, brought his leadership team together at a retreat every three months, determined that they would strengthen their working relationship and solve organizational problems. By the fourth retreat, they had strengthened personal working relationships and addressed most of the issues they could affect. As they continued to meet, it became increasingly apparent that their organization's real problems were from the outside—inadequate resources, poor quality from their suppliers, and inefficiencies in their support organizations. They were powerless to improve these problem areas, and the team retreats only served to remind them of their powerlessness and their unmet expectations.

The major benefits that should be touted from the beginning of the process are better group and individual performance, ease of collaboration and communication, the pride of being part of a winning team, and preparation for future challenges.

To a large extent, organizational improvement is gained through role and goal clarification, better communication, and teamwork. Keep a realistic perspective. Team building will improve the things you can control, but you can't control everything. Here are typical responses that we have heard from individuals who have been involved in team building:

"We understand each other's roles better."
"Our purpose, goal, and direction are clearer."
"We are clearer with one another. Most important, we learned how to listen to each other better."
"I realize that *my* success is dependent on *our* success."

"I realize the importance of group process, not only for our team but in my interaction with my customers."

"We realized that there are many alternatives, not just one right answer."

"My eyes really were opened around the issue of conflict. The principle of win-win problem solving is now a part of me."

"We realized that teamwork helps us to compete better."

"I am more accepting of others' points of view."

"We learned to observe not just surface behavior, but could see and hear several levels down."

7. *A time investment must be made.* Whether it is one meeting, a series of sessions, or an offsite retreat, people should think of the effort as an important investment in the organization's health. This is no trivial expenditure in time, effort, or money. It is not a holiday; rather it is important to managing the organization.

Strong organizations are characterized by leaders who develop strong managers. Strong leaders invest time in their people—in their training, their daily supervision, and their development. These are purposeful activities designed to create a better organization. All management, which is primarily the management of people, requires time—yours and theirs.

8. *An outcome of team building should be realistic solutions and action plans that are followed up, monitored, and rewarded.* A poster on an office wall read, "When all is said and done, there is usually much more said than done." Team building means commitment to keeping the best that we have and improving areas that need to change. This requires responsibilities that are "owned" by the team and supported by a commitment to review and reward progress. A manufacturing team created several effective ways to build on a three-day, offsite team-building retreat that was critical to turning that organization around. They agreed to the following:

- Each participant included at least one team effectiveness objective as part of his or her annual personal performance plans.
- At least 15 minutes were spent during every staff meeting discussing recent behaviors that built on the team effectiveness retreat.
- The management team agreed to a follow-up meeting in six months. For part of the meeting, the members would review group and individual team progress related to teamwork objectives established at the original team-building meeting.

The director's behaviors and practices were internalized by his staff. In turn, each of the director's immediate reports replicated a similar process within each of their own work units. This management team went from having little or no time to consider how to operate, to a period of experimenting with new team behaviors. Today this group has become a well-functioning team that has helped the organization achieve its business goals.

9. *When feasible, enlist the aid of a skilled group and organizational consultant to facilitate the team-building process.* Over the last several decades, the field of organizational development has established itself as a valuable tool for managers. Some team-building efforts can be led by the organization's leader; occasionally, a task force comprised of a cross section within a management group can conduct its own team building. However, it is often wise to enlist the help of an experienced organizational consultant to add structure and an unbiased eye to the process. In addition to infusing expertise, an internal or external consultant will free the manager in charge to participate with his or her team in the activities and become a member of the team.

Training and Developing Your Work Team

Rationale

In this chapter, we have looked at issues relating to the selection of your work team and team building. A third pillar needs to be added: training and development, and coaching your people.

Individual and departmental training and development needs should have surfaced as a result of the diagnostic work that you began as you took over your new position. These needs may be technical, supervisory and managerial, or behavioral and interpersonal. Technical needs relate to the content or expertise of the work itself (e.g., sales training, upgrading financial or computer skills, and increasing state-of-the-art scientific knowledge). Supervisory and management training may include managing performance, employment and selection, planning, delegation, monitoring work, organizing work flow, and time management. All training is designed to improve one or more of the following:

1. Knowledge of information, procedures, principles; what people need to know

2. Skills—what people actually do to apply knowledge

3. Attitudes and feelings about things and people, the way people approach their work and their colleagues

Move quickly to establish people development as a primary organizational value. During the first months on the job, you signal the importance of good personnel selection, orientation, training, and development.

1. You are setting new, often higher expectations of people and of their work.

2. New employees may be entering the organization. They will need to understand the mission, the functions, services or products, and day-to-day operating procedures.

3. Rapid change in work means today's skills will be quickly outdated. Learning must be timely and continuous. New operating procedures and skills are the norm.

4. Competition is ever increasing. Developing skilled contributors and managers is a key competitive strategy.

5. Organizations will have underutilized, marginally performing, or problem employees. In almost all work units, there can be gains of at least 10 percent in individual employee performance given skillful job matching, training, coaching, and overall supervision. The previous director of a major department was convinced that he had to have a staff increase of 15 percent just to "stay above water." When replaced, the new director not only did not increase staff, but in concert with the employees set higher performance standards for each position in the department. This effort was part of an overall performance improvement program (PIP) that the new director initiated and led, a program she began during the three months after moving up to her new post.

Training and Development Guidelines

Both employees and supervisors should have training and development expectations. Some key ones are as follows:

1. The primary responsibility for the employee's professional development always rests with the individual. Individuals must take the initiative to identify and request development and activities, feedback, and appraisals from which they can grow. Make clear to them in written policies and in your interactions that the people who report to you have the primary responsibility to identify their own strengths and weaknesses and determine their developmental goals and activities. Foster initiative and responsibility.

2. You have the following minimum expectations of employees:

- Solid job performance in present assignments.
- Commitment to ongoing professional development and assess-

ment, including expansion of existing strengths or remediation of a performance problem.

- Networking and gaining knowledge of the needs of one's own organization, as well as other organizational functions. Substantial progress toward completing the organization's formal training curriculum or relevant external training is a foundation for further development.

3. The secondary responsibility for professional development rests with the employee's immediate manager, who must provide at least the following:

- Joint agreement with the employee on establishing developmental goals and support for a professional development plan.
- Candid discussions of the individual's performance and career potential.
- Ongoing coaching, counseling, and feedback.

Types of Training and Development

Training and development activities come in a variety of formats, including the following:

1. On-the-job coaching and development counseling from a supervisor or senior coworker who is a master or mentor

2. Job rotation into a job where a new skill must be learned and practiced

3. Project teams and special assignments that help the employee apply new skills and knowledge

4. Replacement assignments during vacation, illness, etc.

5. Lateral transfers to practice a different skill set

6. University executive development programs

7. Technical and management skills training

8. Opportunities to make presentations, which require research or analysis

9. Attendance and involvement in department, division, and staff meetings

10. Serving as instructor, conference leader, or trainer, which provides the opportunity to integrate skills

11. Coaching from specialists in the organization

12. Self-study of manuals, bulletins, reports, and printed material, including home study

13. Attendance at selected conferences, symposia, and workshops

14. Participation in meetings of professional and technical societies

15. Personal counseling, including behavioral skills modeling and modification

16. University course attendance, study groups, and in-house courses

17. Operating responsibility for a new function or task, to practice new skills

Coaching and Counseling

Coaching and counseling is a powerful, flexible approach to elicit subordinates' self-assessment, which, when combined with the manager's feedback, results in mutual understanding, commitment to mutually accepted goals, and a specific plan of action for achieving the goals. The terms *coaching* and *counseling* are generally used synonymously. In the strictest terms, coaching focuses on improving job skills and knowledge. Counseling centers primarily on issues of attitude, motivation, or human relation skills.

Coaching and counseling encourage daily performance monitoring, reinforce good performance, and can be a terrific tool for improving work. Because coaching skills open communications and ensure ongoing feedback, employees generally value the approach. The open flow of communication reduces the tension of more formal performance reviews because there are no surprises. Subordinates know where they stand on a daily basis. Coaching and counseling are the most useful tools in building the helping relationships and empowering behaviors that improve job performance. From the many models for coaching and counseling, we have evolved the following six-step process. Its strengths are simplicity, ease of use, and consistently positive results.

The Coaching and Counseling Process

1. *Establish climate.* Mutually identify specific or discrete performance objectives to meet, and define the performance to be discussed.

2. *Attain the subordinate's self-assessment.* The subordinate should discuss his or her performance with the supervisor or manager, including the following:
   - What have I done that I feel has contributed to the achievement of my own, or department, performance goals or standards?
   - What, if anything, have I done that I could change or do differently to achieve my performance goals and/or standards?
   - If I would change anything, how would I go about addressing my performance goals and standards differently?
   - How can my supervisor or manager best help me?

3. *Provide feedback.* Supplement, correct, or credit performance cited in the subordinate's self-assessment. Reach a mutual understanding of any differences.

4. *Confirm agreement of necessary performance changes.* Explore alternatives to support changes, and redefine or restate expected performance levels.

5. *Establish an action plan.* With the subordinate, plan the developmental activities to help him or her reach the objectives.

6. *Plan for monitoring and review of performance.* The subordinate's developmental progress should be monitored on an ongoing, planned basis, with frequent and open opportunity for feedback and coaching.

If performed well, coaching and counseling should be a positive experience. It should strengthen the supervisor-subordinate relationship and become a natural part of your repertoire of skills and behaviors.

Summary

In this chapter, we have looked at the importance of selecting, building, training, and developing your leadership team and work unit. Doing this well is among your most important activities during your first year as a manager. To a large extent, people selection and their development will determine the pace of bottom-line improvement and overall team effectiveness.

Quick Reminders to Keep You on Track

- Several of your most important responsibilities during the twelve months following your appointment include selecting your leadership staff, molding this group into a highly productive and confident management force, and making available the best possible training/development for your people.

- The choice of your staff is the first pillar of your team's effectiveness. The approach you use to establish your team will be based on a number of factors, including:

  1. Your organization's mission and the ultimate vision you hope to achieve.
  2. The type of work that exists and that will likely exist in the future.
  3. The present type and variety of management talent.

4. Your assessment of how the present staff works together.
5. The talent outside your organization that could fill gaps or strengthen your team.
6. Your evaluation of the extent to which the staff has or will align themselves with you as leader of the function.
7. Your prediction of which managers and staff members will choose to leave on their own during the next year, possibly because they didn't get your job or other important positions.
8. The organization's ability to attract talent based on its prestige, compensation, or opportunities.

- Having considered the preceding points you can assess the organization's needs for key managers and individual contributors and begin to determine whether to retain or select new individuals for your management team.

- Remember that selecting talent is usually the single most important thing you can do to create a strong organization.

- The selection process should begin with a detailed definition of the job, its requirements, and its key factors necessary for success.

- You must determine what incumbents and candidates for positions bring to the position and management team when compared to the key factors necessary for success. Often a difficult decision to make once you have started in your new position is, "Should I keep everyone?" If you decide to terminate someone, remember that you have legal responsibilities that should be reviewed carefully with legal counsel and/or a specialist in human resources.

- If you do decide to terminate one or more people, try to preserve their integrity and self-concept. Whenever possible, provide outplacement counseling and a generous severance package. Such treatment helps the people, but also communicates a lot about you to others.

- You not only will be selecting your management team, you will also need to work with them to become a strong team. This is a second pillar of your team's effectiveness.

- Certain factors characterize well functioning work teams. These factors can become goals for team-building efforts. You might want to have a skilled consultant work with you in your team-building efforts.

- There are situations in which team building is most meaningful. This is especially true when there has been an absence of teamwork or when the organization has undergone considerable change.

- A third pillar of your team's effectiveness is the training, development, and coaching of your people. There are many approaches to this responsibility, and they need to be carefully chosen and tailored.

Summary of Major Responsibilities—Year 1 (Chap. 7)

First Year by Month*

	Preappointment	1	2	3	4	5	6	7	8	9	10	11	12
Moving in: Establishing Yourself in Your New Assignment													
• Entering the Organization	▬	▬	▬	-	-	-							
• Entering Your Boss's World	▬	▬	▬	-	-	-	-	-	-				
Achieving an Impact on the Organization													
• Beginning to Craft Your Vision and Direction	▬	▬	▬	▬	▬	▬	▬	-	-	-	-	-	-
• The Diagnostic Process: The Importance of Good Organizational Information		▬	▬	▬	▬	▬	▬	-	-	-	-		
• Assessing Your Organization's Health — The Nine-Target Model		▬	▬	▬	▬	▬	▬	-	-	-	-	-	
• Selecting, Building, and Developing Your Work Team		▬	▬	▬	▬	▬	▬	▬	▬	▬	▬	▬	▬

*Times are approximate.

Legend
——— Primary period of emphasis
- - - Active but not a period of emphasis

Your Personal Plan of Action for Selecting, Building, and Developing Your Work Team (Chap. 7)

Activity	Suggested Timeframe	Perceived Barriers	Available Resources	Your Projected Timeframe	Completed (✓)
• Defining the key jobs needed in your organization including the following: — Technical and management competencies — Affective competencies — Expected performance levels — Defining conditions under which employees will perform	Begins in the initial weeks after your appointment and is on-going thereafter.				
• The selection process of key individuals—determining what individuals bring to the positions and management team. Multiple approaches include: — Interviews by yourself and others — Observations of on-the-job performance — Referrals from trusted colleagues — Formal technical or executive assessments	Begins in the initial weeks after your appointment and is on-going thereafter.				
• Deciding if any staff need to have their jobs changed or terminated	Begins in the initial weeks after your appointment and is on-going thereafter.				
• Deciding what steps need to be taken and then implementing steps to build a strong work team	Begins in the initial weeks after your appointment and is on-going thereafter.				

Your Personal Plan of Action for Selecting, Building, and Developing Your Work Team (Chap. 7) (Continued)

Activity	Suggested Timeframe	Perceived Barriers	Available Resources	Your Projected Timeframe	Completed (✓)
• Training and developing your work team in one or a combination of the following: — *Knowledge* of information, procedures, or principles — *Skills* necessary for the job — *Attitudes, feelings* regarding the job, work culture. — Establishing training and development guidelines — Determining types of training and development that are appropriate — Implementing ongoing coaching and counseling	Begins in the initial weeks after your appointment and is on-going thereafter.				

8

From Resistance to Renewal: Building Your Management Team's Commitment

*We must all hang together, or assuredly we
shall all hang separately.*
BENJAMIN FRANKLIN, July 4, 1776

Anticipate resistance to your efforts while planning for organizational renewal. In doing so, you can build real commitment through your management team. You will need to:

- Identify those factors in your organization that will help and hinder your efforts.
- Effectively overcome forces and factors that resist change.
- Develop and implement a change strategy that works.
- Learn from others' failed change efforts to increase your chances of your success.
- Deal realistically and effectively with the politics of change.
- Understand your personal political inventory and what to do with it.

In this chapter, there is useful information about:

- What You Should Know About Your Organization's Culture
- Why People Resist Organizational Change
- Key Behaviors and Principles of Effective Organizational Change Efforts
- The Big Three Implementation Strategies
- Learning from Organization Efforts That Fail
- Anticipating the Politics of Change

In this chapter we will look at the forces in organizations that tend to resist change and maintain the status quo. The process of problem solving and strengthening the organization will unnerve some and excite others. Some will fight, while others (your biggest supporters and strongest contributors) will "own" problems and share in the solutions. These winners will turn barriers and problems into opportunities for improvement and renewal. These are the people who will join you in a joint venture to achieve common goals. However, some will drop out while others try to ensure your failure.

A few people usually leave for other jobs after a new leader's arrival. This can be healthy for you and for them. You may lose experience and expertise, but turnover has a way of unclogging career paths for your bright, ambitious people. It also allows you to recruit some new blood. Promotions and new assignments become possible. Those who want to advance have opportunities to grow. Even without promotions, turnover lets you enrich and expand existing job responsibilities because assignments and projects are left uncovered.

When people leave your organization, wish them well. The impression that you leave on those who stay will be positive. Help them see the opportunities ahead even though it is natural for each to feel the loss of a friend and colleague and their expertise. In short, turn voluntary turnover into new opportunities for you and those working with you.

Just as some will choose to leave, some of those who remain will fight you. They will test your skills, strength, and clarity of purpose.

When Dick took over a major department in a financial management company, he felt considerable hostility from about a quarter of the department. Some felt that he wasn't qualified because he came from another functional area. Moreover, his training was in another discipline. Yet he had proven himself a very capable manager and project leader in previous assignments. Besides being talented and a hard worker, Dick had developed a strong relationship with an executive who periodically provided valuable guidance.

At least four internal candidates had applied for Dick's position and were not chosen. Dick dealt with the four straight on. He began to model the behaviors he expected of others. In group and in individual meetings with them, he stated that he valued their talent and experience and that he hoped that they could stay and join his team. Dick acknowledged their disappointment in not being selected and their need to sort out their individual futures. He felt that they could contribute and influence others to do the same.

Two stayed and became valuable members of the department and earned greatly expanded responsibilities. Over a six-month period, Dick had to come to terms with the third individual, who never bought in and never joined the transition. Nor did he demonstrate the management and leadership capabilities expected of the job. Following ongoing, documented coaching and counseling sessions, warnings, and finally a probationary period, Dick eventually terminated the individual.

The fourth individual was the toughest of all. In subtle, often sneaky ways, he not only resisted Dick's leadership but tried to undermine him. He held back and slanted information that Dick needed. Within and outside the department, he missed few opportunities to criticize Dick, but because he used humor rather than outright criticism, he was harder to pin down. He wrote memos pointing out "errors" Dick made. When asked to contribute at executive team meetings, he passed, made a wisecrack, or criticized. Rarely did he build on an idea or contribute positively to the group. He wanted his friends in the department to support him and undermine Dick. But Dick's team members, first indirectly, and then more forthrightly, began to brief Dick on what was happening. They, too, were anxious that the department go forward. A second termination was imminent and was avoided only because the individual in question accepted a position elsewhere days before he would have been fired.

In Dick's experience, two good people chose to help, and they positively influenced others' performance. Two others chose not to contribute. One clearly tried to impugn his new boss. Both would have poisoned the renewing organization.

Yesterday's actions were antecedents for Dick's present success. Dick directly confronted resistance, and as a result he and the organization benefited. Dick insisted that team members must be committed, energetic, and creative. He communicated and modeled from day 1 his view of the people and organization he wanted. Dick knew what he expected of himself and of others—the type of work culture from which the employees and the corporation could benefit—and he succeeded. He got the type of people he wanted and got rid of the malcontents and nonperformers. Now let's look at how you can translate resistance to renewal.

What You Should Know About Your Organization's Culture: A Prerequisite to Organizational Renewal

In recent years the social sciences have viewed groups and work systems in new ways. One key finding has been that, like societies, businesses and other types of organizations have their own cultures. In its simplest form one could define organizational culture by answering the question, "What's it really like around here?" In Chap. 6 we introduced culture as a key diagnostic target in helping you understand your new organization. As you assume leadership, you will have to understand your organization's culture in much greater detail. This knowledge is a prerequisite to organizational renewal and needs to be a priority as you move into your new position and continue in your first year.

Several concepts are important in understanding organizational culture:

1. *Whenever people live or work together, they form a culture.* Culture is a complex web of traditions, values, beliefs, and expectations that exist on an everyday basis. Culture should not be mistaken for the organizational climate, which tends to be transitory and shorter term. Culture describes the social, emotional, and psychological foundation on which decisions are made and actions occur. Companies with strong cultures model by example, matching their guiding principles and vision with the reality of daily behavior.

2. *Every culture develops unwritten expectations and ways of doing things, called norms, that are major determinants of the behavior within that work culture.* Norms range from those that affect how people work together and how power and authority are used to those influencing how people are recognized and rewarded. Norms can also include subtle behaviors such as communication and signs of stress. Whether overt or subtle, understanding the unwritten or "shadow" organization, as it is sometimes called, is a critical skill for the leader who is assuming new responsibilities. If organizational renewal and growth are to be maximized, the influence of norms on *what, how,* and *why* behavior and events occur must be understood.

The best time to begin influencing the climate and culture is during your first several months on the job. This must happen as you help people learn about and understand their culture and the positive as well as negative impact it has on them.

When Andrew was assigned as department head in a medium-sized accounting firm, he had been forewarned about the culture he would inherit. This department had been marginally profitable for the preceding four years. Management had been somewhat laissez-faire, more concerned with work force job satisfaction and autonomy than with productivity. It was a very nice place to work. Predictably, the culture strongly resisted efforts to change.

- Most professional staff maintained the 8½-hour work day, regardless of impending customer deadlines or the workload. Members of the executive team typically were the only ones in the building after 5:00 P.M. Compensatory time was taken liberally, especially for travel. Some would only travel between 8:00 A.M. and 5:00 P.M., even if the travel time extended the trip by a day. If West Coast work required Saturday travel, they took the following Monday off. If Chicago travel would get them home after 7:00 P.M., some would stay overnight in a Chicago hotel, or travel late and take the next day off.
- Supervisors did not assign work; rather, they offered work to employees, who often felt free to reject it depending on their tastes, like or dislike of travel, and matters of convenience. Supervisors had to ask workers whether they would take on work, and often had to beg people to take on jobs that required travel. Frequently supervisors ended up doing difficult or inconvenient jobs themselves.
- By failing at or otherwise resisting work they did not enjoy, some workers had carved out rather undemanding jobs for themselves. Since there was not enough of what they liked to fill a workday, these people were only marginally productive. Profitability was the result of efforts of too few members of the work force.
- Because people expected to work autonomously, some resented attempts to train and supervise. They neither understood nor appreciated the value management brought to the product.
- Some mid- and lower-level managers conspired to keep top managers away from the work, fearful that management might try to control working conditions, work flow, staffing, or hours.

With a mandate to make his department profitable, Andrew had to confront the culture directly. First, he formed a leadership team with the four top managers. They identified the organization's strengths and problems, and began working on the weaknesses. A financial information system was installed that assigned hours to jobs and provided reports to top management that showed which jobs were profitable.

Weekly time sheets tracked the time of particular projects as well as administrative, sales, and product development time. Profitability took on much greater importance as staffing and pricing policies were revised. Employees and mid-managers received monthly reviews of their hours and productivity.

Most importantly, Andrew met with employees individually and in small groups on a regular basis, asking, "What are you doing? What's difficult? How are projects coming? What are the problems? What do you need? What's next?" He did this one, two, three times a week with members of his leadership team, lower-level managers and workers, and in biweekly department meetings. He touched base with everyone frequently, including support staff and work force, and set an example for other managers to follow. He managed by walking around, listening attentively and responding honestly and directly.

Gradually, the culture began to change. People became more attuned to profitability and accountability. Mid- and lower-level managers, more mindful of the expectations, began to ask for more work. Perhaps most importantly, those who most strongly defended the old culture and resented the constant supervision, the accountability, the meetings, and the talk about profitability eventually left the company. Those who replaced them were selected partly for their work habits, partly for the skills they brought, and partly because in their interviews, they indicated that they expected a different culture. The company became hungrier and leaner.

Organizations with unhealthy cultures know it. The managers who are working long hours to pick up the slack left by those under them are resentful. Ambitious mid- and low-level managers are concerned about the organization's health because their livelihoods depend on it—they have tuition, mortgages, and bills to pay.

Find these people. Build around them. Hire people who will support a new culture. In the worst case—and it has happened—you may even have to weed out a lot of the old guard before the culture can change.

3. *Cultures are not powerless.* People are capable of visioning and molding the cultures of which they are a part just as they are capable of being shaped by that culture.

Often during the early phase of a manager's transition, the prevailing feeling of the organization is that problems will continue, that things really can't change. This sense of powerlessness is often found at all levels in the organization. A corollary is an individual's feeling that "others within the organization are better able to improve or effect change and renewal." It is common to hear a middle management group say that if improvements are to occur, then senior management has the power to make it happen. These same senior executives are frequently heard bemoaning their inability to get those below them—

the workers, first-line supervisors, and middle managers—on board. After all, they reason, this is where the work is really done. Certainly, middle and first line management is where the people are who can make ideas succeed or fail.

The workers, on the other hand, who have much more influence and power than they typically recognize, look upward and say, "That's their job, they set the rules, they have the clout." The prevailing sense is that the power and responsibility lies elsewhere and that others are responsible for success. Some use this as a weapon to avoid responsibility and place the blame elsewhere. As Janet, an experienced manager, would often tell her bosses, "You people had better . . ., somebody had better . . ., nobody seems to . . ., somebody ought to . . .," as if everything that needed improving was someone else's responsibility.

In reality, power rests within all of the groups working together to synergize talent and energy with the goal of becoming stronger and better. Excellent leaders at every level of the organization fail to accept "that's the way things are here" or "that's the way it's always been" as the norm. They are able to identify and reverse the forces that resist positive movement and involvement.

When Robert was an assembly line worker in a truck plant, he made frequent suggestions to his foreman for improving efficiency and quality. He didn't complain; he didn't file grievances with the union. Instead, he tried to work constructively with management. When an opening for a new foreman came up, he was promoted to foreman.

Again, he made a number of improvements to increase quality and efficiency, contributions that resulted in his being named head of quality control. From quality control, he was named director of customer service for Western Canada. While visiting one of the regional offices, he spotted a Request for Bids from a large trucking company. Upon inquiring, he learned the Regional Manager did not plan to submit a bid because the customer had never bought their products in the past. Robert asked the manager if there was any objection to his putting a bid together, and within a week Robert had prepared a proposal to sell the customer diesel trucks. For good measure he threw in a 100,000-mile warranty. The customer couldn't resist, and Robert shortly thereafter was made a district sales manager.

From then his career went to plant manager, director of manufacturing, director of sales, and eventually a tenure as president of his company. Special about Robert is that the initiative of one person, his own initiative, could make a difference. No matter what his job, on the production line or as a member of management, he made a difference, and he believed in his company and its products enough to want to try.

Rosemary, president of the largest bank in a large East Coast city, started as a teller. She wrote a training manual for the tellers in her branch. The manual brought her to the attention of management, which promoted her to director of teller training. In whatever job she had, she once told a reporter, she tried to do the best job possible. From there, the promotions just took care of themselves.

Managers typically have many more responsibilities and problems to solve than they can manage at any point in time. Managers, supervisors, and members of the work force who step forward with suggestions, and who offer to get involved in implementing the solutions, are more often rewarded for their initiative. Organizations need energy. They have too few problem solvers, people who are willing to make an extra effort, take some initiative to solve problems.

Those who take initiative, who take some risks to make things better, are usually rewarded by their leadership, eager for help.

The real challenge for newly appointed leaders is to act on the belief that there is hope and power within the organization to renew itself. Both Dick and Andrew found their support from among those who wanted the organization to be more successful, stable, and secure. Robert and Rosemary saw things that needed to be done, and did them. Every organization has those who recognize the need to change, to strengthen the organization, to change the culture. In renewal, the new manager/leader can serve as a visionary, a unifier, and a catalyst of people to improve their individual and team work.

Why People Resist Organizational Change

The following forces that resist change need to be understood so that you can counter their negative effect on the developing culture. We will discuss ways to reverse these forces later in this chapter.

1. *Lack of involvement and ownership in problem solving the organization's critical positions.* Many new leaders are reluctant to involve their people in organizational change. Certainly, to ask them to participate will cede to them some authority and power. Linda, determined to change her organization's work procedures, standards for performance, and to improve the quality of the work in an efficient way, rewrote the procedures over a three-week period and presented them to her group at a department meeting. There was an uproar. People were upset that she had revised them on her own, and even more upset when they read them. Some fought her. Others said that since she wanted to figure out the solutions, she could have *all* the problems as well.

The people who hold the organization's critical positions in management and the work force must feel a sense of ownership for the organization's new ideas. They must participate in developing and implementing those ideas, and their input must receive consideration. Everyone must feel heard if they try to contribute.

2. *Failure to identify the issues to be addressed, and specific action steps to be taken.* A most difficult part of addressing change is to move from the identification of a problem (what's wrong) to the identification of a solution and the action steps, including timetables and milestones for improvement.

A human resources department in an aerospace company had been teaching a technical course for three years. Three trainers taught the course periodically. All three complained about the same problems with the course. They didn't like some of the activities, didn't think the *Instructor's Guide* was adequate, and felt the *Participant's Manual* was too sketchy. Yet in three years not one of them made any changes. Nor had one even asked management for some time to improve the materials. They simply complained and continued to live with the problems.

People need to stop complaining, identify the solution, and take responsibility for selling the improvement to others in the organization and for getting it done.

3. *Escape from accountability.* Given their choice, many people in low or moderately performing organizations would choose not to be held accountable for their work or for efforts to improve the organization. A small device manufacturing company had a serious problem with product reliability. Users blamed the manufacturer. Within the manufacturer, product design people, quality assurance, quality control, project managers, and those who tested the product in the field each blamed someone else for the product failure. No one wanted the responsibility for creating solutions. People need to get involved, take the initiative. They need to get work done and find even better ways to do the job next time.

4. *Not using positive peer support and peer pressure adequately.* Organizational change requires developing a culture that supports change from within. This means that the work force must be convinced that its best interests coincide with what is best for the organization. Some of the most convincing arguments come from colleagues and peers who understand the positive implications in strengthening an organization. Unions are slowly recognizing this as they see jobs flee to Mexico and other countries. Managers need to see this as well.

Management too often keeps the organizational improvement process to itself, often reinforcing a we-they dichotomy that embodies the worst in labor-management relations. Management's authoritarianism and control led to the adversarial conflicts between labor and management in the 1930s–1950s, especially in the autoworkers, steelworkers, and garment workers unions.

When the work force distrusts management, it is very difficult to establish that cooperation. A group of professionals in a small advertising firm shared grievances about lack of consultation on projects, job costing, the control of projects, allocation of company resources, and profit sharing. Once the group realized their common grievances and approached management with their concerns, management could essentially do nothing to placate them. Things had deteriorated to the point that every response management made to solve the problem was viewed with distrust: "There they go again, trying to manipulate us."

One manager's offer to work more closely on projects was viewed as controlling. Management offers of greater autonomy was seen as an attempt to distance themselves from the work force. An offer to a sick employee of sick leave was viewed as an attempt to get rid of an aggrieved employee. A manager's friendly inquiry about a vacation was interpreted as trying to find out how soon the employee would return to work.

A common mistake is not getting the work force involved in the organizational improvement process early enough. To get them involved after they have substantive grievances tends to encourage them to coalesce into a kind of mutually supporting group pitted against management. Better to get them involved early in the process, serving on committees *with* management, and *not* on worker committees which make recommendations *to* management. Build consensus, not conflict.

5. *The pressure that people feel to improve is not great enough.* Generally, the tension or pressure to change and grow is not strong in organizations. People will not change if there is little impetus to change. Organizations can benefit from pressure from within or outside the organization. This *structural tension* or *cognitive dissonance* is the tension that people feel when they realize the difference between what actually exists and what could be. The pressure can come from a variety of sources. External pressure comes from competition, from clients and customers, from leaders and stockholders. Internal pressure can come from leadership, from productivity or profitability data, from peer pressure, or from competition for internal resources.

Individuals often feel their own internalized pressure when they realize the difference between what actually exists and what should be. Those within the organization set internal standards and strive to live up to them. Without tension or pressure to improve, people tend to support the status quo.

Many managers share no productivity or profitability data with their employees. Sometimes the managers have no good data themselves. Some managers insulate their employees from the hard realities. Some don't tell because they don't want to tell employees financial and productivity information when times are good, in fear of greater salary demands. Other managers don't want to alarm employees that their jobs, even their company, may be in jeopardy.

Organizations with little mid- and lower-level pressure to improve often provide employees with too little information. For an organization, especially one that is marginally profitable, to withhold profitability information from employees is to court disaster. Since employees have no reason to believe there is a problem, why should they change? To change their culture, they would have to see the data themselves. Dissonance is created only by real, believable data indicating there is a problem.

6. *Doing too much, too soon.* Organizations are capable of managing only so much change at one time. Change disrupts the work flow, slowing or bringing things to a halt. Well-managed change affects the organization while not seriously disrupting the ongoing work. The key is to work on one or two priorities at a time to build momentum and a pattern of successful implementation. The conclusions from your diagnostic work will provide a firm basis for your priorities.

The goals in the business plan Morgan and his 14-person group developed were ambitious:

- Three new target industries, including one they knew little about but felt had parallels to their base business
- Three new products for old customers, including two that would need considerable organizational time to develop
- The purchase of personal computers for the staff
- A reorganization along product lines
- Naming of new product leaders

Launched with great enthusiasm, by the third month the effort had barely gotten off the ground. Committees no longer met, and Morgan's periodic attempts to raise the issues were met with uncomfortable silence. His organization simply had an inadequate mass of people and resources to do everything they wanted to do at once. They had spread themselves too thin and were overwhelmed. They should have focused their energies on a few needs at a time.

7. *Organizational homeostasis.* Like living organisms, individuals, groups, and organizations tend to level off at a steady state, or revert to earlier norms. This tendency to fall back is called *organizational homeostasis* and is common in all change efforts. Homeostasis manifests itself in several guises. One is the tendency for organizations that have improved their standard of quality to fall back from that standard. A group that adopted a zero defects standard suddenly begins to find exceptions to the standard or to argue that zero defects is an unreasonably high standard that makes the product too expensive, and that the customers will accept a slightly lower standard without complaint.

Homeostasis can also affect how the work is done. Many companies, having spent considerably on new computer systems, software, and training, are stunned to find employees more comfortable with their old ways—including old-fashioned paper and pencil instead of word processing. In one sales group of eight, only two members were using the expensive new sales tracking system, and two of the eight had not even bothered to try it. Without consistent encouragement from leadership and revised work procedures to support the new, organizations tend to revert to former standards, procedures, and methods.

8. *Illusion of impotence.* People tend to attribute much greater power to others than they do to themselves. They often see themselves as isolated and unable to affect change. Individuals often see others as much more able to take action and to overcome barriers. Ironically, people will frequently identify each other as having much more power or influence than they see themselves as having. The key is for many in the organization to feel the ability to influence positive change and work with others to do so.

We've written about the effect the feeling of powerlessness has on an organization. Typically, each person feels someone else holds the power to change things. Even the leader may feel that middle managers, or even the work force, holds the real power to change things.

Depression is a feeling of hopelessness. Nothing is fun, nothing is interesting anymore. We hate to get out of bed, to start the day, to go to bed. There is no energy, drive, or enthusiasm. Organizations, like the people within them, can experience depression. It is the hopelessness engendered by a feeling that nothing really makes any difference, nothing can get better.

Organizational depression is caused by a feeling of powerlessness. When we feel no individual or group ability to affect conditions, a gloom descends over the organization. With power there is hope. Without power the work force slides into depression. Organizations need people who take initiative; initiative must be recognized, appreciated, and rewarded.

9. *Selective perception.* Simply stated, perceiving is believing. Perception gives personal meaning to what we experience. People filter the events around them through the selective screens of their needs and values. They will see and hear what they are predisposed to perceive, and believe their perceptions. It has been said that whenever two people interact, there are seemingly six people present:

- Each person as they see themselves
- Each person as they view each other and the events around themselves
- Each person he or she really is

As a force acting against change or growth, selective perception can be critical since people see what they want to see and what agrees with their perceptions. If people in your organization believe something, they will act as if it is true, whether or not it is actually true. You must deal with what is perceived to be true, not just with the objective truth.

A key to your success will be your ability to create a common perception of the organization's needs and its future. It will do you little good to reassure yourself that the group's perceptions of what exists are not accurate. People will act on perceptions as though they are true. And you must respond. You cannot ignore them simply because you know they are untrue.

10. *Rule of modeling*. Beginning at infancy, we learn how things are done through modeling, habit, and reinforcement. A type of programming occurs. The rule of modeling says that we tend to do first that which has been modeled for us. We will usually act as we have seen others around us behave in the past.

The young manager is fortunate who has worked for an excellent manager. A few months of observing and modeling the behavior of an excellent manager is more helpful than a dozen people with good ideas, or a dozen months spent in school.

Jessica had been on the faculty of a large state university for 12 years, when one of her former students offered her a job as vice president in his rapidly growing company. Eager for a new opportunity, challenge, and the chance to grow, she eagerly took the position.

To Jessica's great surprise, while she was brilliant at product design, sales, and product installation, the management of her function was more difficult. Her university experience prepared her to be a self-starter, and an independent thinker and operator. She was analytical, mentally nimble, quick to solve problems, and a good colleague.

But never in her 12 years of relative autonomy at the University had she ever been managed. Comfortable managing herself, she knew little about the role of the professional manager. She had never hired, supervised, trained, disciplined, or fired an employee, nor had she seen it done well. Never had she had a performance appraisal. She never had a performance plan, never managed one, didn't know how to plan work flow, the work of others, or a budget. While very concerned about her employees and their performance, she was essentially uncomfortable devoting a majority of her time to managing them. She was happier doing her own work.

Fortunately for Jessica, she reported to an experienced, trained manager, who made management his career. As Jessica began to model some of her boss's behaviors, she was able to provide a better model for her own employees, and developed not only a motivated, but also a more organized, rational organization. To help your organization adopt new norms and behaviors, you will have to develop them yourself, and then model them, talk about them, and reward them in others.

11. *Vested interests.* It is often a shock to young managers to learn that people do not do something because it is right and just. Spike Lee to the contrary, people do not always do the right thing, but rather they often act out of self-interest, what is best for them.

When Vanessa became principal of an urban middle school, she was filled with energy for creating a school that would put the needs, concerns, and learning styles of students first. She wanted a new curriculum, new materials, new teaching methods, and new technology to help students. Proposing her ideas to her faculty, she was stunned by their negativity. She had expected they would greet her ideas enthusiastically. She was sure they shared her observations about the school's failures, and would welcome changes that would do the right thing for the kids.

But not every member of her organization saw her ideas as helpful. Applying their own self-interest, many saw Vanessa's plans as essentially disruptive to the organization and to their well-ordered lives. They felt her ideas would require hours of planning, learning new skills, new problem solving, and would not improve student performance materially, or improve the school. They didn't see their own self-interest in the change.

Similarly, when Dennis decided to move his group to larger, more modern quarters, he encountered unexpected opposition from some of his senior employees. Many felt the new space was too expensive, was a longer commute, provided more space than was needed, and was more than the group could reasonably pay for. Again, senior group members did not perceive their benefit in the change, and opposed it.

The most demoralizing experience of Suzanne's 10-year career was an organizational renewal effort initiated by Jay, her new boss. Jay, who had been a successful executive at a large West Coast industry leader, was recruited to Suzanne's East Coast company to improve research and development in an organization whose strength was primarily operations. Jay immediately began by naming six task forces to analyze the organization's strengths and weaknesses, and provide recommendations to an Executive Committee of four. Suzanne's task force met once with Jay, then met on its own, weekly, over the next three months. Suzanne spent an additional four to six hours a week on the task force's work. Over the three-month life of her task, she devoted perhaps 120 hours to her task force, including some evenings and Saturdays spent catching up on her regular work.

Jay had not met with the task force during its deliberations, but at the three-month mark Suzanne's group had finished their report and presented their recommendations. And then there was silence. For three months her task force heard nothing. Another meeting with Jay, and then nothing. No implementation, no feedback, no information about good or bad reaction to the report. Nothing. No explanation, no discussion. Suzanne felt she had been had. People in key positions, vested in the way the organization was operating, became very nervous.

Realize that power and influence usually rest with those who have worked hard to establish their niche in the organization. Those with established interest in the status quo will resist or fight change that might risk the loss of this vested position. Those who see their power unchanged or enhanced will participate in change. Be sure to spend whatever time is necessary to help those with existing interests and power to realize that they can also benefit as the organization changes and grows. To support change, they must believe it is in their best interests.

12. *Lack of monitoring, control, or evaluation tools to maximize follow-up.* Leaders must follow up on decisions, be accountable, and hold others to their responsibilities and agreements. Leaders who do not monitor implementation of plans, exert control when implementation gets off track, or evaluate effectiveness of the plans will fail. Without adequate monitoring and follow-up, all of the effort that went into the planning meetings, information gathering, problem analysis, solution identification, and planning is for naught. It is a waste of time. Worse, the people who invested so much time and optimism, the people who believed in you—believed in the process, invested themselves in it, and sought to persuade the rest of their colleagues to cooperate—will feel betrayed by your failure to ensure follow-through and effective implementation.

Key Behaviors and Principles of Effective Organizational Change Efforts

There are many approaches to changing an organization. Elizabeth, inheriting an agency in disarray, asked for everyone's letter of resignation the day she arrived on the job. She felt that by asking for mass resignations, she would have the leverage needed to rehire only those she wanted to keep, in order to force immediate compliance with policies about which she felt strongly. Second, she felt it was easier to hire back selectively rather than to fire selectively.

One positive outcome of this tactic was that she captured everyone's attention in a hurry. However, she did not anticipate that work would stop and morale plummet. The threat of potential job loss caused great resentment among high and low performers alike. The high performers who were asked to stay were hurt and defensive that they had been forced to go through such an exercise. Many became distrustful, even though Elizabeth had no intention of letting them go. What she did reminded them of their vulnerability, shook them from their feelings of security and complacency. Indeed a number did begin looking for jobs elsewhere. A period of general malaise ensued and Elizabeth had a difficult time reestablishing trust and support for herself. Some who stayed never did recover from the shock to trust her completely.

The most effective approaches to organizational planned change stress high levels of employee participation. The incoming leader will never have a more opportune time to build optimism and hope for the future than during the first six months to one year on the job. Equipped with a knowledge of the typical forces that will undermine change, you can approach renewal with a core of practical primary principles. These *principles* should become *goals* of renewal as well as a *means* to achieve the objective of a fully functioning organization. They directly counter the dynamics and forces resistant to change. They include the following:

1. *Involve people.* Build from employees' individual and organizational strengths. Help them identify opportunities to develop solutions that will assure higher productivity and organizational effectiveness. Your use of a steering committee and task forces during the diagnostic process should get you off to a good start.

2. *Model a true commitment to results.* Managed with energy, enthusiasm and true leadership, high expectations most often beget high results. Leading for results must be a core value pervading all that is done well. There must be no misunderstanding that the primary goal is better organizational performance—derived from better results as individuals, as work teams, and as a total organization.

3. *Apply diagnostic problem solving.* As described in earlier chapters, people gain the best results when they work together on their organizational growth targets. A finely tuned diagnostic process will point you in the right directions. Identify and know what information you need. Devise effective and appropriate ways to know your organizational and business needs, and then sight your vision and goals.

4. *Focus on changing norms and culture as a primary means to achieve desired results.* In the long run your results will come when people's attitudes, behaviors, and actions have changed.

5. *View your organization as a dynamic system.* Realize that activity, decisions, or problems affecting one area or person will almost surely affect other functions and individuals.

6. *Use positive tension and pressure.* Tension is essential for initiating and managing the movement toward change. The concept of positive

tension, as mentioned earlier, is based on psychological principles that have been around for years—cognitive dissonance, discrepancy theory, gap theory, or structural tension. When people perceive a discrepancy or gap between an *ideal* situation that they value highly (e.g., I *really* want to be valued by my team) and the reality of what is (they see me as passive, unhelpful), they will be motivated to change their behavior to achieve the desired state.

The organizational principle of positive tension is potent and releases enormous energy. When responsible employees identify changes that will build a better place to work, you have begun to build positive tension. They will want to reduce the gap between the way things are and the way they could be. A fabric of small groups woven together through collaborative effort is created, and the result becomes goals that are individually and organizationally attainable, valuable, and rewarding to individuals within the organization.

7. *View the role of the leader as catalyst, facilitator, decision maker, visionary, and manager of momentum.* This is the essence of moving up successfully and thriving as a new manager. It is also basic if planned change is to occur during the first year in your new role. The role is challenging and exciting. It is your pot to stir. Remember, your leadership, power, and influence all count; use them.

8. *Lead with a "velvet hammer."* The most successful transitions by leaders seem to be characterized by the leader's well-developed interpersonal skills and behaviors that are tough and courageous. The interplay involves blending the talents of helping professionals such as good listening, respect, and empathy, with those characteristics of results oriented businesspeople. It is difficult but important to coach and counsel an employee, while in the next hour develop bold business plans or discipline or even terminate a chronically unproductive member of your group. This style is leading with a "velvet hammer." It is being humanistic yet determined and results oriented.

The Big Three
Implementation Strategies

The eight behaviors and principles of organizational change work because they counter the forces that slow or prevent change. Here's how you can blend some or all into effective strategies.

Strategy 1. You can add positive forces, norms, or actions to the work environment where previously there was a void or unproductive activities.

Strategy 2. You can decrease or remove negative forces, norms, or actions in the work environment.

Strategy 3. You can add positive forces, norms, or actions *while reducing or removing negative* forces, norms, or actions (a combination of strategies 1 and 2).

Let's take a closer look at these core strategies.

Strategy 1. *Add positive forces that were previously absent or too weak to help.* Sometimes something as simple as adding a resource person, or making a change in work location or equipment can dramatically affect an organization's performance. One small company simply hired an expert technician, which gave the rest of the work force the confidence to pursue a certain line of business. Another organization increased training by 50 percent. One manager began an employee-led quality circle program; another initiated highly visible employee recognition and reward programs and employee appreciation days.

Strategy 2. *Remove negative forces from the work environment.* There are frequently obstacles that get in the way of good individual and team work. Impediments could include certain steps in the work process, certain reporting relationships, or even certain people. These impediments frequently can be managed by asking the following questions:

- What purpose does it (e.g., policy, procedure) serve?
- Do we really need it or need to do it?
- Are anyone's behaviors (including my own) getting in the way?

If you find that impediments exist, reduce or eliminate them from your renewing organization.

Strategy 3. *The most potent strategy of all is when positive norms and forces are added to the system while there is a simultaneous reduction in negative norms and practices.*

A case involving a manager, Judy, demonstrates the effectiveness of strategy 3. When Judy provided much needed focused listening time to individuals at all levels in her department, there was a dramatic change in employee enthusiasm, morale, and productivity. Every Thursday afternoon, for 2½ hours, she welcomed employees into her office. Each took a number, and were guaranteed at least 10 minutes with her to discuss their issues.

Judy also helped communication with a regularly scheduled series of departmental lunch time "table talks" started so that participants could vent feelings and informally generate solutions to persistent issues.

These sessions were designed to mix people from a variety of functions and different levels of work responsibility, which built stronger relationships and better communication across the department. Unlike her precedessor, when concrete suggestions were made, Judy wouldn't commit if she wasn't willing to begin implementing the idea within a short period of time. She always publicly credited the employee for the original idea. These actions resulted in employees who felt valued, capable, and responsible for making things better. The overall effect was to reduce feelings of frustration stemming from poor communication.

Linda was selected as the Western regional sales director for a thriving data management consulting organization. With five district sales managers reporting to her, she commanded a total work force of 85 over a seven state region. On composite measures for sales, productivity, and net profit, the region ranked last of six. Linda was hand selected by the national sales director following six years as a highly regarded account rep and district manager headquartered in the Sunbelt. Linda confronted some difficult practices when she assumed her new responsibility.

- Sales goals were dictated by her predecessor and forced downward to district managers and account reps, with little, if any, opportunity for feedback or negotiation. These people had become cynical about the goal-setting process and regularly undershot their goals. Goals were generally not reasonable.

- Communication within the region was poor. There was a strong feeling of "checking up" versus "checking in" with the account reps and district managers. This resulted in many inaccurate judgments about people and their dedication. Face-to-face contact was infrequent and usually problem or crisis driven.

- The performance management process was poorly administered. Recognition and reward was sporadic and based on loose criteria that the account reps felt were arbitrary and unfairly subjective.

- There was little sharing of "best practices" from person to person. If an account rep developed a new approach or a unique selling proposition, little was done to spread the technique or build on it with others in the region.

Within several days of her arrival as regional sales director, Linda began to implement a strategy of rapid information gathering and relationship building. Her diagnosis was already under way, as were her efforts to establish her presence and credibility. Linda knew of two very experienced district managers in her new region who were regarded as "old pros" with great loyalty to the company. Both were within several years of retirement and had maintained a solid work record. Neither had applied for the regional position, being content to finish their careers without the added pressure that comes with a more senior position. Everyone Linda spoke to in the corporate office said these two could be trusted as reliable sources of good ideas and valuable information.

Linda spent many hours with each of these two district managers during her first few weeks on the job, gaining important insights into the strengths and problems of her region. Without their help, it would have taken several months to gather this information. Both enjoyed serving as sounding boards for her ideas. As Linda began formulating an overall approach to improve performance in the region, she asked for their help. They became loyal and valuable resources for her, forming the nucleus of her leadership team.

Linda designed an approach that would simultaneously reduce negative norms while increasing positive ones. The approach included the following:

- Installing a goal-setting system for each sales district that began with a bottom-up approach. Each account rep identified sales targets, as did, in turn, each district manager. When these did not seem to meet a standard that Linda felt could be reached, she initiated a positive, win-win problem-solving approach to goal-setting.

- Within 10 weeks, Linda had individual, face-to-face meetings with every employee in her organization. She was careful to listen more than speak. When she did speak, she conveyed a message of optimism and involvement. Within a short period of time, Linda had gained an initial impression of each person. She noted who were the complainers and who seemed to be part of her region's problems. It was easy to see who was positive and who made recommendations that could help. Early on, she began to break down the feeling of helplessness that her employees felt. She went right after the dynamics that had paralyzed her region. She was seen as a person with high standards and a willingness to empower the organization by listening to her people's ideas. People felt energized.

- Based on an employee suggestion made in Linda's initial round of individual discussions, a "Regional Performer of the Month" club was begun. Linda asked five account reps and three division managers to develop objective criteria for selecting the monthly winners. From the beginning, Linda invited successful ideas and realized the importance of recognizing people for their contributions.

- A small task force was formed to submit recommendations within two months on training and communication needs in the region.

- Several other employees were asked to work on ideas that would improve the system for measuring and rewarding performance on a semiannual basis.

- Linda volunteered her region for a pilot evaluation sponsored by the corporation for the use of an electronic voice message system. In doing so, she enhanced her image as an advocate for the region, getting her region new resources and recognition.

Today Linda has turned her region around. Sales are up. Her region has gone from sixth to third in performance, and morale is up, as is productivity. People want to work for her.

In the process of renewing the organization, several employees were terminated, including two district managers. Linda's "velvet hammer" was respected because she set high standards, listened, and acted collaboratively with her organization. Only the underperformers feared her. Linda's stock continues to rise in the corporation, where she is seen as firm, fair, dynamic, and supportive manager.[9]

Learning from Failed Organizational Efforts

For every success in renewing an organization, there is a failure. While many elements are needed for success, to fail on just one or two key issues can undermine you.

Even a well-planned, thorough effort can fail. Lauren, with the support of a seasoned consultant, planned a comprehensive diagnosis that identified some obvious and some camouflaged problems. Her staff expended considerable time and effort in problem analysis, decision making, and action planning. The process was generally well designed and executed.

However, one problem was not addressed. Lauren was reluctant to confront her two most strident resistors. She was unable to resolve problems caused by their vested interests. Neither Lauren nor her supporters were willing to be as tough as needed. Win-win conflict resolution wasn't useful because the resistors didn't want to compromise. As Lauren hesitated, her opponents simply stiffened their resistance. Ultimately, time and circumstances demonstrated Lauren's "velvet," but she could not use the "hammer." While some improvements occurred, the pace and depth of change was disappointing to her and her boss. Ultimately unable to control her organization, she was passed over for promotion and eventually reorganized out of her job.

In addition to wasting valuable time and money, unsuccessful efforts can escalate existing problems and further entrench negative norms, apathy, and frustration. Some of the most common traps follow.

Lack of Senior Level Support

As your organization's leader, you have to be fully committed, skilled, and strong enough to improve or turn around your organization. Your boss must also provide unflinching support. If you are hesitant, or your support from above is ambivalent or weak, you stand a better chance of failing.

Perpetuation of Win-Lose Behaviors

Moving an organization is difficult enough without people sabotaging the effort. Decisions that chronically result in winners and losers encourage people to drop out or stand in the way of progress. If you are sure that you have the right people, then do everything in your power to use "I win-You win" (no-lose) problem-solving.

To an extent greater than in most U.S. companies, Japanese management uses the Quaker concept of consensus before action. A Quaker meeting does not adopt a decision until all assent. Similarly, Japanese managers are careful to build on organizational consensus, which helps ensure that the decision has been thoroughly discussed, and will be supported up and down the organization.

Those who choose confrontation and who resist the drive to consensus will either leave on their own or should be removed from the organization. Everyone must be committed to success. Organizations need people who can combine championing good ideas and helping to shape a consensus.

Inadequate Involvement of All Levels of Employees

Time and time again we have seen the status quo perpetuated because employees resent an effort of which they are not a part. Employees at all levels need to help plan and become involved in (not just hear about) the change process. As leader, you can design intra- and interlevel discussions, task forces, and meetings to engender the communication, problem-solving, and information exchange process.

Prewarned is prearmed. If people are not describing the renewal process as "ours," look out! Also make a special effort to involve your support staff, such as secretaries and other hourly or nonexempt workers. Never underestimate their ability to help or hinder an organizational effort. They are well positioned and often more knowledgeable on certain issues than their supervisors.

Inability or Unwillingness of Employees to See the Big Picture

Because they lack information, don't believe in the vision, or are blinded by selective perception, many fail to understand the intent and rationale of a renewal effort. Make sure employees develop a clear understanding of why and how "we" are proceeding as "we" are. Explain the vision and process informally and in scheduled department meetings. Encourage questions. Offer information. Concentrate on communicating the big picture as you work on the various pieces. Act as a broken record. Over and over, offer the vision, explain the process, believe in the goals. Make the dictum for clear communication heard by every graduate.

Falling Victim to Entropy

Organizational energy is hard to define and even harder to measure, but very easy to feel. Energy is essential if you are going to help the organization move forward. Regularly remind yourself of the following twist of a basic law of physics: *An organization in positive motion won't automatically stay in positive motion.* Earlier, we called this tendency to regress *entropy.* Once you have started the process of individuals and groups identifying ways of growing and developing, work doubly hard to perpetuate the effort. At some point (usually during the last quarter of your first year), your organization will achieve and be able to maintain a new level of healthy functioning. Until the organization locks into its new level and pace, keep your foot on the pedal. Manage momentum by continuously tapping the sources of energy within your people.

Insufficient Attention to and by First-Line Managers and Supervisors

As the linking pin between you and the workforce, your first-line managers occupy a unique position. On a daily basis, they are accountable for the performance of the people doing the work. Accordingly, they need to be fully involved in renewal. When you think that you have integrated them into your plans, go one step further. Involve, inform, listen, recognize, and reward them frequently. If they haven't internalized their commitment, if they talk about "they" and "you" rather than "we" and "our," expect breakdowns in the renewal process.

Inappropriate Levels of Expectation

Changing the way things are—the culture, policies, and procedures—takes time. Short-term "highs" can be experienced in training courses, retreats, work team meetings, and individual and group problem-solving sessions. But you are seeking longer lasting results. Depending on the issues uncovered during the diagnostic process, it takes anywhere from 6 to 12 months and sometimes longer to see results that can be sustained. *Set goals just out of reach, but not out of sight.* Organizations that stretch are organizations that grow.

Anticipating the Politics of Change

Politics are part of any organization. University professors lobby for tenure, special research projects and grants, and preferred teaching schedules. Executives jockey for promotions and assignments to key task forces. Airline flight crews want favorite routes and departure times. Teachers and school administrators lobby for assignments to better schools, classes, and rosters. Politics is the process of ensuring, in a human organization brimming with feelings, perceptions, and competing needs, that you get what you want (hopefully not at the expense of others).

For the leader moving up, there are numerous opportunities to take advantage of the political environment. However, the road to political success is strewn with obstacles that can derail your career. Perceptions that change is imminent, and the aftershocks of new leadership, often heighten political behavior. People jockey to gain influence over resources, decisions, and perceptions. The early and continued influencing of people is of prime importance from the announcement of your appointment.

Earlier we talked about a new general manager who, within a few days of starting his new position, was totally engulfed in public and private controversy. His inability to manage the politics of his position inevitably led to his early exit.

Routinely assume that political forces are at work. Never assume that being a solid manager and a strong performer alone will result in your success. Nurture, strengthen, and reinforce your support from subordinates, peers, your boss, and your boss's boss. Be part of their support and networks. Trusting relationships can go a long way toward ensuring your success. Always remember, however, that *your success depends first on the quality of your work.* Your work is your starting point.

We have spent considerable time in this book emphasizing how to build support. You must be able to analyze the political situation, build a strategy to address the prevailing conditions, and implement a specific plan to make the politics work for you. Managed well, you can develop advocates who work in your behalf. One vice president of manufacturing said, "My people began to carry me. I previously had to drag them screaming. Turning it around was hard, but worth it!"

Your Personal Political Inventory

Try the following activity. Inventory those organizational political factors that could help or hinder your transition. Your awareness of these factors or patterns should help you develop a clear strategy and action plan to better manage the politics of your transition.

Complete this assessment as soon as you have some information about your new job, certainly no later than two months after assuming your new position. If possible, do it before assuming your position. Then repeat this inventory every three months during your first year on the job and once or twice a year thereafter. Do it alone or preferably with a confidant or consultant you trust.

Instructions for Part 1. "Your Personal Political Inventory" is designed to help you chart key people and their influence on you. (See Fig. 8.1.) The inventory will allow you to capture a considerable amount of important information. Part 1 consists of compiling data in a variety of categories. The instructions for each category correspond with a numbered column. Part 2 of the inventory consists of integrating the information, searching for patterns of political activity, and identifying potential opportunities or areas of vulnerability.

Column 1. List the names and titles of the 10 to 15 people in the organization who seem most able to affect you politically. Limit your list to those whose behavior or intentions can influence your success or failure during your transitional period. The individuals you list could hold any position and might be individuals from outside the organization, such as people from other departments, clients, customers, suppliers, consultants, and those in professional societies. In addition to the person's name, designate his or her title or position.

Column 2. Code that person's relationship to you. For example, B = your boss, C = colleague or peer, SUB = subordinate, O = other (describe).

Column 3. On a scale from 1 (low) to 5 (high), rate each individual on his or her ability to influence others' opinions of you, whether positively or negatively. As with other codes in this inventory, these are subjective measures. However, they indicate how you perceive others' inten-

Columns ↓	1	2	3	4	5	6	7	8	9
1									
2									
3									
4									
5									
6									
7									
8									
9									
10									
11									
12									
13									
14									
15									

Figure 8.1. Your personal political inventory (Part 1).

tions toward you. Use the code I (for influence), with a number beside it (e.g., I4).

Column 4.   Code each person's general approach with you.

P.   Passive, laissez faire: Seems unconcerned.

PA.   Passive/aggressive: Seems friendly, but is hostile toward you beneath the surface, often by withholding information, evaluating your work, or using humor at your expense.

RA.   Responsibly assertive: Generally acts in an active, "up front" manner. This person generally meets his or her needs without infringing on yours.

S.   Supportive, friendly, loyal: Someone you can count on for support, who gives constructive and discreet help.

A.   Aggressive: Generally goes after what he or she wants with little or no regard for your rights, needs, feelings, or position.

O.   Other (designate).

Column 5. Place a YMR in column 5 for the five people whose work contribution *you most respect.* Limit your coding to five individuals. Do the same with the five whose work *you least respect* (YLR). In the parentheses next to the five YMR and YLR codings, indicate rank on a scale of 1 to 5. For example, YMR (5) indicates the person whose work you most respect and YLR (5) the person whose work you least respect.

Column 6. The information in this column is the converse of column 5. Your coding will depict the five people whom you believe most and least respect your actual and potential contribution. Use MRY for those who you perceive *most respect* your work and LRY for those who *least respect* your work. Rank order the individuals as you did in column 5.

Column 7. Identify up to five individuals who have access to very important information that could affect your performance. Code with an INF for *information.* You may also wish to rank order these individuals. (e.g., INF 1, INF 2, etc.).

Column 8. Identify up to five individuals whom you perceive as having access to critical or important resources other than information, such as people, money, or materials. Code with an R for *resources.* Again, you may wish to rank order the individuals.

Column 9. Using an SM (*support me*), identify the three to five individuals listed on your inventory that you want to have on your side (i.e., supporters of your leadership efforts). Some may already support you, some you'll want to develop.

Now turn to Part 2 and pull your data together.

Instructions for Part 2. Integrate the information from Part 1 to assess your present political environment. Take some time to study your chart. Look for the connecting threads between two or more columns or the items within a column. A useful way to do this is by completing one or more of the following unfinished sentences as you review the information. Feel free to use any of the sentence stems more than once. Try these:

I learned _____ .

I relearned _____ .

I am aware _____ .

I was surprised _____ .

I was pleased_____ .

I was disappointed _____ .

I wonder _____ .

I hope _____ .

I am concerned _____ .

Complete at least five of these unfinished sentences. Take your time to look for the many patterns that exist. The following are examples.

- I realize that I have the support I need from my boss and subordinates but not nearly enough from my colleagues.

- I am aware that some who have access to the resources that I need to be successful are people whom I do not respect in terms of the quality of their work, and with whom I do not have a good relationship.

- I was surprised to see the number of opportunities that I have to increase my influence with others.

Next Steps

- How would you describe the political impact of your new role? Who are the "winners" (those who might be positively affected by your position)? Who are the "losers" (those who might be negatively affected by your position, and who may become the resistors)? Are there others who may be affected by your appointment? How can you align yourself so that winners, losers, and others become at worst neutral and at best your supporters?

- Is there one key person in whom you can confide, who can aid you during the early days? This person may be your boss, a confidant, a consultant, or someone you trust in your new organization. Many organizations have a wily veteran who has survived the comings and goings of many managers, who is wise in the politics and operations of the organization, and knows to keep information confidential. This individual can be a source of great political help and support.

- The type and timing of your oral and written communications affects the political winds. Who can you trust to help? How should you best use his or her talents?

- For purposes of stability, what shouldn't change during your transition into your new role? People? Work assignments? Organizational structures? Certain aspects of the culture? Highly valued or potentially volatile symbols?

- Who are the organizational "high priests" and the opinion molders? How can you get them on your team?

In this chapter we have looked at many issues relating to building your management team's commitment and effecting positive change. In the next chapter we examine ways to stabilize your organization after active periods of change to avoid future stagnation. We also begin to look at work and personal life issues that can benefit you in the process of moving up.

Quick Reminders to Keep You on Track

- Individuals, groups and organizations usually are comfortable with the status quo; they often resist change. Understanding why is fundamental to being able to plan and execute actions that will improve and strengthen your organization.

- An aspect of resisting change centers around resisting your management agenda. There will always be some people who would prefer someone other than you at the helm and a different set of priorities.

- Understanding your organization's culture, i.e., "what it's really like around here," is critical to your early success.

- Several concepts are important in understanding organizational culture.
  1. Whenever people live or work together, they form a culture.
  2. Every culture develops unwritten expectations and ways of doing things, called norms, which are major determinants of the behavior within that work culture.
  3. Cultures are not stagnant; they change.

- The most effective approaches to organizational planned change stress high levels of employee participation. Your first year in managing a function will provide you a great opportunity to build involvement, optimism, and hope for the future.

- Important principles in your effort to achieve the objective of a fully functioning organization include:
  1. Involving people and building from their individual and organizational strengths.
  2. Modeling a true commitment to results.
  3. Applying diagnostic problem solving concepts.
  4. Focusing on changing norms and culture where appropriate.
  5. Viewing your organization as a dynamic system.

6. Using positive tension for initiating and managing the movement toward change.
7. As manager/leader, assuming the role of catalyst, facilitator, decision maker, visionary, and manager of momentum.
8. Leading with a "velvet hammer," i.e., a personal blend of well-developed interpersonal skills combined with tough and courageous leadership.

- Three strategies utilize these principles to effect organizational change.

  1. *Strategy I. You can add positive forces,* norms, or actions to the work environment where previously there was a void or unproductive activities.
  2. *Strategy II. You can decrease or remove negative forces,* norms, or actions in the work environment.
  3. *Strategy III. You can add* positive forces, norms, or actions *while reducing or removing negative* forces, norms, or actions (a combination of strategies I and II). This strategy is usually the most effective.

- Organizational improvement efforts fail for important reasons. The newly appointed manager/leader can learn from the unsuccessful experiences of others in order to avoid making similar mistakes. These mistakes include

  1. Not developing senior management support.
  2. Perpetuating win-lose behaviors in the organization.
  3. Not adequately involving all levels of employees.
  4. An inability or unwillingness of employees to see the big picture of organizational improvement.
  5. Falling victim to homeostasis—not achieving or maintaining momentum to change and improve.
  6. Not creating or maintaining high levels of expectation to improve the organization.

- Organization politics are always at work. They can work for you or against you. You need to employ legitimate approaches that will aid you.

- Your personal awareness of the politics that could affect you is very important. Complete Your Personal Political Inventory several times during your first 12 months as a manager.

Summary of Major Responsibilities—Year One (Chap. 8)

First Year by Month*

	Preappointment	1	2	3	4	5	6	7	8	9	10	11	12
Moving in: Establishing Yourself in Your New Assignment													
· Entering the Organization	──	──	──	- -	- -	- -							
· Entering Your Boss's World	──	──	──	- -	- -	- -							
Achieving an Impact on the Organization													
· Beginning to Craft Your Vision and Direction		──	──	──	──	──	──	- -	- -	- -	- -	- -	- -
· The Diagnostic Process: The Importance of Good Organizational Information		──	──	──	──	──	──	- -	- -	- -	- -		
· Assessing Your Organization's Health — The Nine-Target Model		──	──	──	──	──	──						
· Selecting, Building, and Developing Your Work Team		──	──	──	──	──	──	──	──	──	──	──	──
· From Resistance to Renewal: Building Your Management Team's Commitment		──	──	──	──	──	──	──	──	──	──	──	──

*Times are approximate.

Legend

── Primary period of emphasis

- - Active but not a period of emphasis

Your Personal Plan to Move from Resistance to Renewal: Building Your Management Team's Commitment (Chap. 8)

Activity	Suggested Timeframe	Perceived Barriers	Available Resources	Your Projected Timeframe	Completed (✓)
• Understanding the basics of organization culture	Upon starting your position.				
• Understanding forces or organization dynamics resistant to change	Upon starting your position.				
• Understanding key behaviors and principles of effective organizational change efforts	Upon starting your position.				
• Implementing one of the Big Three Implementation Strategies	Could begin slowly while the organizational diagnosis is being completed. Is most critical when implementing your plan to strengthen the organization following completion of the diagnosis.				
• Understanding why organization efforts fail and applying these principles to your planned change process	Upon starting your position.				
• Dealing with the organizational politics of change — Understanding when the politics of change peak — Completing your personal political inventory	Preferably upon starting your position but certainly no later than two months into the job. Revisit your personal political inventory every three months during your first year and once or twice per year thereafter.				
• Confirming and implementing your organizational political strategy	No later than two months into your new position				

9

Settling into Your Renewing Organization

Nothing is as temporary as that which is called permanent.

ANONYMOUS

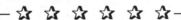

By about the ninth month of your new management position, you should be able to begin helping your organization settle into a much higher level of performance compared to when you started. Also, throughout your first year, there are very important parts of your life outside of work that should thrive but often do not. You will need to:

- Achieve a new, higher, more productive organizational "steady state" as you approach the end of your first year.

- Evaluate how you are doing and whether you like the new position you started less than a year ago.

- Use this personal evaluation as a tool for working well with your boss and helping him or her to help you.

- Understand how you can manage the new responsibilities of your work life and personal life so that they effectively complement each other.

In this chapter, there is useful information about:

- Preventing Future Stagnation
- Fine-Tuning Your Leadership Role and Your Organization
- *SOARING*: Sharpening the Way You Think About Your Work and Personal Life

Preventing Future Stagnation

We have emphasized the newly appointed leader's need to renew the organization. To do so requires great effort and reduces the time available for focusing on the actual work. In most cases, however, skillfully led renewal has an uplifting effect. People feel part of something worthwhile. You will hear barely audible individual and group sighs of "finally!"

But planned organizational growth does take a toll in time, effort, and money. People get tired of meeting to plan and implement change. There comes a point when they want to get back to doing their jobs full-time and slow the pace of change. This cooldown usually comes after some of the major change goals have been achieved, and while enthusiasm for the new vision and direction is still strong. Typically, cooldown occurs during the last three months of your first year. Subsequent changes will fine-tune the major changes already made and will not jolt the system so much.

In his 10 months on the job, Jim, the director of a high-tech research and development center, had overseen the radical streamlining of his organization. He had developed and trained a new executive committee reporting to him. Two of his five direct reports were new. The executive committee had revised the business plan, which resulted in a reprioritization of projects and reallocation of financial and human resources. Resources formerly devoted to postmarketed product redesign were shifted to new product development teams.

The work flow was reorganized and some formerly consolidated functions were decentralized. The planning, design, conduct, analysis, and writing of research projects were divided into five work functions, to be performed by specialists in each function. People would specialize in what they were good at, rather than being responsible for all functions.

Work flow procedures were redesigned, and the standard operating procedures were revised to reflect the new work flow. Much of the new design was technology driven. All professional and clerical staff were supplied with computers. Workstations were introduced into key design functions, and tasks formerly completed in person, often requiring extensive travel time and expense, were now done by fax and by phone.

The executive committee met every two weeks for updates on the renewal. Each executive committee member was involved in at least one task force. Even though consultants were used to facilitate the task forces and conduct much of the information gathering, analysis, and solution identification, the effort had nonetheless consumed about a third of executive committee members' time, and about 20 percent of task force members' time. After eight months, they were dizzy from the pace of change, and many were feeling a discontinuity from their work. Few in the department fancied themselves professional managers. They were successful researchers who had been promoted to leadership positions, and were anxious to get back full-time to their now much streamlined research projects.

Fortunately for Jim, renewal was manageable. He had an experienced and stable work force, good executive committee leadership, and the support from above that allowed him the resources and consultants needed to improve the organization.

Rob, named Director of New Product Development, also hoped for a smooth transition as he took over his responsibilities in a telecommunications equipment manufacturer. But after a preliminary assessment of the 75-person function, he was less hopeful. Pitted against tough Japanese and Silicone Valley competitors, he felt that to become competitive he would have to leapfrog the competition. Projects were in early development that could jump the competition, but to bring them to market quickly, Rob would need a major infusion of cash in order to hire the people and provide the equipment to attain this goal.

Under pressure from investors to reverse recent quarterly losses and a drop in share value of stock, Rob's management was reluctant to provide him the resources needed for the renewal he knew was needed. As one top manager said, "We all have to manage with what we've got. We can't do more than we can pay for."

Rob's direct reports knew that in a competition between maintaining the product flow and rejuvenating the organization, that product flow would receive top management's support. Overwhelmed by their own product deadlines, for which Rob's supervisors would hold them accountable, they had little stomach for a major renewal effort. Like Jim's organization at the end of the renewal process, Rob's was exhausted as well—but it had not yet begun the effort. Already working long hours, under lots of pressure, they had no patience for the extra time and effort needed for examination and renewal.

Rob's needs and the contrasting needs of his managers were both legitimate. Lacking was a well-designed corporate renewal strategy, with agreements from top and middle managers in key functions to make it happen. This strategy would allow the operations people to plan for a slightly longer wait for new products, while product development rebuilt itself. Rob's lesson was painful, one he should have heeded before he took the job. The pace and timing of change are often as important as the "buy-in" and involvement throughout the organization to change. Sometimes two feet are needed on the accelerator to strengthen the organization. Other times intermittent cruising speeds or even pauses should be in order, while the organization tends to the work.

Both these managers, Jim and Rob, were faced with similar situations. Jim's was how to prevent stagnation in an organization wearied by the organizational improvement process. Rob's was how to overcome stagnation in an organization exhausted from the day-to-day work.

Managing the ongoing change will be one of your most difficult challenges, and there is no driver's manual to ensure success. Here are a few rules of thumb:

1. *Try to achieve the difficult balance between combating the forces of stagnation without overextending people so that both the ongoing work and the change process succeed.* This takes constant attention to timelines and progress, communication about delays and problems, openness to suggestions, and sensitivity to people's needs.

Juliette knew her group of data processors was seriously backlogged, yet she knew they needed to have a better way to manage the work. So she decided to ease them into a process of change. They started with a series of once-a-week working lunches in the conference room, which Juliette paid for out of her travel budget. After two meetings, a core group of interested people formed, who continued to meet once a week for Juliette's lunch; others were invited to the open meeting, but Juliette's group committed themselves to continued meeting. As they discussed their needs and wants, they slowly began to evolve a set of goals, and as interest grew, Juliette encouraged them to set a timeline.

She provided the group with consulting assistance from Human Resources to collect the information they needed. The consultant was especially helpful at analyzing alternative solutions and helping the group select and implement the best solutions for them. Visits were scheduled to other companies. The consultant scheduled vendors to demonstrate equipment and new products. A data processing consultant was brought in to evaluate the vendors and their claims. Juliette got her company's Information Systems group to help.

Juliette continued to provide consultants' help and maintained the hiring and training schedule to help the task force's efforts. She remained open to task force suggestions about delays and help with problems. She took their suggestions, and maintained gentle pressure to complete the task. She did not want them to lose momentum, but neither did she want to overwhelm them. She was sensitive to their needs, and was able to keep daily work flowing while gradually adopting changes.

2. *If you are going to miscalculate, err on the side of overpacing, zealousness, and overactive communication.* Goals that make people stretch are motivating. Unreasonable goals are demotivating, since people feel they are impossible to attain. Set somewhat challenging time goals, and stay in close communication with the task forces. It is easier to throttle back than to throttle up.

All managers face daily urgencies, and the urgencies, because they have to be done immediately whether priorities or not, tend to crowd out real priorities. A phone call, for example, is an urgency that is often not a priority task, yet it interferes with priorities.

Tighten time schedules, and pay attention to them so they become urgencies. If task force members know you are concerned about deadlines, task force work will become priorities and urgencies. If, on the other hand, you exert no pressure, the deadlines will slip in the face of other priorities.

When Kevin told his managers and task force members to get the job done "as fast as is reasonably possible," he gave them an open-ended invitation to prolong the task. Impatient about their slow progress, he gave them a deadline.

3. *There is the tendency for things to revert to the way they used to be, if left untended.* Look for the signs of "organizational dry rot." You see them, the growth stultifying disease of "things as they were before, or things as usual." Continue to explore different ways to help people move toward goals.

Be wary of comments such as:

- "We're not ready for this yet. Maybe we should slow down. Things are changing too fast."
- "Why spend the money, it's too expensive. We have spent a lot of time and money and we are not much better off."
- "That's not our job, so-and-so ought to be doing that" (Management, Training, Human Resources, consultants, another department, etc.).
- "Things were better before the changes."
- "Why try this? We considered it three years ago and rejected it/it didn't work."
- "We've never done it this way. I'm not sure it's better."

Keep interest in the changes high. Reinforce them. Alert your direct reports to watch for signs of slippage and to nip them. Where a change is not working out, be prepared to raise the issue rather than to just let things drift back. Actively manage the implementation so changes are reinforced. Identify implementation problems and handle them promptly so those problems do not discredit the renewal process. Be prepared to intervene yourself, or to get a direct report involved in solving burgeoning problems.

Always use your diagnostic and problem-solving skills to "sniff out" what is going on. Stay visible and listen, listen, listen! Get into the work areas. Know your people's names. Be familiar with work processes and equipment. People will appreciate your skilled ear, and you will accumulate valuable information to help you lead your organization more effectively.

Organizational health maintenance is essential! Never forget that what you have gained in the first year of your renewal can be lost in a few weeks if you allow old habits to return. We have seen that bad habits, individual or organizational, are very hard to change. They also easily return. Just as reformed smokers quickly can again become smokers, so can organizational disease quickly recur.

The last two decades have seen an emphasis on personal disease prevention, wellness, and health maintenance. Organizational leaders can learn much from this social phenomena. It is much easier to *maintain* organizational health than to incur the discomfort of organizational surgery and long-term therapy. Organizational health maintenance involves maintaining uncompromising standards and never-ending, everyday effective management.

Derek had worked hard to reorganize the service at his deli restaurant. Working with his experienced employees he had established guidelines for customer service. Some of these guidelines include:

- Because customers like to be acknowledged and order quickly, approach them with a smile and a menu as they are sitting down.
- Take their order as quickly as possible. Regular customers usually know what they want. People hate to wait.
- Get the order immediately to the kitchen. Put your name on the order form so the cook can page you.
- Water, bread, butter, and beverages fill the time while waiting for the order.
- Check on the order from time to time with the cook. Don't let the order get lost.
- If the order is slow, talk to the customer. Assure him/her that they are not forgotten.

- When it is busy, divide the tables among servers so no customers are overlooked.
- If you see a customer looking around, inquire, even if it is not your table. Help each other to keep the customers happy.

In spite of these guidelines, there was constant slippage in service. Derek had to constantly monitor the floor, even with his best servers, to make sure they did not slip back. It required constant vigilance and supervision to maintain the new standards.

Fine-Tuning Your Leadership Role and Your Organization

As you near the end of your first year, step back from your day-to-day responsibilities to reflect on your new role. Reflect on what you have accomplished. Moving up is never easy. You've had to tap dance on a lot of marbles! Personal reflection often results in the awareness that, "I didn't realize that we did that much."

Regular reflection should be standard fare for leaders moving up. Self-analysis is part of being a good diagnostician, problem preventer, and problem solver. Questions such as the following can help you reflect on your organization's progress and your own personal progress.

- How am I (are we) doing?
- Where do I (we) wish to be in the future?
- How should I (we) get there?
- Are there pitfalls of which I (we) should be careful?

At the six-month mark, Suzanne reflected on her accomplishments and disappointments as manager of a small sales team. She had made three new hires. She had structured and led them through a training program. They were reasonably confident they could work with new clients, were actively involved in developing proposals and contracts, and had mounted and successfully carried off an exhibit at the industry's major trade show.

However, Suzanne's list of disappointments was much longer than her list of accomplishments.

1. The sales reporting system was virtually nonexistent. Even though she had designed a system, and required weekly itineraries, and weekly reports on contracts, proposals, and contracts, her people were not accounting for their time and accomplishments, and the

operations department had insufficient information to plan for the upcoming workload.

2. In spite of weekly sales meetings, Suzanne did not have good data on her people's activities. One seemed good at managing old clients, but seemed to have no new leads. One seemed to spend too much time writing sales materials. All seemed to avoid phone work. She felt uneasy that the reassurances she was given at sales meetings did not seem to be operationalized in daily performance activities.

3. In spite of the added sales resources, and the fact she had divided her marketing leads among her sales force, the actual number of sales proposals had not increased from when she was doing the job by herself. To some extent, this was because her salespeople were managing old contracts up for renewal and managed the professional conferences, activities formerly completed by operations staff. This in itself was an indication that her sales force was not sufficiently oriented to new sales.

4. Their reports from sales trips suggested customer interest in a single low-technology, low-priced product. She suspected they were not confident or knowledgeable enough to sell the more complex or higher-priced products.

At the six-month mark, Suzanne began a round of monthly assessments with her direct reports. All were frustrated that the sales information system was not automated, and that sales activity reports were not automated. Similarly, they felt the proposals and contracts were not standardized enough, and required too much effort to complete.

One salesperson, who had formerly been in operations, confessed his discomfort with the sales lead process. Another admitted not having enough leads, but placed the blame on the excessive time required to generate contract renewals, product descriptions, and managing the industry trade show. They had few complaints about Suzanne's own style, except that each felt she was blind to other's lack of accomplishments.

These impressions had become increasingly clear to Suzanne, as her level of discomfort increased. Her six-month self-appraisal was an opportunity for her to turn her heretofore vague discomfort into clearly stated accomplishments and disappointments, to be objective about the disappointments, and begin the problem-solving process. Clearly stated as problems, she proactively addressed the problems and avoided getting blindsided by them later on.

Her instincts to formally assess her performance were correct. Her boss and the operations managers were already aware of the problems in Suzanne's department, especially of the lack of information about sales activity, and the lack of new proposals and contracts. Suzanne's formal self-appraisal allowed her to surface these problems with her boss and solve them *before* he came to her with some ultimatums. Indeed, this six-month assessment may have saved her job. She demonstrated to her boss that she was aware of the problems, was managing them, and allowed her to solicit his help and the help of the operations managers in solving the problems.

At the six-month mark and especially as you near the end of your first year, review your performance.

1. *Prepare a written performance review.* List your accomplishments, disappointments, strengths, and areas for improvement. Send it to your boss and schedule a meeting with him or her to discuss it. Show your initiative, interest, and insight in your abilities, and how you are doing. You'll be helping your boss to help you. It is your responsibility to help your boss be your coach, mentor, and sponsor.

2. *At the six-month performance review meeting, be prepared with questions for which you genuinely desire feedback.* Again, help your boss to help you. Be open to his or her ideas and suggestions. Demonstrate your ability to accept criticism if it is forthcoming. Don't be defensive. Listen, try to understand. Learn from this experience. Show your enthusiasm and pride in what you have accomplished. Thank your boss for his or her help, support, ideas, and feedback.

3. *Selectively solicit input from subordinates, peers, and others in the organization.* By asking for candid feedback, you create a potential reservoir of insight and recommendations. It is okay to be vulnerable with others. Another useful approach is to reserve 15 minutes at the end of your subordinates' performance reviews to ask for ideas on how you can better help them and your organization in general. If you have done a good job establishing rapport and open communication, you will typically receive a wealth of useful ideas.

4. *Consider the following questions as a guide for introspection.*
   - How do I feel about my job now?
   - How do I like the job of manager and leader?
   - Am I underchallenged, or do I feel over my head?
   - Can I do the job the way I feel it should be done?
   - Who have I affected for better and for worse?
   - How have I developed? What do I need to work on next?
   - How does the job fit into what I really value in my life, my family, and my lifestyle in general?
   - What would I change most about the job? Am I able to make changes in the job to achieve a better fit?

5. *Reserve at least a week each year in your schedule to participate in a professional development seminar, workshop, or retreat.* These might be technical and concern the content of your job. Strengthen areas where you feel less confident, broaden areas of strength. Develop your management skills by attending an executive program at a graduate business school or at an association such as the American Management Association. Challenge yourself to be a more complete person by working on your spirit, self-concept, or interpersonal skills. Workshops sponsored by organizations such as National Training Labs (NTL), The Center for Creative Leadership, Outward Bound, and Innovation Associates are generally well regarded and deal with the human side of management.

SOARING: Sharpening the Way You Think About Your Work and Personal Life

Successful leadership also means sharpening your mental outlook, and the way you view yourself, your job, your family, and friends. SOARING is a creative approach to thinking and viewing your personal and professional world. SOARING suggests seven points that successful managers can live by:

S	*Superior leadership* is my daily goal and primary work value.
O	*Opportunities to succeed abound*—I can make them happen, and every day they come my way.
A	*Achievement and success require a positive mindset* which can be learned and developed.
R	*Respond to problems* positively and energetically.
I	*Inform yourself about the common work and personal pitfalls of leaders who are moving up.*
N	*Never fail to develop as a leader.*
G	*Gain an understanding* of the impact of moving up on your family, health, and time.

Let's look more closely at each point.

Superior Leadership

Superior leadership is my daily goal and primary work value. To be a superior leader brings us eye to eye with our true selves—our strengths, weaknesses, concerns, and dreams. To strive to be superior is simultaneously enriching, energizing, and always challenging. To perform at the upper limits of our ability requires complex knowledge, skills, attitudes, and behaviors.

Superior leaders have a master plan, a vision of what they wish to accomplish. Accomplishing that plan is akin to eating an elephant—just one bite at a time. Superior leaders create and operationalize their vision, with activities which, one at a time, help them constantly upgrade their abilities.

Feedback from subordinates, peers, and her boss helped make Carla more aware of her strengths and weaknesses. The weaknesses were, in particular, preventing her from becoming a superior leader, and she knew they would slow her success and promotion.

From her subordinates she learned they needed better systems and procedures to automate elements of the work that were repetitive. They wanted her to provide more frequent and specific feedback, and to tell them when they did a good job more often.

Managers of other departments said they needed better information on her group's work, so those who handled the work knew it was managed in time, and those to whom she sent her work (her clients inside the company) could better plan for what was coming. They also said she was making too many last-minute requests of them, which created timeline pressures that interfered with their normal work.

The feedback from Carla's boss was the most critical, because his impressions would affect her salary, bonus, career advancement, and in fact, whether or not she would continue in her job. At the six-month appraisal, she found her boss had already heard the complaints from her peer managers, who had been going to him with their complaints rather than to her. They felt when they went to her, she listened but nothing ever changed. So in frustration they hoped he would be able to get through to her.

Her boss had some suggestions about her personal attire, the stacks of papers and unfinished work on her desk, her filing cabinets, and even sometimes on the floor. To him, these were symptoms of the lack of organization and planning cited by Carla's fellow managers. He also wanted more accountability from her, so that when he was asked about her work he could report exactly on productivity and short-term accomplishments.

As a result of the feedback at the six-month review, Carla was able to develop a plan of action to strengthen her leadership, which in turn would strengthen her working relationships with her boss and co-managers.

Superior leadership, Carla's aspiration, requires a master plan, and it is difficult to develop that plan without feedback, especially from your boss and your fellow managers who talk to him or her. Rely on others to tell you what you are doing well and what you need to improve. In the final analysis, it is their perceptions of your effectiveness—what they think—that will affect your present and future success.

Superior leaders seek to constantly improve their leadership abilities. For them, managerial effectiveness becomes almost an obsession. Bob uses virtually every moment of his day striving to improve his leadership abilities either by practicing them or reinforcing them. He often listens to management cassette tapes while doing his morning exercises. He rereads his favorite books on management every year, and puts a short synopsis of the ideas he is working with on a 3 × 5 card on his desk as a daily reminder. Every day he is aware of and applies in his work the skills and abilities of a superior leader.

Superior leaders like Bob exercise their best abilities many times a day. They are steady and consistent in their approach to their work. They are logical, consider alternatives, listen to other's ideas, and weigh consequences, yet are confident enough to override logic when their intuition is compelling. They trust their judgment and intuition, and learn who are the others in their organization whose logic and intuition they can trust.

With an unflinching commitment to their beliefs and values, superior leaders set high standards for themselves and others, and have a low tolerance for anything less. Most importantly, they live up to their standards. Bob's daily performance is shaped by his beliefs about good management. He constantly strives to live by his values to achieve his goals, and maintains a remarkable ability to help others to do the same. Superior leaders touch people's lives. Bob has the ability to make every person with whom he comes in contact feel better, more important, more competent, and more valuable and responsible. He knows when to take charge and when to get out of the way. Superior leaders seem better prepared and work harder and smarter than just about everyone around them, because they are well-grounded in their values, beliefs, and the principles by which they live.

Opportunities to Succeed Abound

Opportunities are the constant. The ways each of us thinks, feels, and acts are the variables. We can control the way we view ourselves, others, and the world around us. Opportunities will be there, and we can grab them even when they surface as problems.

Superior leaders are extremely positive, energetic when others are complacent, calm when others are frenzied. Being "on the line" is a challenge to superior leaders who choose to be accountable to themselves first, feeling that if they can manage that hurdle, the rest will fall in place. They look for and find opportunities to shine.

For Brad, every business encounter is an opportunity. Contacts are an opportunity for new business. He is always seeking an opportunity to determine which customer's needs the competition has not identified, is not aware of, or is not meeting well. "You know, Brad," said one potential client, "If I could combine your knowledge of the field with your competitor's technical expertise, we'd have a perfect program." This piece of information gave Brad insight into his competitive strengths, information on where he needed to improve, and an opportunity to suggest a joint arrangement that would get him a part of a contract he thought he had lost.

Another winning attitude Brad has toward his losses is the persistence to know that in a little while his lost contacts will see his competitors' shortcomings and be open to reconsider working with him. So, in effect, all contacts are potential successes, to be maintained.

Similarly, Brad sees lost business as an opportunity. Early in his career, he learned that most angry customers want to be heard. They do not necessarily want you to go away. Rather, they want you to hear their complaints and find a solution. They have already invested much time and effort selecting you, and they do not want you to fail. So Brad uses his company's failures as opportunities to meet with the customer, listen to his or her grievances, solve the problem, and keep the customer appraised of the progress. One unhappy client said, "Yes, I was very unhappy with the job your company did, but I thought your project manager or you would call back. I thought we'd try to analyze what went wrong, and we'd learn from it." Another client said, "Yes, it was a disaster—but it was really our fault. We simply didn't know what we wanted, and we didn't manage you very well. You should have called."

Within Brad's own organization, both successes and failures are similarly an opportunity to grow. It is primarily from his failures that he learns where things should improve. Failure is his most painful feedback, which shows where improvement is needed. A competitor's successes provides Brad with the impetus to pressure top management for more resources, new products, and to pressure his own organization to improve. For him, events both positive and negative are opportunities for growth, improvement, and strength.

Achievement Requires
a Positive Mindset

Achievement and success depend upon a positive mindset which can be developed. Whether it is inborn or learned, some people seem to approach life with an outlook characterized by undefeatable optimism. In the face of disaster they, like Brad, have the knack of finding solutions, for turning problems into opportunities.

More pessimistic leaders tend to view difficult situations as obstacles. They are often more prone to responding negatively to pressure and are often unable to convert tension and anxiety into energy. Those with a more negative mindset often have not learned to control their inner state.

The positive thinker tends to handle stressful situations with positive internal messages such as these:

- Yes, this is a difficult situation, and a solution is out there waiting to be found (*Yes, and* versus *Yes, but*). I need to focus, to think, to control the problem, but the solution is there.

- Solving difficult problems is like walking a tightrope, one careful step at a time.

- I am going to do the best I can even though this is going to be a difficult situation. I will be courageous. (A nationally known news anchor, in a recent interview, confessed to almost daily feeling the fear of failure, the fear in his job, but said success is the ability to fight and, for one more day, overcome the fear.)

- I choose to reduce tension and anxiety by positively focusing on the part of the task I am working on today. (John Wooden, the legendary UCLA basketball coach who won 5 NCAA championships in 6 years, always told his players not to focus on the goal, but the steps. Do each of the things we stress well, and the larger goal (success) will take care of itself.)

- If for some reason I didn't do well today, I will do so tomorrow. My best is the best I could do today, and tomorrow I will strive to do better.

- I will be the ultimate judge of my performance. I am not working to please others, but myself. I work to my own standards of excellence.

- I love difficult challenges; the tougher the circumstances, the better I perform. Challenges provide my opportunity to develop new capabilities, to discover powers I didn't know I had.

- No matter what others say and do, I am always a capable person.

- What is the worst thing that could conceivably happen if I fail? And then what? And what is the likelihood that it will occur?

Respond to Problems

Respond to problems positively and energetically. Here are some reminders that have proven helpful:

- No matter what, I will accept each challenge and my reaction to it. I will work with what life sends me and try to make the best of it.

- I will try to approach my toughest challenges aggressively. I will play to succeed. I want to win, to be the best, to do the best work, to be trusted by my customers to do the best work possible, to get the work. I will work to the limits of my capabilities and succeed.

- *Though my enemies attempt to slay me, and I am in fear, I shall put down my fears and live to fight another day* (St. Anselm's Prayer, posted on the desk of former President Richard Nixon).

- I will include others in my success—I will gain their commitment by giving of myself and helping to empower them, and by giving them credit. I will gain influence and power by sharing it with others.

Inform Yourself of the Common Pitfalls

Inform yourself of the common pitfalls of leaders who are moving up. While the snares seem endless, an important study summarized 10 key reasons for leadership derailment.[1] Here is how they play themselves out.

Specific Performance Problems with the Business. As we have described in this book, managing well is a process of empowering your organization to continuous improvement by mutually identifying specific performance problems, and identifying and implementing solutions. No business can be stagnant. Change is a constant of business. Even as things go well, you must keep your eye on the horizon, on the next generation of goods and services. You must ensure your organization prepares for the future even as you succeed in the present.

Insensitivity to Others: An Abrasive, Intimidating, Bullying Style. Contrary to the business press myths about successful bullies who "win through intimidation," few bullies ever make it to the top. They simply make too many enemies on the way up or expose their Achilles heel—their inability to build a stable, strong, capable staff. There are different kinds of bullies. The stereotype is of the yelling, stomping, threatening bully. But the overcritical manager is also a bully—overscrutinizing his employees, second-guessing their decisions, creating in them the fear to criticize, to make suggestions, or to do anything beyond what they are told to do, for fear of being wrong.

Less recognized but having the same effect is the psychological bully. These are kind, humane, often personable managers who can treat employees like children. They judge the employees' ideas (good, bad) rather than building upon ideas or brainstorming with them. They fine-tune others' ideas in a way that they assume ownership and credit. Their people feel like children—seeking approval of their work and their ideas, rather than colleagues whose input and advice is sought and valued.

All bullies—the loud and brash, the overcritical, and the psychological—have the same effect. They make people feel powerless, childlike, and dependent. They generate resentment and undermine the organization's ability to develop strong capable leadership.

Being Cold, Aloof, Arrogant. The cold, aloof manager thinks he or she has to retain distance from his or her work force. In fact, however, successful managers are accessible, friendly, solicitous of their opinions and input, and grateful for their assistance. They acknowledge that the best ideas frequently come from the work force. Aloofness cuts managers off from the crucial information needed to manage well. Arrogance cuts managers off from the hybridization of ideas that form strong organizations. The arrogance that "I am right, only my ideas are good," discourages employees from taking the initiative to identify and solve problems. They will say, "It is his or her organization, all the ideas have to be his or hers, so let the problems, the solutions, and the consequences be his or hers, too." You will end up with all the problems and all the responsibility, because you are cut off from needed information.

Betrayal of Trust. If an employee comes to you with a request, observation, or confidential information, you must honor the request for confidence, even while you feel compelled to initiate some action. Similarly, not trusting experienced and capable employees undermines their confidence in themselves. "Damn it," said one long-time employee to his boss, "I'm 52 years old, a graduate engineer with over 30 years experience in the field. I need to feel trusted to do this well."

Overmanaging: Failing to Delegate or Build a Team. One of Jo Ann's problems as a manager was that she couldn't let go, didn't delegate. The decisions she got involved with ranged from the trivial to the substantive. She selected the computer cable to link a piece of equipment to the computer system, selected the word processing equipment, decided who needed training and who didn't, signed the checks, edited the product descriptions, made the presentations to major customers, and directed all the firm's most important projects. She hired, fired, supervised, trained, promoted, and reorganized. She was her small organization's manager, accountant, personnel manager, trainer, supervisor, purchaser, head of the support staff, and in charge of buildings and maintenance. Jo Ann did it all, and she was exhausted, angry, and resentful of the load she was carrying.

And carry it she did, not because others couldn't take responsibility, but because she couldn't let go of responsibilities to say, "Okay, it's not the way I would have done it, but it's okay."

In the short term, Jo Ann was helping her organization. She made excellent decisions that invariably helped the organization. But her reluctance to delegate severely constrained her organization. People were reluctant to make decisions on their own because they felt they would get a better decision from Jo Ann. As a result, responsibility upon responsibility and decision upon decision, both trivial and significant, was piled upon her desk. She became a bottleneck to growth, as projects and decisions awaited her attention. By helping, she was unwittingly sitting on the organization's energy, creativity, and competence.

Overly Ambitious: Thinking of the Next Job, Playing Politics. One of Estelle's problems was thinking of her own promotion ahead of the welfare of her organization. She sought influence and contacts too assiduously. It seemed to her employees that her current assignment was merely a steppingstone to her next promotion.

Whether this impression was really her intent or not was immaterial. This was the impression she gave. What did she do? She served on too many corporate and industry committees. It seemed to her employees that she spent more time in meetings outside the department than within the department. Much of the time she did have for the department ended up as time at her desk, preparing reports for her many committee memberships, and doing departmental administrative work.

Her people saw little of her; she had little informal time to chat and brainstorm about problems, and her direct reports felt the time she had available for them was inadequate. She seemed more interested in responsibilities outside the department than in her department's work. How she used her lunchtime also affected those perceptions. Many lunches were so-called "power lunches" with top and middle managers who could help her career. Rarely did she lunch with direct reports and never with her employees. When no power lunch was scheduled, she preferred to eat at her desk, working.

She spent little time chatting with subordinates. There were few "free floating" discussions about the work. Encounters were planned, to the point, purposeful, and functional. Things seemed so impersonal, so businesslike. Her people did not feel she was involved with them, their concerns, or their work.

And she got overly involved with the politics of the organization. Much of what is called politics is the behind-the-scenes gossip, criticisms, second-guessing, and politicking to advance a particular point of view. Politics are often personalized, focusing not on the merits of the idea alone, but explicitly or implicitly on the person advancing the idea.

Politics undermine face-to-face, direct and open communication with the give and take of disagreement, and honest differences among well-intentioned people. Estelle's broad network involved her in corporate politics, even those which would not have normally been her concern were she not so intent on advancing her career.

Failing to Staff Effectively.   Many top managers say that the single most important factor in organizational quality is the quality of the staff. Hire the right people, provide them with the resources and support, and get out of their way.

Staffing is the flip side to delegation. It is difficult to delegate when you feel the work will be problematic. A manager needs people whose judgment and quality he or she trusts. If you don't have them, get some new help.

Joyce, an extremely successful manager, formerly of a Fortune 500 company, built her success primarily through the quality of her hires. She got the best people available—even if they cost more. She hired the best—graduates at the top of their graduating class, from the best schools, alumni from top companies who could bring those companies' procedures and winning strategies to her organization.

Within a year of taking over her organization of 50 people, a third of the professional staff was new. Veterans who were not productive, who were not team players, or whose work required constant supervision were eased out. The new work force not only had an improved work ethic, but their skills reflected where Joyce thought the organization should be headed. Without surrendering any present capabilities, she was able to hire replacements who expanded the capabilities and quality of the organization's products and services.

Unable to Think Strategically.   A successful manager must be capable of planning for the future, as well as managing the work at hand. Strategic thinking means you can think in terms of a one-, three-, and five-year plan. You have goals for your organization's products and services, and operational plans to achieve those goals.

Thinking strategically also means being able to think about the future needs of customers. It is the ability to extend products and services in ways that build customer's thinking and their interest in your products and services. It is the ability to keep customers coming back for repeat business, for future product ideas and needs. In the process, customers will bring their good ideas, and provide a wellspring of product extensions and new product ideas. Sometimes they will even help develop those ideas when the first customer contract is signed.

Anticipating competitive threats and positioning your organization to cope with them is also essential to strategic thinking. Continuous improvement, an eye to new technology, and listening to customers are the keys.

Unable to Adapt to a Boss with a Different Style. We have repeatedly returned to the central issue of your relationship with your boss. After you have taken the job and thought you had negotiated your role and prerogatives, you will have surprises in store for you. In Chap. 3, we discussed a number of issues. By now, you will have faced a few more.

Some of your personal habits may annoy your boss. He or she might value a desktop that is orderly and neat, a reflection of organization and good planning. Your boss might not think the way you dress, the length or style of your hair, or your habits of speech reflect the image he or she wants to project.

Your boss may be a late starter who stays late. If you are an early starter who leaves early, you may not score many points for your hours. He or she isn't there to see your 6:30 arrival, only your 4:00 or 4:30 departure. Check it out with your boss.

You can try to be stubborn and do these things your way. You may not lose, but you will not win. Whatever his or her annoyances, they will crop up again and again, and color his or her perception of your performance.

Keep the things your boss disapproves of in your lifestyle out of sight. Don't bring them to work. Don't talk about them with co-workers, fellow managers, or even with friends at work. For the time you are in the office, they don't exist.

Pay attention to the hints your boss makes, to how he or she may tease you. Raise issues of style directly, if you have a suspicion about how he or she feels. The more issues on the table between you, the smoother the relationship.

Overdependent on an Advocate or Mentor. Overdependence on your mentor can affect your effectiveness. Lisa, a junior manager serving on a corporate task force, impressed Sheila, a senior task force member, and shortly thereafter received a major promotion to a job in Sheila's organization. Sheila appropriately rewarded Lisa's drive, organization, group skills, problem-solving ability, and determination, observed on task force assignments. Working closely together, Sheila rapidly became Lisa's mentor and her strong advocate.

Lisa's problems stemmed not from her working for Sheila, but in doing Sheila's bidding on some difficult assignments. For example, Sheila was dissatisfied with the pace of new product testing and asked Lisa to oversee new project management. As director of project management, Lisa was in the position to push product development very hard, which she did. She shared Sheila's feeling that products were developing too slowly. By doing Sheila's bidding, however, four things, all bad, could happen to Lisa:

1. Sheila's enemies become Lisa's.

2. Lisa, politically much weaker than Sheila, was now tied to Sheila's successes. Should Sheila's career falter, or should she leave for another job, Lisa would be gone too, because she would lose her advocate.

3. Lisa is not perceived as independent or capable in her own right. Her close association with her mentor may deny her the ability to demonstrate her capabilities in her own right and establish herself on her own. She will earn few opportunities that are not linked to Sheila. She will be seen as Sheila's representative in whatever she does.

4. Others in the organization may perceive that Sheila is propping Lisa up, a perception that will further weaken Lisa's effectiveness.

The effective manager has to acknowledge and benefit from the support of managers and mentors. Without people who recognize our talents and nurture us, few of us would move beyond our first job in the company. At the same time, we must attempt to remain reasonably independent of the people who sponsor us, and self-reliant, a difficult balancing act.

Working and surviving, let alone prospering in an organization and outside of work is a complex, risky, and sometimes temporary business. It requires continuous attention. To succeed in management, you have to be smart, creative, and hardworking. Business is so very dynamic. There is always something new to contend with. In management you must simultaneously manage a complex of human, work flow, technology, planning, and competitive pressures that make management at once the most difficult, maddeningly complex, and perhaps the most challenging and rewarding thing you have ever done.

Never Fail to Achieve Your Goals as a Leader

Never fail to achieve your goals to develop as a leader. We spoke earlier about the importance of improving your technical, professional, managerial, and personal competencies. Your knowledge, skills, and attitudes are the "qualifiers," the tickets to get in the door and stay there. Managers mature into superior leaders partly by setting challenging self-development goals. Leaders on the rise who follow through with such plans develop their own skills and ability while communicating a clear message to their people about personal and professional growth.

We suggest updating and reviewing your executive development plans with your boss every six months. See the list of training and development experiences presented in Chap. 7 as a tactical resource.

Gaining an Understanding of the Impact of Moving Up

The seventh and final principle in SOARING is to gain an understanding of the impact of moving up on your family, health, and time. The importance of this principle is so great that we have dedicated the last section of the book to it, Chaps. 10 and 11. Managing your personal life can be the quintessence of tap dancing on marbles. It is slippery, complex, elusive, and full of difficulties. Just when you think things have settled down, you will discover a new set of difficulties. Part 3 is entitled "Managing the Impact of Moving Up on Your Family, Health, and Time." Chapter 10 looks at the "Up Close and Personal: The Impact of Moving Up on Your Family, Health, and Time," while Chap. 11 describes "Achieving a New Life Balance."

Quick Reminders to Keep You on Track

- Since planned organizational growth takes a toll in time, effort, and money, there comes a point when it is best to pull the reins in and slow the pace of change. This usually occurs after some of the major change goals have been achieved, while enthusiasm for the new vision and direction is still strong.

- Managing the pace of change will be a difficult challenge. Here are some helpful hints:
  1. Try to achieve the very difficult balance between the forces of stagnation and overextending people, so that both the ongoing work and the change process can succeed.
  2. If you miscalculate the speed of change, err on the side of overpacing, zealousness, and overactive communication. It is much easier to throttle back than to throttle up in moving an organization forward.
  3. Be attentive and reactive as necessary to the "business as usual" mentality that tends to impede organizational growth.
  4. There are times to slow down or back off on the pace of change. During these periods, concentrate on the work at hand.

5. Keep your ear to the ground and eyes wide open. Maintain your diagnostic/problem-solving approach.
6. Remember that what you gained in the year of renewal can be lost in a few weeks if you allow old habits to return.

- Toward the end of your first year, step back from your day-to-day responsibilities to reflect on your new role. Review your performance, get ideas and input from others, and determine how you really feel about your job. Use SOARING as a way to view yourself, your job, your family, and your friends. Remain in regular communication with your boss; stay in his or her "mental in-basket"; keep his or her expectations of you high.

Summary of Major Responsibilities—Year One (Chap. 9)

First Year by Month*

	Preappointment	1	2	3	4	5	6	7	8	9	10	11	12

Moving in: Establishing Yourself in Your New Assignment
- Entering the Organization
- Entering Your Boss's World

Achieving an Impact on the Organization
- Beginning to Craft Your Vision and Direction
- The Diagnostic Process: The Importance of Good Organizational Information
- Assessing Your Organization's Health — The Nine-Target Model
- Selecting, Building, and Developing Your Work Team
- From Resistance to Renewal: Building Your Management Team's Commitment
- Settling into Your Renewing Organization

*Times are approximate.

Legend
- ——— Primary period of emphasis
- – – – Active but not a period of emphasis

197

Your Personal Plan for Settling Into Your Renewing Organization (Chap. 9)

Activity	Suggested Timeframe	Perceived Barriers	Available Resources	Your Projected Timeframe	Completed (✓)
• Begin taking steps to prevent future organizational stagnation. — Primarily, ensure that there is no slippage of improvements made during the first six to ten months of year one. — Following a major "push" to improve the organization while keeping "normal" work going, more time and energy should be available during the last three to four months of year one to concentrate on "normal work." — Use your fine-tuned diagnostic skills to sense new problems early.	Primarily during months 9–12 depending on the progress of your organizational improvement efforts.				
• Fine-tune your leadership role. — Prepare for a year-end performance review by initiating a written self-evaluation listing accomplishments, disappointments, strengths, and areas for improvement. Send it to your boss without it being requested. — Solicit feedback from your boss during the year-end review — Selectively solicit ideas and input from subordinates, peers, and others in the organization. — Candidly ask yourself how you are doing, how you like your job, and how you can improve your performance and compatibility with the job. — Reserve at least one week to participate in a professional development seminar.	Usually during months 11 and 12.				
• Sharpen the way you think about your work and personal life by implementing the seven-step SOARING model.	During your decision to take your position and continuously thereafter.				

PART 3

Managing the Impact of Moving Up on Your Family and Personal Life

10

Up Close and Personal: The Impact of Moving Up on Your Family, Health, and Time

Let us endeavor so to live that when we come to die, even the undertaker will be sorry.
MARK TWAIN

For almost everyone, moving up means changes at work. In turn, this usually means changes at home, how you use your time and your ability to act on what is important to you. Some handle these changes well. Many, if not most, find the changes a challenge. You will need to:

- Help those close to you understand the personal impact of moving up on your work and life systems.
- Use the six principles in this chapter to strengthen and complement the personal aspects of your life.

In this chapter, there is useful information about:

- The Personal Basis of Moving Up Into a Leadership Role
- Six Principles of Managing the Impact of Moving Up on Your Family, Health and Time
  1. There is a profound relationship between personal wellness, family, health, and executive work effectiveness as you move up.
  2. Major job changes often can trigger major life changes.
  3. Managers who are moving up are in a state of transition which can be understood and managed.
  4. Health and well being in one's personal, family, and work lives affect, and are affected by levels of stress and distress.
  5. Mutual understanding, support, fairness and responsible collaboration within dual career families and partners are essential tenets for leaders on the rise.
  6. The goal is to achieve a new life balance.

The Personal Basis of Moving Up

Moving up often involves a major life transition that spawns events seemingly unrelated to career advancement. Many of the pleasant and unpleasant by-products of career advancement are, however, predictable, part of a total life system. Job changes affect many things:

- Where you live
- The lifestyle of immediate family members
- Your community affiliations and activities
- Your relationship with your spouse
- Your relationship with your children
- The amount of time that you spend at work, at home or with friends
- Your salary and expenses
- Your commuting time
- Available energy and time to maintain your health
- Your friends, colleagues, or associates
- Access to your church, synagogue, or religious and spiritual anchors

- Decreased access to parents, brothers, sisters, or your "roots" in general
- Free time to vacation or do things you love

There are trade-offs and payoffs to every career decision. Moving up will challenge you to minimize the disadvantages and maximize the pluses. Your ability to identify and achieve your desired life balance will be tested and tested again. Bob and Linda Doyle's circumstances are a case in point.

The Case of Bob and Linda Doyle

Bob and Linda's experience is quite typical. One partner, Bob, targeted and achieved a major career goal. Neither Bob nor Linda anticipated or planned for the impact of his promotion on their professional and personal lives. Bob's selection to head the research division for a large international corporation changed their lives markedly. Unknowingly, they quickly lost control over several important areas of their lives, with regrettable consequences.

Bob had an excellent record as a researcher. Over a 12-year period he had proven himself as a scientist and project team leader, developing several new products and successfully tackling every challenge set before him. For the first six years after graduate school, Bob was primarily a bench researcher, participating in the important discoveries which led to the development of several important products. For the next three years, as a project team leader in charge of 5 researchers, his team developed new applications for several company products, increasing the profitability and market reach of those products.

At year 10, a change in companies allowed Bob to take over a research department of about 25 professionals, an opportunity which broadened him scientifically. While he continued to enjoy the time he devoted to his research projects, he now had broader leadership and managerial responsibilities.

He did very well at his science and at managing his team. He inherited experienced, highly motivated people who presented very few personnel or administrative problems. They rarely tested his ability as a manager. The work was well-planned, well-organized; his teams were productive and well-managed. Bob, now one of his company's shining lights, enjoyed management and looked forward to increased management responsibility. Then came his big opportunity.

Bob's promotion to vice president of research was, as he described it, "a high point in my life." He now directed a division, critical to the company's future, responsible for bringing innovative products to the market in the shortest period of time.

Bob knew his new division had some problems.

- Research and development was organized into six distinct departments, which had evolved into small empires with little interdependence, little coordination, and few shared procedures, resources, or policies among them.

- Except for the team he had led, his division had a generally mediocre track record of getting new products to market. The new product pipeline was barely filled. Most new product development was so-called "line-extensions, which consisted of new uses or analogs of old products. What was now in the pipeline looked like products that mimicked products already on the market. There were no market leaders or blockbusters in sight.

- There had been four vice presidents in about 10 years, with little stability at the top. All were solid researchers, but none was an effective manager. Bob's immediate predecessor had been terminated because of an inability to successfully integrate the departments and improve the product pipeline.

- With inefficient work flow and inadequate computer systems, product planning and development were slow, inefficient, and too expensive.

- The organization had some outstanding performers, but was dogged by tolerance for mediocrity. The company was paternal, rarely pressured nonperformers, and never fired them. Accountability was virtually nonexistent, except at the vice presidential level where turnover was endemic.

- Performance of department heads, team leaders, and team members was rarely appraised in an honest way.

- There were inadequate numbers and types of researchers and support staff to meet the goals established by Bob's boss. Quality was lacking in several key areas. Hiring was unsystematic. Good candidates were often snatched up by more aggressive competitors. Training was virtually nonexistent.

Bob's charge, presented clearly to him, was to significantly improve the division's performance. He was to bring more and better differentiated products to the marketplace faster and more efficiently. Given the authority to hire and fire and to restructure the department as he deemed appropriate, his boss's parting words upon Bob's appointment as vice president were, "Revitalize this group once and for all. It has dragged us down for long enough. My job and yours depend on it."

At the time of his appointment, Bob and Linda had been happily married for 11 years. They had a bright son of 10 and a well-adjusted but visually impaired daughter age 8. The children attended good public schools. Their daughter was in an excellent program headed by a caring and experienced special education teacher. Both children loved school and were heavily involved in sports, scouts, and church activities in their midsize suburban town.

Linda had worked as a teacher in a private school for 12 years. She enjoyed her job and was popular with students and staff alike. She was fond of her students, and was respected by parents and fellow teachers. Linda had learned to juggle the difficult task of being a mother, wife, and teacher, and received great family and professional satisfaction. Religious worship, involvement in their children's activities, and physical activities were strongly shared family values.

The family benefitted from a low six-figure income, and were comfortable with their upper middle-class lifestyle. Their 5-year-old suburban tract home had a manageable monthly mortgage payment, and Linda's late model car was paid for. Finances were managed carefully but with enough money to allow for vacations, a tennis club membership, and a growing trust fund to cover the children's college education. They camped about six weekends a year along with a one- or two-week summer outing. Overall, Bob and Linda's marriage was going well. They lived in a comfortable house, were raising two well-adjusted children, had enough money and job security, and both found their jobs satisfying. They shared many common activities, had time for each other, and time for the things they valued and enjoyed. Theirs was a loving, happy marriage.

The promotion to vice president was Bob's big career opportunity. He had prepared himself, interviewed well, and was ultimately selected from four finalists. He was offered the job on a Friday and all but accepted the position on the spot. The company wanted Bob to start within a month. He did say that he would like the weekend to discuss it with his family, and would give a final decision on Monday.

Bob and Linda had discussed the possibility of a job change and promotion on two occasions. Bob didn't think that he would get the position ("I don't have all the management tickets"), but, ever supportive, Linda encouraged him to interview. "If you get the position, we will worry about the details then." As so often happens with an unexpected opportunity, events occurred more quickly than they could prepare for.

Professionally and personally, Bob, Linda, and their children were unprepared for the consequences of their decision. What was seemingly an excellent career opportunity turned into a family nightmare. Bob and Linda did not appreciate the negative effects the change would have on their family "system." Here were but a few changes:

A critical family decision was the one to relocate. The new job was 100 miles away. One possibility was for Bob to commute. But neither Bob nor Linda liked the idea of Bob's commuting over two hours a day each way. He would be home few evenings before 8:00 and would have to leave the house by 6:00. He would see little of the kids, whose bedtime was 10:00, and evening dinner, an important family ritual, would be without Bob. So they decided against commuting. Unforeseen implications of the decision to relocate included:

- *They had to sell an affordable, comfortable home they enjoyed.* Even though their company paid for the move, took over the selling of their old home, and helped them find a new home, it was nonetheless a time-consuming and arduous task. Linda spent a lot of time looking for the right place that was within their price range. Homes in the new area were half-again more expensive, taxes were higher, and the mortgage payment, with higher interest rates, was half again higher.

- *Their daughter would lose the very supportive situation in which she was comfortable and successful, and have to work out a new set of relationships with teachers.* Perhaps more importantly, she would have to find new friends who could accept her disability. Their son was old enough to have strong feelings about leaving his chums who had been his friends since kindergarten, his scouting group, Little League, and his church group. He was very unhappy with the move.

- *Linda had lost a job she loved, her status as a respected professional, and the income that made her feel like she was contributing to her family.* Giving up her job also reinforced feelings of her own vulnerability—that now she was totally dependent on Bob for her support, a feeling that made her angry, and engendered feelings of dependency and powerlessness, which she resented. That she had difficulty finding a new job in a tight job market multiplied her dilemma.

- *Bob, Linda, and their children surrendered strong community ties* to their long-time neighbors, and with friends they had made through the local PTA, Little League, and their church. In their old community, they knew where to get help. They knew and respected their family doctor and dentist. Linda had gone to school with Bill Cole, who repaired their cars. They knew their appliance repairman, plumber, electrician, and roofer, and could get honest, reliable, quality work. They knew their hair stylists, the owner of the hardware store, knew where to get bargains on clothes and appliances, and they could call their banker who would shift funds between their accounts over the phone. These were all the relationships that had taken years to develop and nurture, based upon years of trust and friendship. Now Bob and Linda would have to start over.

■ *They moved away from friends they had known for years, as well as nearby parents and blood relatives.* For years these people had provided emotional support, help with babysitting and child rearing, and the types of daily assistance that made life easier for dual career families. When they were on vacation, a neighbor took in the mail and watered the plants. When the refrigerator broke while they were on vacation, two neighbors threw away the by-now spoiled meat and vegetables, aired out the house, bombed the hoards of flies that had formed, and cleaned the floor of the gooey mess. When Bob and Linda needed help with home repairs, a neighborhood handyman helped out. Uncles, nieces, and nephews helped with painting and decorating. Linda's parents house-sat the kids for two weeks while Linda accompanied Bob on a summer business and vacation trip to Paris. Linda and Bob had a tremendous support network, to which they were tied for daily help.

For Bob and Linda, the relocation was not a happy event. It was creating problems for them in their personal lives that were making the family transition extraordinarily difficult.

As if the relocation by itself were not difficult enough, Bob's difficulties on the job were about to make things worse.

He was not developing the momentum needed to change the organization. The jump from director of a small, smooth-functioning research group to vice president of a much larger, more troubled group was proving to be a bit much to handle. Never professionally trained as a manager, he was not familiar with the formal planning, financial management, and human resources systems necessary to effectively manage such a large organization.

The organization was elusive for him. Direct reports gave him verbal assurances, but rarely committed things to paper. Thus, he had no clear information about project planning, product development timelines, product strengths and weaknesses, or possible problems that might require more time or more money to solve. He couldn't nail his direct reports down. He couldn't get them to make commitments. Everything "depends," nothing was firm. He felt controlled, manipulated, and impotent.

He felt he was failing, and he shared his frustration with his boss. In his disappointment in his own performance, he began to press. He was less approachable, had a shorter fuse, found himself getting angry more often. He felt manipulated by his employees and resented it. He brought that resentment home with him, and felt he was more short-tempered with his kids.

The part of the job he most resented was managing others. As vice president, responsible for a division of over $50 million, he found he

was giving most of his time to others—planning, monitoring, and trou-
bleshooting the work of others, overseeing the work of the organization. He had no time for the science he enjoyed, no time to "do his own
work." He was finding that managing a large organization under stress
required that 100 percent of the time he would pay attention to the
work of others, something he wasn't finding very satisfying.

Nor did he like spending as much time as he had to on the administrative and management part of his job. His entire day seemed consumed by other people's problems. Were they on schedule? What were
their problems? What kinds of help did they need? He feared that he
was quickly losing his scientific edge, a concern experienced by many
technical experts who move into management.

Bob had not fully anticipated that this job change was, in fact, a major
career switch from strong scientist with some management responsibility, to that of research executive with considerable divisional and corporate administrative responsibilities. Because he lacked the experience
of managing a larger organization, Bob underestimated how his time
would be spent. He lacked good models that would allow him to creatively attack management problems with the skill and fervor that he
had previously applied to scientific challenges.

A myriad of problems that had plagued the division for years were
now his. His game plan was rather scatter shot, riddled with gaps and
inconsistencies. Within two months after starting, Bob began to question the wisdom of his decision to move up. Pressures built at work and
were compounded by the normal difficulties establishing roots in a new
community. In a matter of less than a year, the Doyles' tidy world was
coming undone.

What went wrong and how could it have been prevented? For the
remainder of this and the next chapter, we will suggest principles that
can help you, your spouse, and family through the experience of professionally moving up. These principles can increase your ability to anticipate the personal and family life implications of being a leader on the
rise. Before looking at the principles, let's look at the issues often
associated with making successful adjustments.

Typical Areas of Personal Conflict[1]

Earlier in this chapter we listed important considerations related to
your personal and family life that you should look at very closely as you
think about moving up. The following is an expanded list of the areas
most frequently affected when you take on bigger and tougher responsibilities. You might want to create your own checklist or use your list to
help you anticipate and plan the management of issues that could

become troublesome. Which were most closely associated with the
Doyle family? You? Your primary relationships? Your family?

- Housing—location, type, cost
- Family members—spouse, children, parents, siblings
- Time—at work, home, traveling, commuting, vacation, leisure
- Finances—income, expenses, investments
- Friendships—at work, home
- Lifestyle
- Recreation, hobbies
- Education, schools
- Marriage, love relationships with significant others
- Material possessions
- Work style
- Religious affiliations
- Community activity
- Health, fitness
- Are there others that fit your personal circumstances?

_____

_____

_____

_____

_____

_____

The Six Key Principles of
Managing the Impact of
Moving Up on Your Family,
Health, and Time

1. *Personal wellness, family health, and work effectiveness* are strongly interdependent. Understanding "personal/family/work systems" will
   help you better manage the process of moving up.

2. *Major job changes often can trigger major life changes.* The impact of these
   changes are best addressed through careful individual and family

reflection, communication, and clarification of personal/family priorities and values.

3. *Managers who are moving up* are in a *state of personal transition.* The process of personal transition can be understood and effectively managed by individuals and by families.

4. *Health and well-being in one's personal, family, and work life* affects and is affected by levels of stress and distress.

5. *Mutual understanding, support, fairness, and responsible collaboration* within dual career families or with partners are essential for leaders on the rise.

6. *The goal* is to achieve a new life balance.

Let's examine each of these six key principles more closely.

Principle 1

Personal wellness, family health, and work effectiveness are highly interdependent. Understanding how personal/family and work systems interact will help you better manage the process of moving up.

A system is any complex of elements in which each element has an effect on the others. Computer systems, machines, weather systems, rocket systems, body systems, and ecological systems are each comprised of multiple elements, each one affecting the others within the system. Borrowing this concept, social scientists have begun to appreciate the importance of personal, family, and organizational systems. The actions of one member in a system affect others who belong to the system.

Social scientists have found that human systems are similar to technological systems, with one critical difference: Technological systems can generally function independently of each other. A computer system does not affect a weather system or body system unless they are deliberately or naturally linked (such as a computer system and a machine, a machine and a person, the body systems and the ecosystem). Human systems, on the other hand, are integrally linked. They are fully interdependent. What happens in one system of a person's life inevitably affects the others. What happens at home affects your work and your well-being; what happens to you personally affects your family life and work. Human systems are a single, interdependent system, try as we may to keep them separate.

For Bob Doyle, as is true for you and every other leader going through change, when one system changes, it affects the others. Changes in Bob's work system dramatically affected the personal and family system of the Doyle family. Several elements within each system were affected.

Bob's Personal Health/Wellness	Doyle Family Health and Wellness	Bob's Work Effectiveness
• Physical	• A sound family unit	• High motivation
• Mental	• Common core values	• Compatibility with the job
• Emotional	• Differences respected	• Responsibility and authority
• Spiritual	• Cooperative efforts	• Adequate resources
	• Love	
	• Shared activities	

Figure 10.1 illustrates the interrelationships between your systems. During transition, each system ebbs and flows as you manage the transition through your successes and problems. Also represented are forces in the environment that help or hinder you. These forces are dynamic, constantly tugging and pulling each individual system, its subsets, and the relationships between systems.

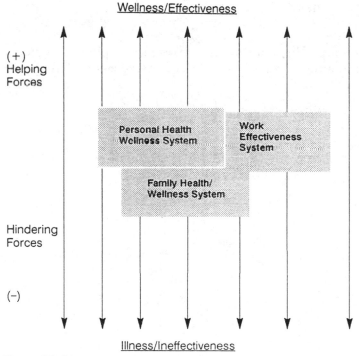

Figure 10.1

Figure 10.2 illustrates the manager in his first year following a major promotion successfully plowing tremendous effort, attention, and energy into his work system, to the detriment of his family and personal systems.

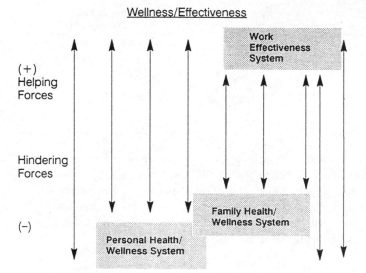

Figure 10.2

Figure 10.3 shows the transitioning manager keeping all systems under control at a high level of wellness and effectiveness. Things are going very well.

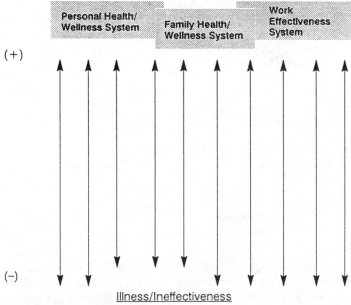

Figure 10.3

In Fig. 10.4, approximate your present situation. Draw your own boxes in relation to the wellness and effectiveness, illness and ineffectiveness scales.

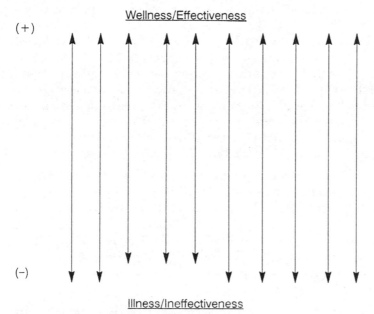

Figure 10.4

What can you conclude about your own systems' effectiveness?

_____

_____

_____

_____

_____

The following guidelines will help you effectively manage the relationship between your personal, family, and work effectiveness systems:

1. _Know what is important to you, what you value, and what has priority at any given time._ Consciously strive to gain consistency and congruence between what you _say_ is important and what you actually _do._

Think about the Doyles as a family of individuals. What was most important to them? In what ways were their most important values compromised by Bob's job change? What preventive steps could they have taken to minimize the negatives? Job changes are times for heightened family communication and for creatively addressing opportunities and problems. The key is to know what should and shouldn't be changed and how to compensate effectively when compromises are unavoidable.

One family, similar to the Doyles, consciously planned a series of activities to learn about the opportunities and recreational resources in their new community. They did this together each weekend for several months until they made new "connections." Another set of parents took their children with them to a new city on two occasions in advance of their move to explore the community and visit their new schools and church. Some families continue certain rituals and customs that have great meaning to their marriage and family, such as

- Playing and reading with young children at their usual times.
- Arranging special "alone time" with children and spouse.
- Making arrangements for frequent reunions with friends and family.
- Structuring time to ensure that cherished activities are maintained. Whether it is religious worship, working on a car, bowling, aerobics, playing tennis or golf, or volunteer community service, schedule what is of value to you and do it.

2. *Realize that you have a finite amount of time and energy.* Heighten your awareness about how you use your time and energy. Engineer your time. Take charge of your time and energy by taking care of real priorities, not simple urgencies. You can't do everything you are asked to do. Protect your real priorities, and learn to say no to the rest.

If you need help on how to manage your time better, talk with people who seem to use their time well. Get at least one new idea per week. Read books and articles written on this subject, and adopt a few of these ideas to your situation. Never accept that you have no alternatives. One group of friends helps each other generate ideas and alternatives to their problems when they seem to be stuck. Don't forget to assign work to your children. For example, a third grader and kindergartner who pack their lunches for the next school day with minimal supervision save at least 20 minutes of time for mom or dad and become more responsible in the process.

Select your child-care support well and treat them as an extension of your family. Make sure they know your expectations and needs. Provide fair and competitive compensation as well as recognition and reinforcement for a job well done so you can count on their long-term help.

3. *Avoid spreading yourself too thin.* Too many commitments ultimately reduce your effectiveness. Check the number of "have to's" in your life.

High achievers often overextend themselves. This is often because of enthusiasm and involvement in their job, but also because of ineffective delegation skills, unwillingness to say no, and lack of a support network. Sometimes people just feel guilty and do too many things themselves. It is not uncommon to see managers of both genders trying to be all things to all people. Our contemporary lexicon includes the terms *Superwoman* and *Superman, Supermom* and *Superdad.* Do it all, want it all, have it all, lose it all.

4. *Realize that every choice you make has payoffs and trade-offs.* Every action has pluses and minuses. When priorities are in conflict between self, family, and work, make the best decision possible and don't criticize yourself for what you are unable to do. Make yourself a mental or written note to catch up with someone or something at a subsequent time if you can't spend the time now.

Our society is supercharged with options. Obligations weigh heavily on our choices. Try to make your best choices and avoid the tendency to try to be perfect and satisfy everyone.

5. *Use your diagnostic skills at home and at work.* Be aware that extra time and energy in one area of your life likely has implications in another area. When work is dominating, something else (often spouse, children, favorite activities, personal wellness, or alone time) is usually suffering. *Recognize early warning signs.* Try to be aware of signals around and within you. Are you spending quality time in what you do, or are your efforts and relationships superficial? Do you see as many smiles as before? Do you give and get as many heart-felt hugs from your spouse, partner, children? Are you offering or accepting offers to spend special time with those who are really important to you, or are you always too busy?

6. *Don't let hobbies and interests go unattended.* How long has it been since you've done things that you really enjoy? Are you laughing and enjoying life as much as you used to or you would like?

Hobbies and recreation serve as life's cushions. They not only help to absorb the stress of daily life, but they provide an energy reserve. They aid in preparing for the tougher challenges we face. But hobbies and recreational activities are often the first to go under pressure. This creates a troublesome cycle, since leisure time provides for necessary relaxation and unwinding. Do your best to preserve and respect your leisure time.

7. *Maintain a high trust and supportive relationship with at least one other person or group.* Mutually beneficial relationships characterized by trust, sharing, and good listening are invariably healthy and therapeutic.

Life is tough enough. To go it alone is to miss much of what life is about. Most managers who are successful at work and in other aspects of their lives are quick to credit their life partners, family, and close friends as essential for their success.

8. *Build frequent "pitstops" into your work and lifestyle.* No racer has ever won the Indianapolis 500 without periodic stops to refuel and check key parts. The same is true with people. Envision the balance that you desire in your life and then design ways for it to happen. Taking the time to catch your breath and gain perspective increases your clarity, commitment, and energy to achieve your goals.

Principle 2

Major job changes often can trigger major life changes. The potential and actual impact of these changes is best addressed through careful individual and family reflection, communication, and clarification of personal and family priorities and values.

This principle is closely related to principle 1. Think about the case of the Doyle family. One decision resulted in shaking the basic foundation on which the family system existed. Bob Doyle's promotion was, on the surface, a peak event, the high point of his career. But Bob, Linda, and their children did not take the time to consider the effects of this promotion on each individual family member and on the family as a whole. If they had, the Doyles might have anticipated many potential problems. The decision affected key areas of their lives. With reflection, they might have made a clearer choice whether to pursue and then accept (or not accept) the promotion. The entire family could have been involved in thinking through the pros and cons, the trade-offs and payoffs and creative ways to deal with anticipated problems. Communication and involvement dramatically increase the possibility of commitment and buy-in.

Here are some additional guidelines:

- Confide in and involve those that you love and who love you in how, when, and if you will move up. Even when answers are not clear, keep talking and working on good solutions—they will come.

- Diagnose, plan, and solve problems both individually and as a family.

- Be sensitive to the hopes, fears, and concerns of a mate and of children, particularly if a relocation is required. This will be a time of adjustment. It will include broken, new, and interrupted relationships. It will be strange and can be very scary.

- If the downside of your management appointment appears too great, be careful that your ego and need for "stroking" are not the overriding factor in making your decision to move up. Get input and feed-back from those you trust.

- When relocations are involved, be certain to

  Think through what it would really mean for everyone affected. Anticipate potential issues. Revisit typical areas of personal conflict.

  Rehearse the move. What needs to be anticipated? Talk to others who have experienced relocations and learn from them. Research good books and guides (available from realtors, corporate reloca-tion services, and contemporary bookstores).

  Identify and respond to the needs of each family member.

  Investigate the new geographic area ahead of time and repeatedly, if possible. Involve the family. Go there to shop, go to movies, and visit other places that you are likely to frequent or rely on.

  Ask questions, questions, and more questions—minimize your sur-prises.

  Maintain emotional bridges to your old home. This could include taking items of emotional meaning from your existing home or staying in touch with those who are important to you.

  Plan and then make the move as a family.

  Anticipate the costs and financial realities of a move. Relocations are expensive. There are both obvious and hidden costs; identify as many as possible in advance. Tap into books, local civic groups, and people who already live in the area.

  If needed and appropriate, request exceptions to your company's relocation package to help cope with the many expenses of mov-ing. These are frequently granted if requested.

  Try to meet new colleagues and neighbors in advance. They can be very helpful to you and remove some unknowns.

  When a second career of a spouse or partner is involved, dedicate yourself to successfully reestablishing his or her career. In doing this, utilize your company's resources and connections with other organizations in the area.

Principle 3

Managers who are moving up are in a state of transition. The process of transition can be understood and effectively managed by individuals and by families.

We have examined some of the issues of which the Doyle family was unaware and highlighted some of the family and work systems im-plications that upwardly mobile leaders face. We have begun to view executive change in different ways. William Bridges, in his masterful

book *Transitions—Making Sense of Life's Changes,* points out that our lives
are composed of hundreds, even thousands of transformations,
changes, or transitions that shape who we are and where we are going.
Quoting Oscar Wilde, Bridges notes "The gods have two ways of dealing
harshly with us—the first is to deny us our dreams, and the second is to
grant them."[2]

Bob Doyle was granted his dream. He sighted the job that he wanted,
went after it, and was selected for it. But Bob Doyle and his family did
not appreciate the dynamics of personal transitions. People do not
automatically change. Some have difficulty operating on any new channel. For others it is easier and essentially a matter of fine tuning. Some
have trouble letting go of what exists, while others catastrophize what
will be. Many individuals seem to shift smoothly from the conclusion of
one job to the beginning of another. For the many who encounter
difficulty in moving up or in changing jobs, homes, or responsibilities,
there is often a lack of understanding and subsequent difficulty in
managing the transition process. Typically, there is a period of orientation, disorientation, and reorientation. Many of our life's anchors are
uprooted or shaken. We are challenged to maintain or establish new
support in our lives.

Bridges views life transitions as having three stages, which occur in a
predictable sequence:

1. An *ending*

2. A period of confusion and sometimes distress, which he entitles the
   neutral zone

3. A *new beginning*[3]

We have already seen that a seemingly single transition is usually connected to many other issues in our lives—work, love, family, friends,
leisure time, material possessions, etc. Bridges's sequence of phases
helps to explain what is happening and how we can deal more constructively with it.

Endings.   Every transition begins with an ending. Some endings are
chosen. Others begin because of unavoidable circumstances or when
something goes awry; job termination is an example. In all cases, there is
a disembarking or leaving from something that was to something that is,
whether anticipated or unknown. Before new roots can be established,
old ones must come out. Even when you are looking forward to a new
beginning, the effects of ending your previous situation (at work and at
home) should not be underestimated.

What were some of the endings that the Doyles experienced?

_____

_____

_____

_____

_____

What endings have you experienced recently in one of your own life transitions, and how did you deal with them? Did you effectively antici-pate your reactions to the ending experience?

_____

_____

_____

_____

_____

How would you deal differently in the future with your endings? Write a self-prescription of at least two or three ideas that could work for you.

_____

_____

_____

_____

_____

The Neutral Zone.   Bridges describes the neutral zone as a period of seemingly unproductive "time out" when we feel disconnected from events, people, activities, or things that we have come to know. This is an uncomfortable and confusing time. People frequently feel mixed up and disoriented. It is a particularly frustrating and sometimes depress-ing time because we aren't sure what will come next.

The neutral zone is frequently associated with heightened anxiety and anticipation. For managers on the rise, it often occurs during that period between ending one position and starting the new and expanded role. During this period, many managers slow down long enough to reflect and say, "My God, do I really know what I am getting into?" This is sometimes a period of self-doubt when our deepest fears emerge from our subconscious. In a moment of anxiety during a two-week hiatus before stepping into a new leadership role, one newly appointed branch manager said, "Why am I doing this? I was so happy doing my previous work. I'm not sure that I can handle this."

The neutral zone is an important time, and it is crucial that you anticipate it. It may be nature's way of signaling a time out. On the surface, it may be an unproductive period. Bridges calls it a time of inattentive activity. Others have described it as a period of healing and a phase of developing new potential, energy, and direction. Its importance should not be underestimated; nor should its existence be unexpected.

Describe your experiences with your own neutral zone. Tap into recent endings and beginnings and think about what was going on between these two stages. List a few of your personal observations.

_____

_____

_____

_____

_____

_____

_____

_____

Bridges suggests how to find meaning in the neutral zone experience and how to shorten it.[4]

1. Find a regular time and place to be alone.

2. Begin a personal log of neutral zone experiences.

3. Take this pause in the action of your life to write an autobiography or autobiographical thoughts. This may often lead to more reflection and clearer personal insights.

4. Take this opportunity to discover what you really want. This is an excellent period for clarifying what is really important in your life.

5. Think of what would be unlived in your life if it ended today.

6. Take a few days to go on to your own journey, a personal rite of passage.

New Beginnings.　Bridges indicates that we come to new beginnings only after an end, and when activities are being started.[5] While this is a period of great challenge and questioning, it is also an opportunity for new energy, direction, and success.

Principle 4

Health and well-being in one's personal, family, and work life affects and is affected by levels of stress and distress.
To consider the concept of stress and distress, consider the following statements. Test yourself by indicating whether each statement is true or false.

1. Stress and distress have just about the same meaning.
2. People in management positions usually feel the effect of stress more than those in technical or clerical positions.
3. People work best when their stress levels are low.
4. Most causes of stress (stressors) and distress are unpleasant.
5. It is generally better to be under- rather than overstimulated.
6. Two clear indicators of stress are poor concentration and poor job performance.
7. Most stress is related to an impending feeling of things to come.
8. A good predictor of long-term stress management is the ability of a person to adjust and adapt to immediate challenges and un-anticipated alarming agents.
9. From a health and fitness point of view, your body can separate stressful and distressful experiences at work from those at home.
10. The primary way to manage daily stressors is to have releases, such as exercise, hobbies, and outside interests.

Although it may surprise you, all 10 of these statements are false.

Let's start by looking at the nature of stress. Stress is any reaction of the mind, body, and sometimes behavior to stressors or causes of stress. Everyone needs a certain amount of stress or stimulation. Without it we would not be alive. Thus, a key to understanding stress is becoming aware of our stress and using it constructively.

Each of us has an ideal stress level. We also have a range or "stress comfort zone" in which we function best and are most comfortable.[6]

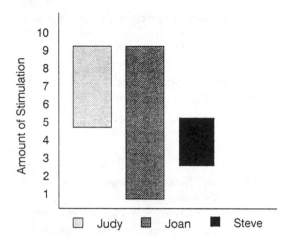

Figure 10.5. Hypothetical comfort zones.

The comfort zone has two endpoints. One point is the level that, when exceeded, indicates that we are too busy, too involved, or the intensity of our experiences is too great. In short, we are overstimulated in either the number or seriousness of our present life and work events. Conversely, when we fall below our minimal endpoint in our stress comfort zone, we usually are not challenged enough, bored, or involved in activities that are not important to us.

When we go over the edges of our personal comfort zone, we experience distress. Too much or too little stimulation equals distress. Contrary to stress, which can mobilize us and is often a useful reaction of the mind or body, distress has negative aspects. When we are aware of our stressors and use them well, we feel challenged, alert, and alive. As we approach the endpoints of our comfort zone, we usually begin to have different feelings. They are not necessarily bad, but often act as warnings that we are not at our peak. As we slide past our comfort zone, from either end, many telltale symptoms begin to appear.

As you can see in Fig. 10.5, Steve, Joan, and Judy all have different hypothetical comfort zones. Joan has the largest range and shares the highest upper limit with Judy. Steve is comfortable within very limited boundaries. Judy has a fairly large range with a very high limit.

A Further Look at Stressors.[7]   We mentioned previously that stressors are the cause of stress or potential distress. The following are characteristics of stressors:

1. They can be generated from within yourself (undue worry or fear) or from outside sources (pressure or conflict involving a new job or boss).

2. They can be pleasant (an appealing, challenging work promotion or work assignment) or unpleasant (little hope of meeting a tight time schedule).

3. They can be few in number or can build up and be many.

4. They can be low or high in intensity.

5. They can be short (a major project with a short timeframe) or long in duration (ongoing work or home responsibilities).

6. They can be old (have been with you for a long period) or new and less familiar to you.

7. They are changeable. A stressor with certain characteristics can affect us dramatically at one point in time but not much or at all at other times.

What Leads to Distress?   Let's look at circumstances that typically cause a person to move from effective use of optimal stress levels toward distress.

1. Transitions of all types are likely to be associated with distress. Job changes are a prime example. Increases in management responsibility, changes in colleagues, subordinates, or boss, relocations, loss of respect, and alterations in schedules are others.

2. Doing too much—overtaxing or overloading yourself in either the number of events or intensity of tasks—often leads to distress. This can occur at work or home. Individuals who are moving up in management are especially susceptible to overloading.

3. A person can be very busy but feel understimulated because the work or life in general is boring.

4. Doing work of little perceived value, being involved in activities that are unimportant to you or for which you do not understand the purpose, can lead to distress. A percentage of professionals who become managers for the first time frequently are criticized by peers for leaving their professional roots and joining management. In certain technical and scientific professions, people often identify more with their profession than with their employer. Distress often occurs when individuals feel they will lose their expertise when they become a manager.

5. Role confusion or conflict can lead to distress. The person feels down because of differences in perceived ability and actual responsibility or authority level (either too high or too low). Distress also occurs when there are unresolved conflicts in responsibility and authority with others. This often happens to newly appointed man-

agers in organizations that do not effectively define responsibilities and accountability.

6. A loss of someone personally or professionally important can lead to distress. This is true even in positive situations when an individual is promoted or takes a better job in a different organization.

7. Unresolved issues are the residual feelings we all carry with us when emotional issues are left unfinished. These can be current issues such as recent unresolved disagreements with coworkers, or issues from the past that remain bothersome.

8. Perceived differences between what should be and what is can lead to distress. We previously discussed cognitive dissonance, the feeling of tension, when we realize that there is a difference between what we really value and what we actually do. Losing out on a promotion creates dissonance between your own and others' beliefs about you. Having less money than you need to support the lifestyle you want creates a discrepancy between your real and the ideal income needs. If you are a manager moving up, there will be differences between what you are experiencing and what you expected would occur.

Symptoms of Stress Moving Toward Distress.   As we move toward a state of distress, there are indicators or signals to be aware of, such as:

Headaches, neckaches, and backaches

Sore and tense muscles

Feelings of anger, even rage

Generalized feelings of anxiety

Loss of sleep and feeling chronically tired

Abnormal levels of perspiration

Constipation or diarrhea

High blood pressure

Violent behavior

Problems with perception, thinking, and concentration

Difficulty in getting along with others and generally being touchy

Boredom with activities that used to be enjoyable

Identifying these areas enables you to recognize them, identify their causes, and realize your own comfort zone. To use stress more constructively, try the following activity.

Your Personal Stress Inventory

1. Look at Fig. 10.6 to get the "big picture" of this activity.

2. List up to 15 significant personal stressors (at work, home, big or small).

3. Place the appropriate information next to the stressors on your list that matches the topic(s) on the top of the form. If you have no response to a topic, leave it blank. After listing your stressors, work on one inventory topic at a time.

4. After completing your stressor listing and filling in the various columns, look for unique situations or patterns. For example, how many of your stressors have existed for a long time, or how many are work related versus home related?

5. Take 10 minutes to summarize your thoughts and feelings. Complete as many sentence stems (see pages 225 and 228) as you would like. You may use any one stem as many times as you wish.

6. Finally, think about the positive and negative implications of your inventory as it relates to the quality of your work, your life outside of work, and its impact on how you work and relate to others.

I learned

_____

_____

_____

I relearned

_____

_____

_____

I realized

_____

_____

_____

I was surprised

_____

_____

_____

	List up to 15 significant personal stressors.	Who is involved in stress?	Where in your body do you feel the effects of stress?
1.			
2.			
3.			
4.			
5.			
6.			
7.			
8.			
9.			
10.			
11.			
12.			
13.			
14.			
15			

Figure 10.6. Personal stress inventory.

When? Always? Often? Seldom?	When the stressor occurs, do you feel in or out of control? 1-in control to 10-out of control	Yes or no—is there at least a glimmer of hope for handling this well?	What are the three highest priority stressors that you feel you should work on?

Figure 10.6. (*Continued*)

I wonder

_____

_____

_____

I hope

_____

_____

_____

The Three Major Strategies for Stress Management.[8]   The three major strategies for stress management are managing our stressors, managing our stress filter, and managing our coping response. Used in concert, they can be the cornerstone for better health and fitness as well as personal and professional effectiveness.

Managing Our Stressors.   Figuring out how to manage the intensity of our stressors is an important task. Many factors, including your personal needs, the number of events, and responsibilities in your life, are important when managing stressors. Here are some suggestions:

1. Take personal responsibility for your pace of life and for major life changes. Do not blame circumstances or other people.

2. Be aware of your comfort zone and your minimal, optimal, and maximum levels of stimulation. Know your low and high limits.

3. Continually work to attain a good fit between your needs, your work challenges, and your home environment. Try to reduce the gaps and discrepancies between what you want to do, need to do, and have to do.

4. Try to predict the effects of major life changes, including job changes. Remember the experience of the Doyle family. Transitions are often stressful.

5. If you can, avoid clustering too many major life changes within a short period of time. Too many changes overload and reduce our ability to cope effectively.

6. Engineer your time and effort. Provide yourself enough time to regroup after big events.

7. Do not let emotional issues go unresolved for long periods of time. Therapists call this "unfinished business." Important unresolved issues have a gnawing, debilitating effect on us.

8. Be clear about what is important to you and what takes highest priority in your life. Take time for introspection. Strive for consistency between your values and your actions.

9. Choose the tasks and challenges that are most important to you. There will be more than enough—you don't need to handle those that have little or no meaning. Learn to say no to the things you "should" do that you don't really want to do.

10. Work on improving your stress awareness through introspective activities (such as the "Personal Stress Inventory"), discussions with people you trust, spiritual or religious activity, and seminars and workshops on personal development.

Managing Your Stress Filter.   Try as we might to manage our stressors, the unpredictable nature of life and the charged pace of our world force us into trying situations. You can sometimes reduce their harmful effects by developing a good stress filter. A personal stress filter consists of the qualities that reduce the negative effects of stressors on your physical, mental, and emotional well-being. How many items from the following list do you already do? How many could you do more effectively?

1. Maintain good health habits in relation to eating, resting, and exercising. People who are worn down, physically weak, or constantly tired are susceptible to stressors.

2. Assume a take-charge approach to your life. Be personally responsible for who you are, how you feel, what you are thinking, and the way you act. Believe that you can change aspects of yourself that need changing.

3. Each week come up with at least one additional way to build your psychological, emotional, and spiritual strength.

4. Learn to express your feelings. With your spouse or a trusted friend, open up. Don't sit on a powder keg of feelings. Stored feelings, old and new, are very unhealthy.

5. Be patient with your own and others' imperfections. Many high achievers try to be perfect. It is okay to make mistakes. Perfection and striving to improve yourself are two very different concepts.

6. Surround yourself with people whom you trust as a friend and intimate. Be open to help and support. Be there for others.

Managing Your Coping Response.   Here are a few examples of effective coping responses.

1. Take enough risks so you are challenged, but not so many that you are overwhelmed. Set goals just out of reach but not out of sight.

2. Choose to accept a certain amount of stress. Push yourself to be more flexible and patient with adversity. Acceptance of what is happening to you or around you is the first step to adapting to situations. As a manager, it is important to realize that there are certain things you can't control.

3. There are other times when it is wise to pull back or remove yourself from a stressor. Leave the scene for a while, take a vacation, change responsibilities, change where you live; end a romance, marriage, or friendship that simply isn't working.

4. Change how you relate to the stressor. Experiment with new behaviors. Where you would typically back off, jump in, and vice versa. Be more assertive, more honest, say no to new demands, accept compliments, be more open, be more empathetic and understanding, develop new skills, stop acting so angry, be more diplomatic, stop "game playing," don't be so critical of yourself or others, and allow yourself to get close to others.

5. Change the stressor. Sometimes you can change what is bothering you. Modify one or more stressful features of your immediate environment. For example, fix or replace something that is bothering you about your new job, through discussions with your boss, peers, or those working for you. People often accept as gospel their written job description or what they are told the job is. Good win-win discussions and trade-offs with others are very helpful. What is a chronic stressor for one person is sometimes a delightful challenge for others.

6. Accept the situation and work to reduce the stress. When the situation cannot be changed, use stress-reducing options such as exercise, a talk with someone important to you, counseling or therapy, more sleep, or relaxation techniques such as meditation, biofeedback, brief solitude, or a religious activity.

Stress can have a positive effect on your life unless it reaches the point of becoming distress. Stress is a natural part of living in our complex society. As we pointed out previously, everyone needs a certain degree of stress to be stimulated, motivated, and challenged. The key is to have stress without distress—to keep the positive effects of stress working for you.

Principle 5

Mutual understanding, support, fairness, and responsible collaboration within dual-career families are essential for leaders on the rise.

Think back to the case study of Bob and Linda Doyle. Try to recall some of the issues that the Doyles faced. Describe how their decisions helped or hindered each of their careers and their family cohesiveness. What could the Doyles have done more effectively to manage their dilemma?

_____

_____

_____

_____

_____

_____

In a *dual career* couple, each individual pursues a separate career alongside a commitment to their loving relationship. The following are the most common mistakes when facing major changes in either partner's career:

- Partners think and act in a self-centered manner and lack concern for the effects of change on others in the family. Or they ignore their own needs and do what they think others need.

- They do not take time to anticipate the effects and decide if they are willing to accept the predictable pros and cons of events. As we have seen, these include important issues such as uprooting children from school, loss of friends and key relationships, or the loss of one partner's job.

- They don't ask each other for help, assistance, and support. They figure things out alone and often act without the other's support and counsel.

- They take on too many obligations and changes at one time, trying to do too much in too short a period of time.

- They don't clarify expectations, goals, and needs with each other. It is all too common for one spouse (traditionally the husband) to announce his job change to his mate, with so much pressure that the spouse feels obligated to go along, despite how she or he may feel.

- They fail to get help from outside the family for domestic maintenance and children's needs. Third-party help often becomes essential to help families cope with the change in the household's day-to-day operations.

- They don't plan for emergencies and have backup plans for situations that are not part of regular (and almost always harried) schedules. Typical disrupting events are sickness, trips out of town, and unanticipated late days at the office.

- They don't take time to get away from the pressures and recharge their relationship together.

Suggestions for Helping Dual-Career Families Cope during Periods of Transition

- The cornerstone of successful dual-career families is mutual respect for each other's careers and collaboration and support between the partners.

- Dual careers require cooperation, not competition.

- Communication needs to be free of secret agendas. It should be open and clear. If one is feeling something, it should be said, no matter how trivial or selfish it may seem. Better to state feelings before the transition than after you are already in the eye of the storm.

- Uprooting often causes guilt. Guilt is predictable. Face it head on and talk it out.

- Keep the emphasis on flexibility, creativity, innovation, compromise, and commitment to problem solving. Look for win-win solutions.

- If relocation is necessary, carefully plan a process to reestablish both careers as part of the decision for one partner to accept a new position. Progressive employers know this is an issue today and often help the spouse or partner make a successful move.

- In advance, agree not to accept new positions, despite the benefits for one partner, if the disadvantages for the other partner or for other family members are too severe.

- Explore the new community together.

- If children are involved in relocation, or if one or both parents are going to be spending more time on work because of a promotion, plan for special time with children, individually and together with brothers and sisters.

- Provide for outside help with household, maintenance, and child-rearing needs.

- Plan to spend extra time taking care of your personal health and fitness during periods of transition.

- Plan for a special vacation with your loved ones after the initial peak work period following a promotion.

- Build backup or contingency plans for emergencies, for those periods when your packed schedules begin to fall apart.

In this chapter, we have examined the possible impact of assuming new or increased management responsibilities on the personal aspects of your life. In so doing, we have described the first five of six principles that can aid the newly appointed manager in finding success at work, at home, and in other important life areas. In Chap. 11, we explore the sixth principle and a key goal of this book: achieving a new life balance as you move up.

Quick Reminders to Keep You on Track

- Being promoted, the process of moving up, is a major life transition that spawns events that are seemingly unrelated to your career advancement. Many aspects of your life can be affected by job changes, and as a result there are trade-offs and payoffs to every career decision.

   The case of Bob and Linda Doyle points out the many, and often predictable, areas of personal conflict that may arise when one is promoted.

   These areas of personal conflict can occur even if you remain in your present work site and home. The situation often becomes more complex when factors such as dual careers, relocations, and other significant lifestyle factors come into play. The good news is that you can take many steps to manage personal and family problems that surface as a result of your promotion.

- *There are six key principles of managing the impact of moving up on your family, health, and time.*

   1. Personal wellness, family health, and work effectiveness are strongly interdependent. Understanding "personal/family/work systems" will help you better manage the process of moving up.
   2. Major job changes often can trigger major life changes. The impact of these changes can be addressed through careful individual and family reflection, communication, and clarification of personal/family priorities and values.
   3. Managers who are moving up are in a state of transition. The process of transition can now be understood and effectively managed by individuals and by families.

      Transitions usually begin with an *ending,* then move to a period of confusion and sometimes distress called the *neutral zone.* The transition period ends with a *new beginning.*
      Completing your personal stress inventory and applying accepted stress management strategies and techniques can add a lot of

strength and resiliency as you work through the first 12 months of your new job.

4. Health and well-being in one's personal, family, and work life affect and are affected by levels of stress and distress.

   Understanding concepts such as stress, distress, your personal comfort zone, and what leads to distress can help you effectively manage the work, personal, and family aspects of being promoted.

5. Mutual understanding, support, fairness, and responsible collaboration between dual career partners are essential for leaders on the rise.

   Relationships and families can either be weakened or strengthened, depending on how well you work together to solve problems that may arise during the first year of your new job.

6. A key goal is achieving a new life balance as you move up.

This primary goal of *Just Promoted!* is the subject of Chap. 11.

Summary of Major Responsibilities—Year 1 (Chap. 10)

First Year by Month*

	Preappointment	1	2	3	4	5	6	7	8	9	10	11	12

Moving in: Establishing Yourself in Your New Assignment
- Entering the Organization
- Entering Your Boss's World

Achieving an Impact on the Organization
- Beginning to Craft Your Vision and Direction
- The Diagnostic Process: The Importance of Good Organizational Information
- Assessing Your Organization's Health — The Nine-Target Model
- Selecting, Building, and Developing Your Work Team
- From Resistance to Renewal: Building Your Management Team's Commitment
- Settling into Your Renewing Organization

Managing the Impact of Moving Up on Your Family and Personal Life
- Up Close and Personal: The Impact of Moving Up on Your Family, Health, and Time

*Times are approximate.

Legend

——— Primary period of emphasis

– – – Active but not a period of emphasis

235

11
Achieving a New Life Balance

Time is at once the most valuable and the most perishable of all our possessions.
JOHN RANDOLPH, early member of Congress

I believe the true road to preeminent success in any line is to make yourself master of that line.
ANDREW CARNEGIE

In order to achieve a new life balance as you move up, you will need to:

- Understand what is really important to you, what you value most in your life and how your new management position fits into your life style.

- Understand how you presently spend your time and effort, and how moving up affects your time and priorities at work, home, and other aspects of your life.

- Be creative and committed to a custom-designed action plan that affords you opportunities for success at work, at home, and in other aspects of your life that you value.

☆ ☆ ☆

In this chapter, there is useful information about:

- Spending Your Time: Your Real and Ideal Self
- Your Personal Values Ranking
- Your Personal Time Inventory
- A Personal Implications Check
- Striving for Balance: A Personal Action Plan

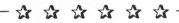

People feel best about themselves when what they value most in life is consistent with the way they actually live, when their real self matches their ideal self. Psychologists call it self-actualization. It is a level of mature personal satisfaction, each of us at our best, characterized by a sense of harmony and balance in the way we live. Gaining this balance and maintaining it is hard work. How we balance our time, including work time, family time, personal time, spiritual time, and recreational time, is one manifestation of self-actualization. How we *intend* to use time and how we *actually* spend it is our primary measure of balance in our lives. Using time as we wish is one of the biggest challenges in successfully managing the personal side of moving up. After all, the point of managing a career is learning how to plan and work toward a lifestyle that has professional and personal meaning to you and those closest to you.

Spending Your Time: Your Real and Ideal Self

Achieving your ideal lifestyle balance among career, family, and personal goals is a challenge that, left unresolved, will leave you confused and unhappy. More importantly, a lifestyle dominated by work can be unhealthy and hurtful to those you love and care about, your family and friends. The challenge of management will stress your daily schedule and the way you use your time.

In most companies, the bosses are the earliest in and the last out. They are under the stress of deadlines, responsibilities, and quotas. As never before, you must learn to balance your "wannabees" with your "haftabees," what you want to do with what you have to do. It is a journey that only few survive unscathed, with marriage intact, children secure, body healthy, self at peace, and career assured.

Try the following activity, called a Personal Pie Chart. The chart reflects how you spend your time and how you would like to allocate time in key life areas. This is a self-assessment activity that is especially valuable to help you appraise how well your ideal and real self are in sync. Try this activity several times in your first year as a manager. It is not uncommon to see the graphic change from the beginning to the end of a major career transition.

Step 1.   Rank the following key aspects of your life in order of relative importance. No ties are allowed—force yourself to distinguish and rank from first to last, starting with what is of highest value to you:

- Work time
- Family time
- Religious and spiritual time
- Recreational and vacation time
- Unplanned and spontaneous time
- Community time
- Self-maintenance time
- Sleep
- Other time (your choice)

1. _____

2. _____

3. _____

4. _____

5. _____

6. _____

7. _____

8. _____

9. _____

For even finer tuning, you might want to take any one of the areas and break it down (including a forced ranking) further for a closer view. The following are examples.

Family Time

Spouse

Daughter(s) and son(s)

Parents, brothers, and sisters

Extended family

Close friends

Maintenance Time

Home repairs

Shopping

Doctors

Cleaners, repair shops, bill paying, finances, cooking, cleaning

Work Time

Time on own tasks

Managing others

Product development

Client and customer time

Community

Church activities, neighborhood, activities, associations, children's school activities, children's recreation, scouts, clubs

Politics

Recreation

Reading, sports, and hobbies

Relaxing

Traveling

Listening to or playing music

Step 2. Using the blank pie graph in Fig. 11.1, draw your best estimate of how you would ideally like to spend your time. Use either a typical week or month as your frame of reference. An example is shown in Fig. 11.2. Start by counting actual hours, and then translate hours into percentages. You might wish to keep a daily time log for two or three weeks to determine an average over that period.

Step 3. On the blank graph in Fig. 11.3, draw your best estimate of how you are presently spending your time. An example is shown in Fig. 11.4. Use either a week or a month as your frame of reference.

Step 4. Compare your graphs. As you contrast your ideal (Fig. 11.1) and real (Fig. 11.3), consider the following questions:

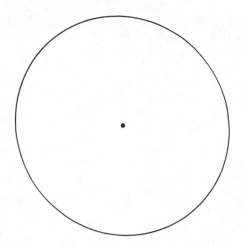

Figure 11.1. A blank Personal Pie Chart.

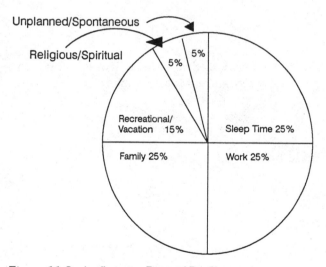

Figure 11.2. An illustrative Personal Pie Chart.

- What are the major differences between the two?
- Are you pleased with the way you are allocating your time? What seems right?
- Are there discrepancies between what you believe or say is important and the way your time is apportioned?
- As you review your charts, ask yourself about the quality of the time that you spend. For example, are you really attending to what you are

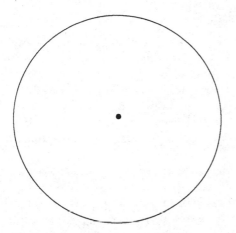

Figure 11.3. A blank Personal Pie Chart.

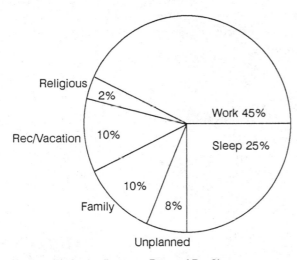

Figure 11.4. An illustrative Personal Pie Chart.

doing, or are you going through the motions? When are you at your best? Your worst? What, if anything would you change? As you concentrate on your new leadership position, are there important elements in other parts of your life that you are letting go? If so, can you think of ways to remedy the imbalance?

- Where might you add time to one by taking time from another area?

By reflecting on your active and ideal graphs, your view of how you balance your personal life should be getting clearer.

Your Personal Values Ranking

Some key value areas are very important to you, and others less. During periods of intense work, such as during the first year of increased leadership responsibility, important areas of our lives outside of work are often compromised. In the short term, this may be understandable. If you follow the guidelines discussed in preceding chapters, you should reduce the negative impacts in your life. However, you get into trouble when you are not aware of the short- and long-term trade-offs that a major job transition requires.

You can also face health or personal problems when circumstances at work get out of control or unanticipated pressures and stressors become a regular part of your daily work. What is seemingly a short-term strain because of the transition into your new responsibilities can easily and inadvertently become a long-term imbalance that can negatively affect your attention to family, health, and other activities you value.

Rank order the following from most important (entry 1 on the list below) to least important (entry 10) to you. Again, no ties. Do a forced ranking.[2] This activity will help form the basis of your personal time inventory later in this chapter.

A   Spirituality and religious practice
B   Wealth: Getting it, holding it
C   Family strength
D   Social relations, friendships
E   Achievement, accomplishment
F   Love
G   Health and fitness
H   Personal power
I   Intellectual pursuits and wisdom
J   A beautiful home
K   Personal appearance and beauty
L   Leisure and recreation
M   Community involvement
N   Others

1. _____

2. _____

3. _____

4. _____

5. _____

6. _____

7. _____

8. _____

9. _____

10. _____

11. _____

12. _____

13. _____

14. _____

You will use your top seven ranked values to do a more in-depth check when completing your personal time inventory.

Your Personal Time Inventory

This activity is designed to give you a clear view of consistencies or discrepancies in your most important values and how you use your time. Be as accurate and candid as you can.

I	II	III	IV	V
Top seven Personal Values	Ranking of the same values in terms of actual effort over the past 4–6 months	↑ or ↓ dedicated time over next 4–6 months	major motivation to increase or decrease dedicated time	Predicted outcome if you don't increase or decrease dedicated time
Highest	Highest			
1	1			
2	2			
3	3			
4	4			
5	5			
6	6			
7	7			
Lowest	Lowest			

Figure 11.5. Your personal time inventory.

Instructions

Column I. In forced ranked order, place your top seven personal values as identified earlier.

Column II. Taking the same seven values, rerank them based on your own assessment of the effort with which you have addressed these values over the past four to six months. We are not necessarily looking at the amount of total time dedicated to each (although this is probably an important indicator), but rather your evaluation of committed quality time and effort allocated to each value. Some values may require less dedicated quality time to be ranked higher. All, however, have certain requirements to maintain their relative ranking.

Column III. As you view column II, do you want to increase (↑) or decrease (↓) the amount of dedicated quality time allocated to each value over the next four to six months? Use the symbols ↑ or ↓ to designate.

Column IV. Given your choice to increase or decrease the amount of dedicated quality time, summarize in a key word or phrase your primary reason or motivation for doing so.

Column V. Referring to columns I through IV, what is your prediction of the consequences if you don't either increase or decrease (whatever your choice) the amount of dedicated quality time to the ranking in column II? Again, use a key word or phrase.

As the next step, using some of the sentence stems identified in earlier exercises, summarize your reactions to the data that you generated on your personal time inventory.

I learned _____ .

I relearned _____ .

I realized _____ .

I was surprised _____ .

I hope _____ .

I wonder _____ .

A Personal Implications Check

You have now had the opportunity to inventory, diagnose, and compare your life's time balance in both a real and ideal manner in the form of graphs and a customized "Personal Time Inventory." You have looked at what is important to you and how you are actually using your precious, finite time. You have reviewed your most important values. Because of the tremendous time pressures when assuming increased management responsibility, most managers develop discrepancies or imbalances between what is most important to them and the way they actually use their time. Our desired life balance is constantly taxed, especially when more than one area of high personal value is compromised by work requirements. The personal implications check examines the interplay among life balance, consistency between ideal and real use of time, and your most important values.

Step 1. Review information from your time graphs (Figs. 11.1 and 11.3), and time inventory (Fig. 11.5) in terms of key information as well as important discoveries.

Step 2. List at least three points that you like about how your life is presently structured and how you use your time. State them in the form of concise statements beginning with any of the following sentence stems:

I am aware_____ .

I realize _____ .

I am pleased that _____ .

I am clear that _____ .

I plan to continue _____ .

For example,

- I am aware that I have been able to pay a lot of attention to my children.
- I am happy that my wife and I have continued our Sunday morning time together.
- I am pleased that I haven't gained any additional weight since I moved up to my new job.

Step 3. This is similar to step 2, but look only at what you regard to be negative trade-offs in your present lifestyle and how you use your time. Use the following sentence stems, and identify at least three issues.

I am aware_____ .

I realize _____ .

I am disappointed _____ .

I am concerned _____ .

I plan to discontinue _____ .

For example,

- I am aware that I am not giving enough time to my spouse.

- I am concerned that we will not like our new home and community as much as our last.

- I am disappointed that I don't have enough time to take walks with my spouse or play tennis with my foursome.

Column 1 Positive Awareness	Column 2 Positive Implications	Column 3 Negative Implications
e.g. Attention – CHILDREN		
e.g. Sunday		
e.g. Steady Weight		

Figure 11.6. Positive personal implications check.

Column 1	Column 2	Column 3
Negative Awareness	Positive Implications	Negative Implications
Spouse/Time		
New Community		
Time for Walks or Tennis		

Figure 11.7. Negative personal implications check.

Step 4.   Identify a key word or phrase to represent each of the positive and negative sentences that you completed in steps 2 and 3. Then write that word or phrase in the first column ("Positive Awareness," "Negative Awareness" in Figs. 11.6 and 11.7).

This activity can be done alone or shared with trusted family members or friends. It is intended to help you examine the implications (positive and negative consequences) of some of the key actions in your present life and work style. Take your time and use your best diagnostic and predictive skills. Use logic, but listen to your feelings above all.

Striving for Balance: A Personal Action Plan

Having completed the previous activities, you are now equipped to pull together your awareness and insights in the form of a personal action plan. In so doing, you will have completed a cycle that includes the following:

- Heightened awareness of important work and life values as well as the way you are allocating your time in regard to these personally relevant areas

- Increased insight into the positive and negative implications of your work and life style in comparison to a desired ideal situation

- Made decisions about what is important for you to maintain, change, or possibly remove from your work or life style to achieve a desired life balance

- Commited to actions that should align your work and nonwork life

In short, you are striving for a self-prescribed balance in your work and life style. Doing so requires that your wisdom, logic, intuition, and feelings are working as one. In this way, you can focus more attention and assign higher priority to those areas of your life that are important to you, and over which you choose to exert control.

My Personal Action Plan[3]

Step 1
- Review your conclusions from this chapter's three activities: the personal pie graph, personal time inventory, and personal implications check.

Step 2
- Crystallize your insights from these previous activities into clearly stated objectives.

- Identify one or two work and/or life value areas that you wish to change. Your primary criterion should be, "Is this important to me in bringing my life closer to the balance that I desire?" Remember, work on no more than two at a time. Go for success and guard against doing too much in too little time.

As examples, we will use the following work and life factors:

- Extended hours of work
- Not having time to coach my son's baseball team
- Very little time alone with my spouse.

Use the SMART formula for writing your personal behavioral objective.

S	Specific:	The objective should be to the point and should be behavioral in nature.
M	Measurable:	You should be able to observe clearly when the objective is achieved
A	Attainable:	The objective should be possible to attain. Stretch yourself. A good guideline is "just out of reach but not out of sight."
R	Results Oriented:	The objective is truly worth taking on; it is of value to you.
T	Time Bound:	There should be a clearly identified time element involved. Goals and objectives without a tight time standard generally become unfulfilled wishes.

Personal objectives generally can be written in one sentence, two at the most. For example,

By June 1 of this year, I am going to leave the office by 6:00 p.m. every day.

Beginning this spring season, I am going to be the assistant coach for Steve's baseball team and miss no more than one practice every two weeks and no more than two games the entire season.

By December 1 of this year, my spouse and I will take a one-week vacation together without business calls, briefcase, or the children.

I will be home for dinner with the family every day that I am not out of town.

Write your personal work and life balance objective(s) here (remember, two at the most).

1. _____

2. _____

Step 3. Identify what keeps you from doing this now (barriers), and write down how you are going to overcome these barriers (enablers). What might help you to achieve your objective (e.g., people, commitment, money, creative approach, information)?

Barriers	Enablers

Be honest with yourself. Is this goal a "should" or a "want"? Do you feel you should (ought to) do it, or is it really an important value to you (want to)? Check one of the following three categories of personal motivation.

_____ *High motivation:* I am determined to achieve this objective, no matter what.

_____ *Medium motivation:* I'll do better, and do the best I can.

_____ *Low motivation:* It is something I think I should do, but my feelings aren't really there.

Go back to your barriers, and, after reflection, answer four more questions.

Who can help and support my efforts?

_____

_____

What other factors or resources could help me?

_____

_____

Can I mobilize myself? What are my next immediate steps?

_____

_____

What additional actions will I take to help myself?

_____

_____

Step 4. Write a contract with yourself to help strengthen your commitment and resolve. It can usually be written in one or two paragraphs. In its shortest form, it is a restatement of the personal change objective that you wrote in step 1.

Address the contract to yourself, and indicate the date that you write it at the top. Be sure to be specific in terms of what and how you wish to change the work and life factor that you have identified. Remember to state the date by which your important change will be made.

Step 5.   Give the contract to someone you trust, and ask that person to give it or mail it back to you on your designated due date. Doing so helps you stick to your goal. For some it works because of the added support, and for others because they respond well to pressure.

The personal change model that we have outlined is not new. It has been adapted over the years. We know it works. We present it here because leaders on the rise are simultaneously strong and vulnerable. They are in new leadership positions because they have either forged their own course and/or have been hand picked to take on tough, important challenges and responsibilities. Managers in positions of increased responsibilities are typically highly committed and dogged in their determination to be successful in their new roles.

But leaders in transition are also vulnerable because they can spread themselves too thin and try to be too many things to too many people. Others lose sight of aspects of their lives outside of work that are of equal or greater importance. Some need a gentle, others a thunderous reminder of personal, health, and family priorities. Their career success can blind them to what is happening in other areas of personal value. Our strengths, when used to excess, can become our greatest weaknesses, planting the seeds of failure in other life areas.

Summary

This book has addressed the three major aspects of moving up into a new level of management responsibility:

Moving in: Establishing yourself in your new management assignment

Achieving an impact on the organization

Managing the impact of moving up on your family and personal life

We hope that as you work through the difficult and unfamiliar challenges of the first year in a new management position, you will function effectively from the outset and achieve success in other vital parts of your life by using the principles and suggestions in this book.

Quick Reminders to Keep You on Track

- People feel best about themselves when what they value most in life is consistent with the way they actually live. Using time as you wish is one of the biggest challenges in successfully managing the personal side of moving up.

- Some key personal values have great importance to you but mean less to others. During periods of intense work, such as that experienced during the first year of increased leadership responsibility, important areas of your life outside of work might be compromised.

- What is seemingly a short-term strain because of the transition into your new responsibilities can easily and inadvertently become a long-term imbalance that can negatively impact your attention to family, health, and other activities you highly value.

- Completing an activity like the personal implication check can help you examine the interplay among your life balance, consistency between ideal and real time use, and your most important values.

- Completing and adhering to a Personal Action Plan can help you achieve the kind of work and life balance you desire.

Summary of Major Responsibilities—Year 1 (Chap. 11)

First Year by Month*

	Preappoint-ment	1	2	3	4	5	6	7	8	9	10	11	12
Moving in: Establishing Yourself in Your New Assignment													
• Entering the Organization													
• Entering Your Boss's World													
Achieving an Impact on the Organization													
• Beginning to Craft Your Vision and Direction													
• The Diagnostic Process: The Importance of Good Organizational Information													
• Assessing Your Organization's Health — The Nine-Target Model													
• Selecting, Building, and Developing Your Work Team													
• From Resistance to Renewal: Building Your Management Team's Commitment													
• Settling into Your Renewing Organization													
Managing the Impact of Moving Up on Your Family and Personal Life													
• Up Close and Personal: The Impact of Moving Up on Your Family, Health, and Time													
• Achieving a New Life Balance													

*Times are approximate.

Legend
—— Primary period of emphasis
- - - Active but not a period of emphasis

253

Your Personal Plan for Managing the Impact of Moving Up on Your Family, Health, and Time and for Achieving a New Life Balance (Chaps. 10 and 11)

Activity	Suggested Timeframe	Your Projected Timeframe	Completed (✔)
• Read Chapter 10 in preparation for completing activities in Chapter 11 with special emphasis on understanding the following concepts: — Typical areas of personal conflict and confusion during the process of moving up — The six key principles of managing the impact of moving up on your family, health, and time	Before accepting your new position and several times for review during year one.		
• There is a profound relationship between personal wellness, family health, and work effectiveness.			
• Major job changes can trigger major life changes.			
• Managers who are moving up are in a state of personal transition which can be understood and managed by individuals and families.			
• Health and well-being in one's personal, family, and work lives affect and are affected by levels of stress and distress.			
• Mutual understanding, support, fairness, and responsible collaboration within dual career families are essential tenets for leaders on the rise. — The goal is to achieve a new life balance.			
• Complete and evaluate your real/ideal graphs and values ranking.	Before accepting your new position and several times for review during year one.		
• Complete and evaluate your personal time inventory.	Before accepting your new position and several times for review during year one.		
• Complete and evaluate your personal implications check.	Before accepting your new position and several times for review during year one.		
• Complete, evaluate, and implement "Striving for Balance" a personal action plan.	Before accepting your new position and several times for review during year one.		

Notes

Chapter 2

1. See also Michael Lev, "How Grey Got the Account for Domino's," in *Wall Street Journal*, April 25, 1991; *New York Times*, April 25, 1991, section C, p. 17; *New York Times*, June 20, 1990, section C, p. 11.
2. See also "A Humble Hero Drives Ford to the Top," *Fortune Magazine*, vol. 117, no. 1, January 4, 1988; "Ford's Don Peterson," *Fortune Magazine*, vol. 120, no. 5, February 11, 1991.

Chapter 4

1. The source of this parable is not known. The authors first encountered it as part of course material at Hoffman-La Roche Inc., Nutley, N.J.
2. Barbara Buell and Robert D. Hoff, "Hewlett-Packard Rethinks Itself," *Business Week*, April 1, 1991, pp. 76–79.
3. Dr. Bernard Gifford, "Apple's Vision: The Learning Society," a speech delivered during the Apple K–12 Solutions Forum, February 1991, p. 1.
4. Richard Wellins and Jill George, "The Key to Self-Directed Teams," *Training and Development Journal*, April 1991, pp. 26–31.
5. Keith H. Hammonds, "Corning's Class Act," *Business Week*, May 13, 1991, pp. 68–76.
6. "25 Who Help the U.S. Win," *Fortune Magazine*, vol. 173, spring-summer 1991, pp. 34–46.

Chapter 7

1. Andrall E. Pearson, "Muscle-Build the Organization," *Harvard Business Review*, July-August 1987, pp. 195–97. Used with permission.
2. Adapted from James H. Shonk, *Working in Teams*, (New York: AMACOM, 1982), pp. 8–16. Used with permission.

Chapter 9

1. Adapted from Michael M. Lombardy and Cynthia D. McCauley, *The Dynamics of Management Derailment* (Greensboro, N.C.: Center for Creative Leadership, Technical Report 34, July 1988).

Chapter 10

1. Adapted from Sidney B. Simon, Leland W. Howe, and Howard Kirschenbaum, *Values Clarification* (New York: Hart Publishing Co., 1972), p. 15.

2. William Bridges, *Transitions—Making Sense of Life's Changes*, p. 43. © 1980 by Addison-Wesley Publishing Company, Inc. Reprinted with permission of the publisher.

3. Ibid., p. 9.

4. Ibid., pp. 121–31.

5. Ibid., pp. 134–50.

6. Adapted from Walt Schafer, *Stress, Distress and Health* (Chico, Ca.: Responsible Action, 1978), p. 47. Used with permission of the author. Schafer also authored *Stress Management for Wellness*, 2d ed. (Fort Worth, TX: Harcourt, Brace Jovanovich, 1992).

7. The information about stressors and what leads to distress on pp. 222–224 is adapted from Walt Schafer, *Stress, Distress and Health*, pp. 27–65. Used with permission of the author.

8. The three major strategies for stress management on p. 228 are adapted from concepts and principles the authors first encountered in Walt Schafer, *Stress, Distress and Health*, pp. 149–79. Used with permission of the author.

Chapter 11

1. Adapted from Sidney B. Simon, Leland W. Howe, and Howard Kirschenbaum, *Values Clarification* (New York: Hart Publishing Co., 1972), pp. 228–31.

2. Adapted from *Values Clarification*, pp. 112–15.

3. Adapted from Leland W. Howe and Mary Martha Howe, *Personalizing Education: Values Clarification and Beyond* (New York: Hart Publishing Co., 1975), pp. 342–47.

Additional Readings

Career Development

Bridges, William. *Transitions, Making Sense of Life's Changes.* Philippines: Addison-Wesley, 1980.

Burack, Elmer, and Mathys, Nicholas. *Career Management in Organizations: A Practical Human Resource Planning Approach.* Lake Forest, Illinois: Brace-Park Press, 1980.

Dalton, Gene, and Thompson, Paul. *Novations: Strategies for Career Management.* Glenview, Illinois: Scott, Foresman & Co., 1986.

Derr, C. Brooklyn. *Managing the New Careerists.* San Francisco: Jossey-Bass, 1986.

Greenhaus, Jeffrey. *Career Management.* Chicago: Dryden Press, 1987.

Gutteridge, Thomas G., and Otte, Fred. *Organizational Career Development: State of the Practice.* Washington, DC: ASTD Press, 1983.

Hall, Douglas T., and Associates. *Career Development in Organizations.* San Francisco: Jossey-Bass, 1986.

Kaye, Beverly. *Up Is Not The Only Way: A Guide for Career Development Practitioners.* Englewood Cliffs, New Jersey: Prentice-Hall, 1982.

Leibowitz, Zandy, et al. *Designing Career Development Systems.* San Francisco: Jossey-Bass, 1986.

Raelin, Joseph. *The Salaried Professional.* New York: Praeger, 1984.

Schein, Edgar H. *Career Dynamics: Matching Individual and Organizational Needs.* Reading, Massachusetts: Addison-Wesley, 1978.

Sonnenfeld, Jeffrey. *Managing Career Systems.* Homewood, Illinois: Irwin, 1984.

Storey, Walter. *Career Dimensions I-III.* San Diego: University Associates, 1986.

Leadership

Astin, Helen S., and Leland, Carole. *Women of Influence, Women of Vision: A Cross-Generational Study of Leaders and Social Change.* San Francisco: Jossey-Bass, 1991.

Argyris, Chris. *Increasing Leadership Effectiveness.* New York: Wiley, 1976.

Autry, James A. *Love and Profit: The Art of Caring Leadership.* New York: William Morrow, 1991.

Badaracco, Joseph L., Jr., and Ellsworth, Richard R. *Leadership and the Quest for Integrity.* Boston, Massachusetts: Harvard Business School Press, 1989.

Bass, Bernard M. *Leadership and Performance Beyond Expectations.* New York: Free Press, 1985.

Special thanks to the Center for Creative Leadership for their bibliographic assistance in the leadership, systems leadership, teams/teamwork, and mentors/ mentoring areas.

Bellingham, Richard, and Cohen, Barry. *Ethical Leadership: A Competitive Edge.* Amherst, Massachusetts: Human Resource Development Press, 1990.

Bennis, Warren. *On Becoming a Leader.* Reading, Massachusetts: Addison-Wesley, 1989.

Birnbaum, Robert. *How Colleges Work: The Cybernetics of Academic Organization and Leadership.* San Francisco: Jossey-Bass, 1988.

Bolman, Lee G., and Deal, Terrence E. *Reframing Organizations: Artistry, Choice and Leadership.* San Francisco, California: Jossey-Bass, 1991.

Bruce, James S. *The Intuitive Pragmatists, Conversations with Chief Executive Officers.* Greensboro, North Carolina: Center for Creative Leadership, Special Report, 1986.

Burns, James M. *Leadership.* New York: Harper & Row, 1978.

Campbell, David P. *If I'm in Charge Here Why Is Everybody Laughing?* Greensboro, North Carolina: Center for Creative Leadership, 1984.

Caroselli, Marlene. *The Language of Leadership.* Amherst, Massachusetts: Human Resource Development Press, 1990.

Chaffee, Ellen E., and Tierney, William C. *Collegiate Culture and Leadership Strategies.* New York: Macmillan, 1988.

Cohen, Michael D., and March, James G. *Leadership and Ambiguity, 2nd ed. Boston, Massachusetts: Harvard Business School Press, 1986.*

Conger, Jay A. *The Charismatic Leader: Behind the Mystique of Exceptional Leadership.* San Francisco: Jossey-Bass, 1989.

Convey, Stephen R. *Seven Habits of Highly Effective People: Restoring the Character Ethic.* New York: Simon & Schuster, 1989.

Davis, Stanley. *Managing Corporate Culture.* Cambridge, Massachusetts: Ballinger, 1984.

Drucker, Peter F. *The Effective Executive.* New York: Harper & Row, 1969.

Eichinger, Robert W., and Lombardo, Michael. *Twenty-two Ways to Develop Leadership in Staff Managers, 1990.* Greensboro, North Carolina: Center for Creative Leadership.

Fisher, James, and Tack, Martha, eds. *Leaders on Leadership: The College Presidency.* San Francisco: Jossey-Bass, 1988.

Friedman, Stewart, ed. *Leadership Succession.* New Brunswick, New Jersey: Transaction Books, 1987.

Gardner, John W. *On Leadership.* New York: Free Press, 1990.

Greenleaf, Robert K. *Servant Leadership: A Journey into the Nature of Legitimate Power and Greatness.* New York: Paulist Press, 1977.

Helgesen, Sally. *The Female Advantage: Women's Way of Leadership.* New York: Doubleday, 1990.

Hersey, Paul, and Blanchard, Kenneth. *Management of Organizational Behavior: Utilizing Human Resources,* 5th ed. Englewood Cliffs, New Jersey: Prentice-Hall, 1988.

Janis, Irving L. *Crucial Decisions: Leadership in Policymaking and Crisis Management.* New York: Free Press, 1989.

Kaplan, Robert E. with Wilfred H. Drath and Joan R. Kofodimos. *Beyond Ambition: How Driven Managers Can Lead Better and Live Better by Growing Personally.* San Francisco: Jossey-Bass, 1991.

Kellerman, Barbara, ed. *Leadership: Multidisciplinary Perspectives.* Englewood Cliffs, New Jersey: Prentice-Hall, 1984.

Kets de Vries, Manfred F. R. *Prisoners of Leadership.* New York: Wiley, 1989.

Kilmann, Ralph, and Covin, Teresa. *Corporate Transformation: Revitalizing Organizations for a Competitive World.* San Francisco: Jossey-Bass, 1988.

Koestenbaum, Peter. *Leadership: The Inner Side of Greatness.* San Francisco: Jossey-Bass, 1991.

Kotter, John P. *A Force for Change: How Leadership Differs from Management.* New York: Free Press, 1990.

Kouzes, James, and Posner, Barry. *The Leadership Challenge: How to Get Extraordinary Things Done in Organizations.* San Francisco: Jossey-Bass, 1987.

Lamb, Robert. *Running American Business: Top CEOs Rethink Their Major Decisions.* New York: Harper & Row, 1987.

Lansing, Alfred. *Endurance.* New York: Avon, 1976.

Levinson, Harry. *Executive.* Cambridge, Massachusetts: Harvard University, 1981.

Lindsey, Esther H.; Homes, Virginia; and McCall, Morgan W. Jr. *Key Events in Executives' Lives.* Greensboro, North Carolina: Center for Creative Leadership, 1987.

McCall, Morgan, W., Jr.; Lombardo, Michael M.; and Morrison, Ann M. *The Lessons of Experience: How Successful Executives Develop on the Job.* Lexington, 1988.

McClelland, David C. *Power: The Inner Experience.* New York: Irvington, 1979.

Maccoby, Michael. *Why Work: Leading the New Generation.* New York: Simon & Schuster, 1988.

Mintzberg, Henry. *The Nature of Management.* New York: Harper & Row, 1973.

Peters, Thomas. *Thriving on Chaos: Handbook for a Management Revolution.* New York: Knopf, 1987.

Peters, Thomas, and Austin, Nancy. *A Passion for Excellence: The Leadership Difference.* New York: Random House, 1985.

Quinn, Robert. *Beyond Rational Management: Mastering the Paradoxes and Competing Demands of High Performance.* San Francisco: Jossey-Bass, 1988.

Rost, Joseph C. *Leadership for the Twenty-first Century.* New York: Praeger, 1991.

Sayles, Leonard R. *Leadership: Managing in Real Organizations,* 2nd ed. New York: McGraw-Hill, 1989.

Schein, Edgar. *Organizational Culture and Leadership.* San Francisco: Jossey-Bass, 1985.

Srivastva, Suresh, ed. *Executive Integrity: The Search for High Human Values in Organizational Life.* San Francisco: Jossey-Bass, 1988.

Taylor, Robert L., and Rosenbach, William E. *Leadership: Challenges for Today's Managers.* New York: Nichols, 1989.

Tichy, Noel, and Devanna, Mary Anne. *Transformational Leader.* New York: Wiley, 1986.

Vroom, Victor, and Jago, Arthur. *The New Leadership: Managing Participation in Organizations.* New York: Prentice-Hall, 1988.

Waterman, Robert, Jr. *The Renewal Factor: How the Best Get and Keep the Competitive Edge.* New York: Bantam, 1987.

Yukl, Gary A. *Leadership in Organizations,* 2nd ed. Englewood Cliffs, New Jersey: Prentice-Hall, 1989.

Zaleznik, Abraham, and Kets de Vries, Manfred F. R. *Power and the Corporate Mind.* Boston: Houghton Mifflin, 1975.

Mentoring and Coaching Employees

Arndt, Sheril. "Mentor Programs Help Boost Production," *National Underwriter (Life/Health/Financial Services)*, Vol. 93, No. 15, April 10, 1989, pp. 17–18.

Ball, Aimee Lee. "Mentors & Proteges: Portraits of Success," *Working Woman*, Vol. 14, No. 10, October 1989, pp. 134–142.

Bernstein, Beverly J., and Kaye, Beverly L. "Teacher, Tutor, Colleague, Coach," *Personnel Journal*, Vol. 65, No. 11, November 1986, pp. 44–51.

Buonocore, Anthony J. "Reducing Turnover of New Hires," *Management Solutions*, Vol. 32, No. 6, June 1987, pp. 5–10.

Burke, Ronald J., and McKeen, Carol A. "Developing Formal Mentoring Programs in Organizations," *Business Quarterly* (Canada), Vol. 53, No. 3, Winter 1989, pp. 76–79.

Carsrud, Alan L.; Gaglio, Connie Marie; and Olm, Kenneth W. "Entrepreneurs—Mentors, Networks, and Successful New Venture Development: An Exploratory Study," *American Journal of Small Business*, Vol. 12, No. 2, Fall 1987, pp. 13–18.

Dunbar, Donnette. "Desperately Seeking Mentors," *Black Enterprise*, Vol. 20, No. 8, March 1990, pp. 53–56.

Fagenson, Ellen A. "The Mentor Advantage: Perceived Career/Job Experiences of Proteges Versus Non-Proteges," *Journal of Organizational Behavior* (UK), Vol. 10, No. 4, October 1989, pp. 309–320.

Jacoby, David. "Rewards Make the Mentor," *Personnel*, Vol. 66, No. 12, December 1989, pp. 10–14.

Kizilos, Peter, "Take My Mentor, Please!" *Training*, Vol. 27, No. 4, April 1990, pp. 49–55.

Lawrie, John. "How to Establish a Mentoring Program." *Training & Development Journal*, Vol. 41, No. 3, March 1987, pp. 25–27.

Mendleson, Jack L.; Barnes, A. Keith; and Horn, Gregory. "The Guiding Light to Corporate Culture," *Personnel Administrator*, Vol. 34, No. 7, July 1989, pp. 70–72.

Morse, Michele Block. "Friends in High Places," *Success*, Vol. 34, No. 10, December 1987, pp. 58–62.

Noe, Raymond A. "Women and Mentoring: A Review and Research Agenda," *Academy of Management Review*, Vol. 13, No. 1, January 1988, pp. 65–78.

Odiorne, George S. "Mentoring—An American Management Innovation," *Personnel Administrator*, Vol. 30, No. 5, May 1985, pp. 63–70.

Orth, Charles D.; Wilkinson, Harry E.; and Benfari, Robert C. "The Manager's Role as Coach and Mentor," *Organizational Dynamics*, Vol. 15, No. 4, Spring 1987, pp. 66–74.

Ragins, Belle Rose. "Barriers to Mentoring: The Female Manager's Dilemma," *Human Relations*, Vol. 42, No. 1, January 1989, pp. 1–22.

Reich, Murray H., "The Mentor Connection," *Personnel*, Vol. 63, No. 2, February 1986, pp. 50–56.

Thomas, David A. "Mentoring and Irrationality: The Role of Racial Taboos," *Human Resource Management*, Vol. 28, No. 2, Summer 1989, pp. 279–290.

White, Harvey L. "The SELF Method of Mentoring," *Bureaucrat*, Vol. 19, No. 1, Spring 1990, pp. 45–48.

Willbur, Jerry. "Does Mentoring Breed Success?" *Training & Development Journal,* Vol. 41, No. 11, November 1987, pp. 38–41.

Wilson, James A., and Danes, Lois M. "Is Mentoring Only for the Chosen Few?" *Executive Excellence,* Vol. 5, No. 12, December 1988, pp. 8–9.

Zak, Michael G. "A Mentor for All Reasons," *Personnel Journal,* Vol. 67, No. 1, January 1988, pp. 46–51.

Organizational Strategy and Change

Argyris, Chris. *Strategy, Change, and Defensive Routines.* Boston, Massachusetts: Pitman, 1985.

Harris, Philip R. *Management in Transition.* San Francisco: Jossey-Bass, 1985.

Humphrey, Watts S. *Managing for Innovation: Leading Technical People.* Englewood Cliffs, New Jersey: Prentice-Hall, 1987.

Kanter, Rosabeth M. *When Giants Learn to Dance: Mastering the Challenge of Strategy, Management, and Careers in the 1990s.* New York: Simon & Schuster, 1989.

Kilmann, Ralph H., and Kilmann, Ines. *Managing Beyond the Quick Fix: A Completely Integrated Program for Creating and Maintaining Organizational Success.* San Francisco: Jossey-Bass, 1989.

Kilmann, Ralph H.; Saxton, Mary J.; and Serpa, Roy. *Gaining Control of the Corporate Culture.* San Francisco: Jossey-Bass, 1985.

Kirkpatrick, Donald L. *How to Manage Change Effectively.* San Francisco: Jossey-Bass, 1985.

Lippitt, Gordon L.; Langseth, Petter; and Mossop, Jack. *Implementing Organizational Change.* San Francisco: Jossey-Bass, 1985.

Mills, D. Quinn. *Rebirth of the Corporation.* New York: Wiley, 1991.

Naisbitt, John, and Aburdene, Patricia. *Re-inventing the Corporation: Transforming Your Job and Your Company for the New Information Society.* New York: Warner Books, 1985.

Pascale, R. T. *Managing on the Edge: How the Smartest Companies Use Conflict to Stay Ahead.* New York: Simon & Schuster, 1990.

Pennings, Johannes M. *Organizational Strategy and Change.* San Francisco: Jossey-Bass, 1985.

Rock, Milton L.; Rock, Robert H.; and Kristie, James. *Corporate Restructuring: A Guide to Creating the Premium-Valued Company.* New York: McGraw-Hill, 1990.

Schaffer, Robert H. *Breakthrough Strategy: Using Short-Term Successes to Build the High Performance Organization.* Cambridge, Massachusetts: Ballinger, 1988.

Schuster, Fred E. *Schuster Report: The Proven Connection Between People and Profits.* New York: Wiley, 1986.

Scott Morton, Michael S. *Corporation of the 1990s: Information Technology and Organizational Transformation.* New York: Oxford University Press, 1991.

Tichy, Noel M., and Devanna, Mary Anne. *Transformational Leader.* New York: Wiley, 1986.

Waterman, Robert H. *Adhocracy: The Power to Change.* Knoxville: Whittle Direct Books, 1990.

Waterman, Robert H. *Renewal Factor: How the Best Get and Keep the Competitive Edge.* New York: Bantam Books, 1987.

Wilkins, Alan L. *Developing Corporate Character: How to Successfully Change an Organization Without Destroying It.* San Francisco: Jossey-Bass, 1989.

Stress and Stress Management

Albrecht, Karl G. *Stress and the Manager: Making It Work for You.* Englewood Cliffs, New Jersey: Prentice-Hall, 1979.

American Hospital Association. *Stress! You've Got It! What Are You Going to Do About It?* Chicago: American Hospital Association, 1977.

Bernstein, Albert J., and Rozen, Sydney C. *Dinosaur Brains: Dealing With All Those Impossible People at Work.* New York: Wiley, 1989.

Buck, Vernon E. *Working Under Pressure.* New York: Crane, Russack, 1972.

Carnegie, Dale. *How to Stop Worrying and Start Living.* New York: Simon & Schuster, 1972.

Cooper, Cary L., and Marshall, Judi. *Understanding Executive Stress.* New York: PBI, 1977.

Forbes, Rosalind. *Corporate Stress.* Garden City, New York: Doubleday, Dolphin Book, 1979.

Gherman, E. M. *Stress and the Bottom Line.* New York: AMACOM, 1981.

Gmelch, Walter H. *Beyond Stress to Effective Management.* New York: Wiley, Wiley Self-Teaching Guides, 1982.

Gowler, Dan, and Legge, Karen. *Managerial Stress.* New York: Wiley, 1975.

Howe, Leland W., and Howe, Mary Martha. *Personalized Education: Values Clarification and Beyond.* New York: Hart Publishing Co., 1975.

Kaufman, Harold G. *Professionals in Search of Work: Coping with the Stress of Job Loss and Underemployment.* New York: Wiley, 1982.

Kiev, Ari. *Strategy for Handling Executive Stress.* Chicago: Nelson-Hall, 1974.

Kiev, Ari, and Kohn, Vera. *Executive Stress.* New York: AMACOM, AMA Survey Report, 1979.

Levinson, Harry. *Executive Stress.* New York: Harper & Row, 1970.

London, Manuel, and Mone, Edward M. *Career Management and Survival in the Workplace: Helping Employees Make Tough Career Decisions, Stay Motivated, and Reduce Career Stress.* San Francisco: Jossey-Bass, 1987.

McQuade, Walter, and Aikman, Ann. *Stress: What Is It, What It Can Do to Your Health, How to Fight Back.* New York: Dutton, 1974.

Moos, Rudolf H. *Human Adaptation: Coping with Life Crises.* Lexington, Massachusetts: Health, 1976.

Schafer, Walt. *Stress Management for Wellness,* 2nd ed. Forth Worth: Harcourt, Brace & Jovanovich, 1992.

Schafer, Walt. *Stress, Distress and Health.* U.S.A.: Responsible Action, 1978.

Selye, Hans. *Stress without Distress.* Philadelphia: Lippincott, 1974.

Stress, Work, Health. Chicago: American Medical Association, 1980.

Simon, Sidney B.; Howe, Leland W.; and Kirschenbaum, Howard. *Values Clarification.* New York: Hart Publishing Co., 1972.

Yates, Jere E. *Managing Stress: A Businessperson's Guide.* New York: AMACOM, 1979.

Systems Leadership

Beer, Stafford. *Diagnosing the System for Organizations*. New York: Wiley, 1985.

Bennis, Warren, and Nanus, Burt. *Leaders: The Strategies for Taking Charge*. New York: Harper & Row, 1985.

Bennis, Warren. *On Becoming a Leader*. Reading, Massachusetts: Addison-Wesley, 1989.

Berman, Melissa A., ed. *Corporate Culture and Change: Highlights of a Conference*. Conference Board Report No. 888. New York: Conference Board, 1986.

Bruce, James S. *The Intuitive Pragmatists: Conversations with Chief Executive Officers*. Greensboro, North Carolina: Center for Creative Leadership, Special Report, 1986.

Conger, Jay A. *The Charismatic Leader: Behind the Mystique of Exceptional Leadership*. San Francisco: Jossey-Bass, 1989.

Davis, Stanley M. *Future Perfect*. Reading, Massachusetts: Addison-Wesley, 1987.

Davis, Stanley. *Managing Corporate Culture*. Cambridge, Massachusetts: Ballinger, 1984.

Gardner, John W. *On Leadership*. New York: Free Press, 1990.

Hage, Jerald, ed. *Futures of Organizations: Innovating to Adapt Strategy and Human Resources to Rapid Technological Change*. Lexington, Massachusetts: Lexington, 1988.

Jaques, Elliott. *Requisite Organization: The CEO's Guide to Creative Structures and Leadership*. Arlington, Virginia: Cason Hall, 1989.

Kilmann, Ralph, and Covin, Teresa, eds. *Corporate Transformation: Revitalizing Organizations for a Competitive World*. San Francisco: Jossey-Bass, 1988.

Kotter, John. *The Leadership Factor*. New York: Macmillan, 1988.

Peters, Tom, and Austin, Nancy. *A Passion for Excellence: The Leadership Difference*. New York: Random house, 1985.

Roy, Robert H. *The Cultures of Management*. Baltimore: Johns Hopkins University, 1977.

Sayles, Leonard R. *Leadership: Managing in Real Organizations*, 2nd ed. New York: McGraw-Hill, 1989.

Schein, Edgar. *Organizational Culture and Leadership*. San Francisco: Jossey-Bass, 1985.

Schein, Lawrence. *A Manager's Guide to Corporate Culture*. New York: Conference Board (Research Report #926), 1989.

Tichy, Noel, and Devanna, Mary Anne. *Transformational Leader*. New York: Wiley, 1986.

Tregoe, Benjamin B., et al. *Vision in Action: Putting a Winning Strategy to Work*. New York: Simon & Schuster, 1990.

Waterman, Robert, H. *The Renewal Factor: How the Best Get and Keep the Competitive Edge*. New York: Bantam, 1987.

Teams and Teamwork

Belbin, R. Meredith. *Management Teams; Why They Succeed or Fail*. New York: Wiley, 1981.

Bowers, David G. *Systems of Organization: Management of the Human Resource.* Ann Arbor: University of Michigan Press, 1976.

Dyer, William G. *Team Building: Issues and Alternatives.* Reading, Massachusetts: Addison-Wesley, 1977.

Eddy, William B. *The Manager and the Working Group.* New York: Praeger, 1985.

Ends, Earl J. *Organizational Team Building.* Cambridge, Massachusetts: Winthrop Publishers, 1977.

Francis, Dave. *Improving Work Groups: A Practical Manual for Team Building.* La Jolla, California: University Associates, 1979.

Goodman, Paul S. *Designing Effective Work Groups.* San Francisco: Jossey-Bass, 1986.

J. Richard Heckman, ed. *Groups That Work (and Those That Don't): Creating Conditions for Effective Teamwork.* San Francisco: Jossey-Bass, 1990.

Herrick, Neal Q. *Joint Management and Employee Participation: Labor and Management at the Crossroads.* San Francisco: Jossey-Bass, 1990.

Isgar, Thomas. *The Ten Minute Team: 10 Steps to Building High Performing Teams.* Boulder, Colorado: Seluera Press, 1989.

Johansen, Robert. *Groupware: Computer Support for Business Teams.* New York: Free Press, 1988.

Larson, Carl E. *Teamwork: What Must Go Right, What Can Go Wrong.* Beverly Hills: Sage Publications, 1989.

Olson, Margrethe H., ed. *Technological Support for Work Group Collaboration.* Hillsdale, New Jersey: L. Erlbaum Associates, 1989.

Reddy, W. Brendan, ed., with Kaleel Jamison, *Team Building: Blueprints for Productivity and Satisfaction.* Alexandra, Virginia: NTL Institute for Applied Behavioral Science. 1988.

Rosen, Ned A. *Teamwork and the Bottom Line: Groups Make a Difference.* Hillsdale, New Jersey: L. Erlbaum Associates, 1989.

Shronk, James H. *Working in Teams.* New York: AMACOM, 1982.

Stewart, Alex. *Team Entrepreneurship.* Newbury Park, California: Sage Publications, 1989.

Tjosvold, Dean. *Working Together to Get Things Done: Managing for Organizational Productivity.* Lexington, Massachusetts: Lexington Books, 1986.

Varney, Glenn H. *Building Productive Teams: An Action Guide and Resource Book.* San Francisco: Jossey Bass, 1989.

Work and Family

Freidman, Dana E. *Family Supportive Policies: The Corporate Decision Making Process.* New York: Conference Board, Conference Board Report, No. 897, 1987.

Friedman, Dana E. *Linking Work-Family Issues to the Bottom Line.* New York: Conference Board, Conference Board Report, No. 962, 1991.

Peters, J. L. et al. *Work and Family Policies: The New Strategic Plan.* New York: Conference Board, Conference Board Report, No. 949, 1990.

Sekaran, Uma. *Dual-Career Families.* San Francisco: Jossey-Bass, 1986.

Index

About the Authors

EDWARD BETOF, Ed.D., is Assistant Vice President and Director of Human Resource Planning and Development for the U.S. Pharmaceuticals Division of Hoffmann–La Roche, Inc. Ed has also directed the Drug Regulatory Affairs and the Pharmaceuticals Project Management departments, and the Center for Professional Development at Hoffmann–La Roche. Ed previously worked for the Reliance Insurance Companies as Director of Human Resource Planning and Development and was a worldwide management consultant for Sperry Univac. Ed began his career as a teacher, coach, and educational administrator, and consulted extensively to public and independent schools, and was an adjunct faculty member at both Temple and Penn State Universities.

FREDERIC HARWOOD, Ph.D., is Vice President of Barnett International (a division of PAREXEL International Corporation), a management consulting firm specializing in productivity improvement, systems design and integration, and the design and management of training, primarily in the pharmaceutical and health care industries. He has over 15 years of international consulting experience, mostly in the management of multinational research and development, and has held management positions in the U.S. and Germany. A graduate of the University of Minnesota, he was on the faculty of Temple University for 16 years, where he chaired the Adult Education Program.